L.P.

# COLLECTING AUTOGRAPHS AND MANUSCRIPTS

# COLLECTING

# AND

UNIVERSITY OF OKLAHOMA PRESS

# AUTOGRAPHS

# MANUSCRIPTS

 by CHARLES HAMILTON

*Illustrated with more than Eight Hundred Facsimiles
and other Reproductions*

*Second Edition*

NORMAN

Books by Charles Hamilton

*Cry of the Thunderbird:* The American Indian's Own Story (New York, 1950)
*Men of the Underworld:* The Professional Criminal's Own Story (New York, 1952)
*Braddock's Defeat* (editor) (Norman, 1959)
*Collecting Autographs and Manuscripts* (Norman, 1961)

INTERNATIONAL STANDARD BOOK NUMBERS:
    0–8061–0873–8 (cloth); 0–8061–1156–9 (paperback)

LIBRARY OF CONGRESS CATALOG CARD NUMBER: 61–9007

TO DORIS

# PREFACE

AN AUTOGRAPH LETTER OR DOCUMENT is far more than a scrap of writing signed by a famous or unknown person. It may provide a new interpretation of a decisive battle, a vital clue for biographers, or a thought to change the course of history.

This book will tell you about autographs and give you some ideas on what sort of collection you can create.

Once you start on this most intimate and challenging of all pursuits, you will find great excitement in exploring behind the scenes of history, literature, science, and the arts.

You will also help to preserve our cultural heritage!

New York City

# ACKNOWLEDGMENTS

No AUTHOR EVER RECEIVED MORE CORDIAL HELP than was accorded me by the autograph collectors of America. Not one said "no" to my request to quote previously unpublished or little-known material, even when publication might affect a document's value.

For permission to publish material or reproduce facsimiles I should like to express my thanks to Robert K. Black, Richard Maass, Samuel Moyerman, Dr. Bernard L. Pacella, Warren A. Reeder, Lucius S. Ruder, Nat Stein, and Justin G. Turner. My thanks are due also to Gordon T. Banks, Rex Beasley, the Reverend Cornelius Greenway, Morton Dean Joyce, Professor Jack Pollman, Fred C. Schang, and H. Keith Thompson.

Further I wish to express my gratitude to the Alderman Library and the C. Waller Barrett Library of the University of Virginia, the International Grapho Analysis Society, Inc., the Library of Congress, the McLellan Lincoln Collection of Brown University, the New-York Historical Society, the New York Public Library, and World-Wide Photos.

Especially I wish to acknowledge my indebtedness to Elsie O. and Philip D. Sang for their magnanimity in permitting me the liberal use of their collections.

For providing me with interesting or unusual anecdotes I am indebted to Paul Appel, Dr. Maury A. Bromsen, Louis Cohen, Alden S. Condict, my brother Bruce Hamilton, and R. F. Kallir.

I am particularly grateful to W. B. Thorsen, editor and publisher of the *American Book Collector* in Chicago, and Pearl Ann Reeder, editor of *Hobbies*, also of Chicago, for permission to use excerpts from articles which first appeared in their publications.

To Charles Smith for his splendid artistry in designing several montage illustrations and offering important layout suggestions I should also like to express my thanks.

To the late F. H. Sweet, of Battle Creek, Michigan, I owe my gratitude for his unstinting co-operation and friendly advice. I especially appreciate his many helpful suggestions when, some years ago, I started in business.

My thanks are also due to Daryl Brooks for aid in preparing the Index and to Roselle S. Morse for her meticulous reading of the proofs.

Of immense help was the assistance of Eleanor Daniels Bronson in reading the manuscript and offering scores of valuable suggestions, nearly all of which I accepted.

For accomplishing with success a most arduous task, calling for ingenuity and scholarship, I should like to thank my secretary June Baxter, who worked tirelessly on the lists of Revolutionary War generals and Washington's aides. Both my assistant Catherine C. Unold and my secretary Judith Irby were immensely helpful during long hours of dictation, when they recorded with rather disconcerting accuracy the chapters which I dictated, often late at night. I am grateful, too, for the intelligent typing of the final draft done by Miss Unold. To my secretary Judith Irby I should like to express my deep appreciation for the way in which she labored with me over the manuscript, suggesting many corrections and deletions and insertions. Her critical ability greatly improved this book.

Most particularly I wish to thank my wife Doris for her continuous encouragement. Her reading and rereading of the manuscript, always with the proffer of many useful suggestions, was a great spur to my efforts and has made this a much better volume.

*Charles Hamilton*

# CONTENTS

ILLUSTRATIONS

COLLECTING AUTOGRAPHS AND MANUSCRIPTS

# 1 HOW TO BUILD AN
IMPORTANT COLLECTION

FREQUENTLY I AM ASKED: "What is the best way to build a collection of autographs which will have permanent value and importance?"

To form a significant collection takes intelligence and courage and good taste, plus a modest outlay of money. In no other field of collecting can you build a really distinguished collection for so small an investment. With an assemblage of stamps or coins, the difference between a collection which costs one thousand dollars and a collection which costs one million is enormous and obvious. But in autographs, the taste and knowledge of the collector play so vital a role that a thousand-dollar collection may be more valuable historically and more intriguing than its million dollar counterpart.

If you are not familiar with autographs, and are not certain of what you wish to collect, you should seek the advice of a dealer or experienced collector. If you plunge in boldly without guidance you may, it is true, ultimately emerge with a great collection, as did J. P. Morgan, who started by assembling the signatures of Methodist-Episcopal bishops and ended by founding one of the greatest manuscript libraries in the world. But if you lack the shrewdness of Morgan you may find yourself with a collection of unrelated odds and ends fit only to feather a magpie's nest.

A few months ago a letter came to me from a retired salesman who was for half a century an avid seeker-of-autographs, tracking down material from Maine to California. For years he was a familiar sight to antique and curio dealers. They set aside autographs for his annual visit. As a traveling salesman, his opportunities were unique, and he had searched out remote corners of the land, quietly gathering "treasures" into his net. Everywhere attics were opened to him. Now he had retired and wished to sell his immense accumulation of rarities—a collection that filled more than a dozen cartons!

The thought of exploring those magic cartons lifted the floodgates of my imagination. I have no strength to resist the unknown! Putting aside other tasks, I wrote, asking him to visit me. A few days later he walked into my reception room carrying a bulging valise. His tall, sparse frame, distinguished face, and quiet manner inspired confidence and I felt a tingle of excitement as I opened the valise.

The first document I looked at was a very ordinary land deed, the second was a worthless invoice, the third was a clerical copy of an old will. They might all have come from the same barrel! Of the first forty or fifty documents not one was worth so much as a dollar.

"Do all the cartons contain similar material?" I asked.

"They do!" His answer was confident and prompt.

How could I tell this fine old man that his lifetime of collecting would net him nothing? For years he had been putting his money into these documents believing that someday—and this was that day—they would prove a magnificent investment. Still holding one of the valueless old papers in my hand, I studied him out of the corner of my eye while I searched for the words that would let him down gently.

"Tell me," I said, "did you ever go to an autograph dealer?"

"No, sir! I didn't!" He chuckled. "Cut out the middleman—that's my motto! I went direct to the source—bought up the stuff before it could get to the big dealers."

"Well, I won't deny that some of this material has a certain antiquarian interest. Doubtless there are collectors who might prize it highly. But it is not exactly the sort of thing an autograph specialist would handle."

"What do you mean, not exactly?" His voice faltered.

"You see," I went on, "my clients are interested in old letters about battles or whaling or Indians. They want letters full of excitement and action. They want documents and letters of famous men—authors or Presidents or composers or scientists. And I'm afraid you have nothing like that, have you?"

He shook his head. "I thought just any old document was valuable. Why, some of these papers go back as far as 1800."

"The year 1800 is old, so far as you and I are concerned, but for documents it is recent. European documents are valued for their age only if they are dated before 1400. In America, the dividing line between old and modern is 1650."

"Then my collection has no value?" His voice fell to a whisper. "It cost me a fortune, really a fortune. My basement is full of cartons of documents like these, gathered from towns and cities all over the United States."

"Their main value is sentimental. But perhaps you could sell them back to the antique and curio dealers from whom you got them."

"No," he observed sadly, "I bought them from so many different places. Hundreds of different places."

As he left my office, he said, "If I had known fifty years ago what I have learned in the past ten minutes, it would have saved me thousands of dollars."

In contrast I recall a visit to the safe-deposit box of my friend R. F. Kallir who, after cautioning me that nothing was for sale, admitted me to his holographic sanctum deep in the vault of a bank. Here were preserved the treasures he had gathered during three decades of wise and tasteful collecting. What delight was mine as I held the original manuscripts of compositions by Beethoven, Bach, and Schubert. Curiously, in the metal box which housed some of his great documents was a shaving-brush case filled with ducats, an unexciting form of wealth compared with the yellowing pages on which Mendelssohn's quill first set down the "Spring Song."

Here was a collection formed in utter defiance of the fads of the moment! A few, a very few, of his letters and manuscripts were acquired by private purchase; some were picked up at auction; but most were obtained from dealers who, I venture to say, would be glad to buy them back at five or ten times the selling price! Kallir had never hesitated to pay a high sum if the autograph warranted it. In paying a price which caused less astute collectors to flinch, he would say: "Perhaps the price is high today, but I will set the item aside, and soon it will be worth more than I paid for it."

This faith in one's own judgment, and the courage to pay a high price when others quake and back away, is the mark of the great collector!

Consider that only a few years ago a letter of a Civil War soldier describing a battle or a visit to Lincoln was "high priced" at three or four dollars. Today it would fetch ten or twenty times as much! The collector who invested in such treasures before they became a "vogue" is now the owner of an important collection, built at a modest cost, yet of great historic interest.

On the other hand, if you pass up rarities or desirable specimens in the hope of "finding a cheaper one later," you may be disappointed. Recall the poignant lament of the impecunious Eugene Field:

*At Davey's in Great Russell Street were autographs galore,*
*And Mr. Davey used to let me con that precious store:*
*And sometimes I read what warriors wrote, sometimes a king's command,*
*But, oftener still, a poet's verse writ in a meager hand;*
*Lamb, Byron, Addison, and Burns, Pope, Johnson, Swift and Scott—*
*Yet, when Friend Davey marked 'em down, what could I but decline?*
*For I was broke in London in the fall of '89!*

Like fine paintings or gold coins, important autographs are an excellent hedge against inflation. A letter of Lincoln or Goethe or Napoleon or Wagner can be transmuted into money in any nation of the world. How many refugees escaped from Nazi Germany, stripped of their jewels and real estate and paintings and cash, and with "nothing but a few old family papers" in a battered portfolio or suitcase! The "family papers"— you guessed it!—were priceless autographs which enabled the fortunate possessors to start life afresh in the New World. If Marshal Goering, who had a passion for choice manuscripts, had known how many rare letters of Martin Luther and Voltaire and Beethoven were smuggled out under the very noses of Nazi officials, he would doubtless have stood sentinel at the border himself!

While I believe that the collector who is essentially an investor, and to whom autographs have no emotional appeal, would be happier gambling with stocks and bonds, I cannot escape the conviction that, in general, fine autograph letters and documents are a sounder investment than gilt-edged securities. When the collection of autographs and manuscripts formed by the Earl of Ashburnham was dispersed at auction after his death in 1878, the Stowe, Barrois, and Libri manuscripts, which had cost the Earl the staggering sum of £22,000, fetched the much more staggering amount of £102,000, proof of the Earl's astuteness as a collector. After the stock market crash in 1929, nearly all of the gilt was rubbed off the gilt-edged bonds, but autographs held their values reasonably well. In the worst depression year of 1933 some autographs actually hit new highs! Of how many stocks can this be said? In 1928–29, the composer Jerome Kern sold his collection of autographs and rare books at auction. It fetched more than one million dollars, many times the sum he had paid for it. Unfortunately for Kern, he put the proceeds of the sale into the stock market and lost nearly every cent. In 1935, a collector declared: "The stock market wiped me out. I had nothing left but my collection of rare autographs. These still held much of their original value, and, by selling them, I was able to get started again and make a come-back."

While other hobbies may be interesting and educational, autographs

*International Grapho Analysis Society, Inc.*

Autograph Letter Signed, of Franklin D. Roosevelt. ". . . I too collect autographic letters but for historical reasons."

are sought not only by connoisseurs and collectors, but by avid scholars to whom they are indispensable for research, and by libraries, institutions, museums, and historical societies. Without autographs, there can be no literary, scientific, or cultural history. The heritage of the written word is the basis of our civilization.

Assuming that you wish to protect your investment in autographs and collect letters and documents which will increase in value, here are a few suggestions:

*Do not specialize, but gather five or six different collections simultaneously.* Just as the intelligent investor in stocks seeks diversity, so should you. Suppose that thirty years ago you had formed half a dozen different collections, say in music, science, World War I, Napoleon, and American Western autographs. Except for World War I, in which prices have declined in the past two or three decades, all of your purchases would have held their worth, and those in music and science would have increased phenomenally, so that taken as a whole your collection would be vastly more valuable than when it was first assembled.

With a diversified collection you have another important advantage. You will be able to pick up many more "safe" buys. Instead of paying premium prices for items badly needed to fill out your specialty, you can wait and get material for your various collections when it appears for sale at a fair price. You will have a wider choice from which to buy. You will find, too, that a general collection, formed in half a dozen different fields, will be more interesting to your friends. Let me make clear, however, that I do not recommend a hodgepodge collection of odds and ends in every field from Spanish monarchs to Russian poets and French scientists and American pugilists. Pick five or six special fields which interest you and stick to them. If you find yourself leaning toward one subject, specialize!

A few years ago, collectors were urged to specialize, but most of the outstanding collectors of today are distinguished for extensive knowledge and wide interests. Elsie O. and Philip D. Sang, of River Forest, Illinois, have an insatiable appetite for any letters which are remarkable, and have assembled vast collections on Russian history, the Civil War, American Judaica, and the Revolutionary War. Almost as indefatigable is Lucius S. Ruder, of Clearwater, Florida, a collector of autographs on the Confederacy, Colonial currency, early steamboats and railroads, and Anthony Wayne and the Indians of Ohio. No less universal in his taste is Justin G. Turner, of Los Angeles, into whose collecting net have come innumerable letters of the Revolutionary and Civil wars, together with many autographs about such specialized topics as Arnold's journey to Quebec, the Paxton boys, and the XYZ Affair. While showing a keen interest in medi-

Two noted American collectors, Nathaniel E. Stein and Richard Maass, examine a rare collection of original Presidential checks which they assembled for a bank display. Both collectors have many other autographic interests.

cal letters and documents, Dr. and Mrs. Richard H. Hamilton (who, I regret, are not related to me) also have a large enthusiasm for other autographic fields. The collection of signed photos owned by the Reverend Cornelius Greenway, of Brooklyn, New York, is perhaps the greatest in the world, but he has not neglected other aspects of collecting. Even more diversified is the collection of Warren A. Reeder, of Hammond, Indiana. A noteworthy general collection emphasizing political leaders and formed on a very small outlay is that of my friend Barry Jones of Melbourne, whose encyclopaedic knowledge enabled him to become the biggest quiz-prize winner in Australian history.

*Buy letters with interesting or important contents.* Collectors and scholars like the dramatic, and routine documents seldom provide any historic fireworks. Avoid mere signatures cut from documents and pedestrian commissions and land grants. For the price of a cut signature of Washington, actually nothing more than tangible evidence that he knew how to write his name, you can buy three or four significant Revolutionary War letters by persons unknown to fame, yet whose penned thoughts are of historic value.

Generally a scholar is not interested in a routine document signed by Napoleon; but a letter of one of his marshals or generals, commenting on an important military event and available at half the price, would intrigue the chronicler of "the Man of Destiny." For a modest outlay, say five or ten dollars a month over a period of a few years, you can build a significant collection of theatrical letters by well-known stage personalities, such as Henry Irving and Joe Jefferson. Or you might prefer to assemble a collection of letters by noted French composers—perhaps Saint-Saëns and Massenet, whose autographs are inexpensive yet appealing.

*Never hesitate to pay a record price for an autograph.* If a letter or document is of surpassing historic or literary or scientific significance, and if you are confident that it possesses a unique quality, do not hesitate to pay an awesome price for it. Here is the advice of the great book and autograph collector Thomas J. Wise, who made a fortune as an amateur dealer: "I never buy a book or autograph at 'what it will fetch,' but at what I consider its value. And I judge its value by three things: (1) its intrinsic merit; (2) its rarity; and (3) its condition. For this reason I sometimes pay record prices—prices which other people shrink from; and on the other hand I sometimes refuse to buy a thing at the current price 'it will fetch.' In the long run I have found myself pretty well on the right side of the account."

*Study your own fields of collecting carefully.* Once you have mastered the facts about your own collecting interests, you will be in a position to recognize good values. With specialized knowledge you may occasionally acquire choice letters for a tenth or even a hundredth of their value. Naturally it requires intelligence and knowledge "to beat the dealer at his own game," but there is no greater thrill, and few dealers begrudge their clients a bargain.

*Buy only from reliable sources.* You will find that autographs turn up in unexpected places, but your main sources will be autograph dealers, rare book dealers, auction houses, and antique and curio dealers, with an occasional offering from a private collector or the owner of a family heirloom. All of these sources are important, but you should not rely on the judgment of one to whom autographs are nothing more than occasional or incidental commodities. The autograph dealer gains his livelihood from buying and selling manuscripts and letters, and may, in the course of a single year, handle fifty or one hundred thousand documents. He is familiar with all aspects of collecting. He needs only a glance at the ink to identify a Spring forgery of Washington or a Cosey forgery of Lincoln. A facsimile is obvious to him. He understands the rarity and value of what he sells and is not apt to charge too much or too little. If you place your trust in an autograph dealer, you will find that he can be of enormous aid to you in building your collection. Once he understands your aims as a collector, he will be glad to advise you and to assist you in locating fine items at fair prices. You need have no fear of forgeries or facsimiles when you buy from a recognized autograph dealer. Equally worthy of your confidence are the many rare book dealers who make a regular sideline of autographs and who are familiar with handwritings and values.

At auction, however, you must take the risks described in the terms of sale in the front of every catalog. There is no guarantee of authenticity, such as is furnished by autograph and rare book dealers. Everything is sold "as is," and the prices are generally top retail figures. Very few dealers buy for stock at auction, mainly bidding on behalf of their clients, so that the amounts fetched are often very high. Still, fine items at times go for startlingly low figures, so that it is not a good idea to generalize about auction prices, other than to say that they are unpredictable. If you are tempted to enter the lists and tilt with experts at auction, make a comparison between the prices fetched at auction and the prices in dealers' catalogs. You will then discover whether the game is worth the candle.

There are many rackets in the auction world, most of them not familiar to collectors and sometimes not to dealers. The collector who elects to bid without a dealer's help is almost certain to pay a high price for whatever he buys. In England, collectors rarely bid personally at auctions and this has led to an unfortunate practice known as the "K. O." or knockout, by which dealers gang up and buy material at the lowest price, afterwards holding a private auction among themselves, in which the proceeds above cost are divided equally.

The knockout has never prevailed in America, but an even worse racket exists among dishonest dealers. As all experienced collectors know, auction prices are uncertain. Beware, then, of the dealer who consistently forecasts auction prices with accuracy!

Recently an old-time New York auctioneer said to me: "When I was new in the rare book business, I attended a sale of manuscripts. Another dealer, bidding for a client on a ten per cent commission, was sitting with me and, since he was obliged to leave before the end of the sale, he left a bid with me for one lot, scribbling his instructions, 'Pay ninety dollars.' I had examined the lot before the sale and thought that five dollars would be a high price for it, and that is exactly the sum at which it was knocked down to me. When I took the material and the bill to the dealer, expecting his congratulations, he shouted, 'You idiot, now I get a fifty-cent commission instead of a nine dollar commission! I wanted you to bid that lot up to ninety, for I told my client it would fetch one hundred dollars. He would have thought it a bargain at ninety!' "

The dealers who give their clients ridiculously high estimates of value and then employ a confederate to bid them up to, or near, the estimate are, fortunately, few. But you may encounter another problem if you decide to submit your bids by mail direct to the auction house. You will receive on request a catalog which provides a printed form to make bidding easy. You merely fill in the number of the lot (or item), the first word of its description, and the top amount you are willing to pay. Presumably you will get the lot for a one-bid advance over the highest floor bid or next highest mail bid. But many auctioneers have a knack for "picking bids off the wall," and you will probably have to pay the full or nearly full amount of your bid. It is a well-known jest in the trade: "To get a good price, the expert auctioneer needs only two bidders, one of them alive." The fraudulent practice of picking bids off the wall is confined mainly to the United States and does not prevail among the leading auction houses of England.

Most antique and curio dealers are entirely honest, but autographs are not a specialty with them, and their knowledge may be very limited. Unless they sell with a guarantee of authenticity, it is wise to buy only inexpensive items from them.

*Avoid being stampeded into collecting currently popular autographs.* Not long ago I was chatting with an English dealer who was in quest of the fashionable authors of today [1960], such as Ernest Hemingway, James Joyce, William Faulkner, Dylan Thomas, and Robert Frost.

"I usually sell any of the popular favorites the moment their autographs come in," I commented drily.

"But these men are not 'popular' favorites," protested my visitor. "They are modern classics."

"Possibly," I answered. "But they have today the identical status which half a century or so ago was held by Richard LeGallienne, Charles Dudley Warner, George W. Cable, and Charles W. Stoddard. And which, when you and I were young, was occupied by those once-upon-a-time giants John Galsworthy, Joseph Hergesheimer, H. G. Wells, James Branch Cabell, and Arnold Bennett."

Whether or not my associate was convinced of the vacillation of literary taste and its effect upon autograph values, I cannot say. But I have been wary about venturing a positive opinion on my contemporaries ever since I read the list of Lord Byron in which he tried to anticipate posterity's evaluation of the poets of his age. Modestly, he omitted his own name from the list. At the top, he placed Rogers and Crabbe. In the center, Moore and Campbell. At the bottom, Wordsworth and Coleridge. The writers of no consequence—Shelley, Keats, and Blake—were omitted. Posterity has accepted Byron's critical evaluation, but reads it upside down!

If literary autographs are subject to fluctuation, historical material is no less changeable. At the turn of the present century, the popular hero was Napoleon. Rare items were pounced upon the moment they appeared. The presses creaked and groaned as they turned out volume after volume on the immortal Corsican. Today there is a new hero—Lincoln. To those in the grip of the Lincoln craze, it seems impossible that there can come a time when interest in him will subside.

Five decades ago, the demand for scientific and Western autographs was negligible. Fine letters of Edward Jenner and David Crockett found no buyers while collectors competed savagely for autographs of theatrical personalities. Daniel Boone documents were offered in lots, but high prices were paid for letters of Sir Henry Irving. Today a routine document signed by Boone would fetch more than one hundred fine letters of Irving!

A final example of the vagaries of historical autographs will suffice. After the first World War, the letters and documents of its outstanding figures—Foch, Hindenburg, Pershing, for example—were sought by collectors, and big prices were paid for fine examples. The second World

*From the collection of the Reverend Cornelius Greenway*

View of the Russian moon-strike, signed by Premier Khrushchev.

War introduced a new set of historical figures, and collectors lost interest in the earlier group. Today the favorites are Dwight D. Eisenhower and Sir Winston S. Churchill; and the once tremendous personalities of David Lloyd George and Clemenceau are nearly forgotten.

The moral? Follow your own bent and your own taste. Get as far away from collecting fads as you can. If you wish to gamble against future changes in taste, plunge in boldly with the courage of your convictions. It is an exciting and often rewarding game to speculate on who will some-day be President, or who will be regarded as a great author or composer in ten or twenty years.

There is always a renaissance of interest and a bull market in auto-graphs of any personality whose centennial or bicentennial is being cele-brated. Anticipate such an event by five or ten years and your collection is sure to increase markedly in value. In 1976 we will celebrate the bicen-tennial of the Declaration of Independence and there will be a great surge of interest in Washington and Jefferson and other leaders of the Revolutionary era.

If you collect autographs which interest you personally, your collec-tion will turn out to be a splendid investment. Certainly it will be a great cultural experience and will give you much happiness. And, if your col-lection is historically important, it will aid the cause of scholarship and human knowledge.

# 2 THE ART AND TECHNIQUE
## OF MAKING "FINDS"

PICTURE AN OLD SHOP—a bookshop, let us say—in a small town. Presided over by a sleepy proprietor, it is heaped high with old volumes, unsorted and in gay disorder. In a dark and dusty corner, redolent with crumbling morocco, is a pile of slender quartos and fragile pamphlets, among which you glimpse the yellow of old papers and the curled creaminess of ancient parchment. Seemingly, the old books and documents are of little consequence.

Almost certainly they *are* of little consequence. Seldom does a choice item come to a small dealer and, when it does, he is almost certain to recognize it—or he will, the moment you try to buy it—and ask five or ten times its value. Unless you have a great deal of leisure, say four-and-twenty hours in every day, you would do well to make your "journey to Serendip" in the big cities and the shops of the larger dealers.

A real find is, or should be, the supreme goal of every autograph collector, for the find is to the avid collector as the knockout is to the prize-fighter, the bull's-eye to the archer, and the grand slam to the bridge enthusiast. To pretend otherwise is to have no pulse for the chase.

There was once, I am told, a soulless dealer who deliberately placed sleepers in his catalogs. When any collector ordered them, he removed him at once from his mailing list. "I absolutely refuse," he cried, "to send my catalogs to those who are looking only for bargains."

We are all of us searching for bargains!

Most dealers welcome the collector who is astute and alert, with a keen eye for finds. I am fully in accord with my friend Lou Cohen, of Argosy Book Shops. When a scholar, rummaging through Lou's many floors of choice books, discovered at fifteen dollars a unique vellum copy of Junius' *Letters* worth several thousands, he bought it, and announced the fact to Lou. Thereupon Lou hung a colorful banner in front of his shop, proclaiming the discovery of a magnificent find on his shelves and urging other collectors to try their luck.

Whoever buys a sleeper from me has my permission to blow trumpets and beat drums to celebrate my error and his triumph!

That sleepers have turned up by pure chance in unexpected places is not to be denied. A box of paving tiles bought in a rummage sale in Kent contained the entire Lord Fairfax correspondence. The accidental collapse of a ceiling in Lincoln's Inn revealed the Thurloe papers, long sought by historians. The letters of Madame Roland were discovered in a heap of decaying vegetables. There is a well-authenticated story of the old gentleman who, losing patience with a long-stuck cabinet, fiercely kicked it open. Inside was a collection of deeds bearing the signatures of Richard III and other notables.

Rare autographs have been discovered even in bird's nests. A canon at an English cathedral noticed one day that the jackdaws flying over his garden carried in their beaks what appeared to be rolls of paper. One such roll was dropped at his feet and the canon, to his astonishment, found that it was a valuable Anglo-Saxon manuscript. Other choice documents were traced to the jackdaw's nest. Investigation showed that the bird was pilfering rarities through the window of a long-sealed muniment room in the cathedral.

Recently a cache of letters from James Madison to Noah Webster turned up in a secret compartment of a Colonial bureau purchased by a curio collector in Ogunquit, Maine. The letters, which I obtained from the lucky owner, were far more valuable than the bureau!

One of the most spectacular sleepers of modern times was discovered by Paul Appel, a book dealer of Long Island, who gambled twice the amount offered by another dealer for a pile of cartons in a Mount Vernon storage house.

"This was my great find, my 'Tamerlane,'" Appel told me. "I was intrigued by a pair of dueling pistols and a first edition of *Huckleberry Finn,* but I hoped there would be something more in this mass of material to justify the price I paid. The very last carton I opened was crammed with Mark Twain letters—140 of them—together with letters to Mark Twain from his brother Orion and from his mother. I knew at once that I had made a great discovery. My judgment was confirmed when the collection finally went to the University of California for twenty thousand dollars!"

Pure luck, all of these discoveries, and never to be duplicated. I certainly do not recommend that you knock down the plaster of your ceiling or ferret through piles of old vegetables or climb trees to reconnoitre the nests of rooks and jackdaws. No; if you count upon luck to make your finds, you may live to be as old as Methuselah and never light upon anything rarer than a cut signature of Longfellow.

In his delightful *Romance of Book Collecting*, J. H. Slater affirms that finds "must necessarily be made by the rarest of accidents." "Bargains, real bargains!" observed Andrew Lang in a letter of advice to a young American collector, "are so rare that you may hunt for a lifetime and never meet one." And Eugene Field, in gossiping enviously of a friend who had picked up a rarity on a twenty-five cent shelf, exclaimed, "Some men have a genius for that kind of luck."

Lay it not to serendipity, friends Slater, Lang, and Field! Discovering sleepers is a science—an exact science—and the prize falls to the knowledgeable, the swift, and the decisive! Consider the consistent "good fortune" of such great huntsmen as Dr. A. S. W. Rosenbach, to whom sleepers came with almost unbelievable frequency. What set the Doctor apart from his fellows? Courage, resourcefulness, speed, alertness—yes, all of those! But most important, technique! Dr. R. was a master in the art and technique of making finds. Like the clever fisherman whose creel is always full, Rosenbach landed the big ones in the same pools where others fished in vain.

Let's start with the assumption that you are interested in looking for "finds" and that you have already ransacked the old trunk in your attic and found nothing but three receipted coal bills and a buffalo robe packed in mothballs.

Where do you go from here?

The first thing you need is knowledge—the factual background which will enable you to recognize a sleeper when you see it cataloged or when you hold it in your hands.

*Study books of facsimiles and learn to recognize as many famous handwritings as possible.* Scores of sleepers remain undiscovered simply because they have no signature. Unsigned poems and manuscripts and annotated volumes are often met with. A collector browsing among the bookstalls along Charing Cross picked up a little volume of classical dramas. It bore copious marginal notes in a sloppy handwriting. The collector recognized Shelley's rugged scrawl and bought for a sixpence what was worth several hundred pounds.

A scout[1] once offered me an early New England document signed by Thomas Welde. "I bought it at an auction," he explained.

___

[1] A "scout" is a part-time or full-time dealer who makes his living by searching out

"What do you want for it?"

"Fifty dollars," replied the scout, naming what he believed to be the highest price he could possibly get.

I knew that Welde was one of the authors of the famous *Bay Psalm Book*, the first volume printed in the English-American colonies. It was published in 1640, the very date on this old legal document. The body of the document was not written by Welde, but the handwriting struck me as vaguely familiar.

No sooner was the purchase completed than I checked the script against a facsimile of John Eliot. I discovered that I owned a document entirely in the hand of the famous Apostle to the Indians. Eliot was the translator into Natick of the *Indian Bible*, the first Bible to be printed in North America. He was also, with Richard Mather, one of the three authors of the *Bay Psalm Book*. I promptly sold this rare autograph document for the very reasonable price of $750.

Signature of John Eliot.

On another occasion I fared better. This time it was my wife, Doris, who made the initial discovery. In the window of Charles Hollander's Hobby House only a few blocks from our shop she spotted an unsigned quarto document dated from Greenville, Ohio, in 1795, and priced at $1.50. Doris knew that William Henry Harrison had been at Greenville as aide-de-camp to Anthony Wayne during the Indian campaign which resulted in the opening of the Old Northwest, and she suspected that this document might be in the handwriting of the future President.

It had been in the window, she learned, for several weeks, and thousands of people had looked at it as they passed.

"I have twelve others similar," admitted Hollander, "and you can have the entire group of thirteen for twelve dollars. I had a stroke of luck. One of my customers found them in an old trunk in New Jersey, and I swapped a few old newspapers for them."

Later that afternoon Doris beamed as she handed me the small bundle of documents. "What do you think of *these*?" she asked.

"Do you know what they are?"

"Yes, they're in Harrison's handwriting, aren't they?"

"Well, almost," I said. "These are Anthony Wayne's original orders to his troops, entirely in his handwriting, all dated during his famous expedition against the Indians."

Within a few days I had sold the thirteen documents at the modest

material which he sells to collectors or dealers. If he visits private homes in quest of autographs, he is known as a "bell ringer" (in England, a "knocker"). The scout may carry his entire stock in a valise, and his office is usually his home or apartment.

*From the collection of Lucius S. Ruder*

A manuscript general order written by Anthony Wayne.

price of $1,450, less than the amount I would have been willing to pay for them!

*Of great importance is the ability to distinguish authentic handwriting from facsimiles.* While you often see facsimiles put forward as originals, it is also true that originals are occasionally mistaken for worthless reproductions or copies. Several years ago an elderly scout entered my office one morning with a small bundle of documents under his arm. "I think these will interest you," he said, handing the collection to me.

It was a group of letters written by and to Horace Mann, the noted educator. Included were several unsigned manuscript fragments.

Fanning with my thumb through the documents, I realized that the collection represented the remnant of the personal papers of Horace Mann. There were no letters of really important people.

"And where are the letters of Hawthorne, Emerson, and Thoreau?" I asked. Startled at my question, and momentarily at a loss for a reply, the old scout finally told me that he had purchased the family papers of Horace Mann from a descendant. He paid only a small sum for them, and subsequently took them to two of America's greatest libraries. The manuscript librarians had both gone carefully over the collection, buying all the Hawthorne and Thoreau material, as well as other literary items, and leaving only this small group.

We quickly settled upon $450 as a fair price.

Among the papers was a three-page fragment, a portion of which had been replaced and was labeled, "facsimile." On looking closely at the writing, I saw that it was original, and in the hand of Thoreau. As I began reading the manuscript, my mind traveled back a quarter of a century to my high school days. I recalled my teacher of American literature saying, "I should like to shake the hand of any student who can read that tiresome book, *Walden*, from cover to cover." A week later I shook his hand. I had discovered that he and I were marching to different drums. I never suspected, however, that I would derive financial as well as spiritual profit from my reading of *Walden*. A quick check confirmed my belief that the fragment was a portion of the original draft, containing several unpublished passages. The importance of the find may be judged from the fact that, although the Huntington Library owns a part of the manuscript of *Walden*, very few other fragments are known to exist. I sold these precious pages for many times their weight in gold. They are now in the C. Waller Barrett Collection at the University of Virginia.

Here is what happened when I failed to follow my own advice. I had acquired a large collection of autographs, mostly unimportant, and among them were two letters of Benedict Arnold dated from Ticonderoga in 1775, written on opposite sides of a folio sheet. The letters were labeled "copy" at the top and seemed to be in a clerical hand. They were enclosed in a fifty-year-old folder, on which was written, "Copies of letters by Benedict Arnold." Since the collection in which I found them was undistinguished—certainly not likely to contain any rarities—I failed to look at the letters with my customary thoroughness and priced them as early clerical copies.

A few days later a dealer was browsing through my files and ran across the Arnold letters. "These seem to be in Arnold's hand," he said.

"The handwriting looks like Arnold's," I agreed. "But you can see that they are labeled as copies."

Requesting that I bring him a facsimile of Arnold's writing, the dealer made a comparison. There was a striking similarity.

"It's your discovery," I said. "You can have the Arnold letters for fifteen dollars, the price marked on them."

Still uncertain, the dealer turned them down. That night I checked the letters carefully and confirmed beyond doubt that they were Arnold's own drafts of two very important letters. I sold them for $250. They would be worth two or three times that much today.

*Learn as much as possible about your particular fields of interest.* If your fund of knowledge exceeds the dealer's, you will be in an admirable position to pick up sleepers. Concentrate on minute details and tuck away in your memory as many little knickknacks of information as possible. If you collect books from the libraries of Presidents, you should know that Jefferson identified his books by printing the initial *T* in front of the book signature letter *I* [J], and placing the letter *J* or *I* after the book signature letter *T*.

You should learn, for instance, that a letter of Attorney General James Speed merely signed by him may be in the hand of his clerk, Walt Whitman. Some of Washington's letters were written by his aide-de-camp, Alexander Hamilton. Normally a letter merely signed by Auguste Rodin, the French sculptor, would not be so desirable as a full handwritten letter, but there are exceptions when the body of the letter was penned by his secretary, Rainer Maria Rilke, the German poet. It is useful to know that Meriwether Lewis, the explorer, was Jefferson's private secretary, and that Jonathan Swift was the secretary of Sir William Temple.

It will help you, also, if you know a little about "lost" manuscripts. There is still an unlocated manuscript of Key's "The Star-Spangled Banner." It is worth about ten thousand dollars! Even a century of searching has not dimmed the hope that a manuscript copy of Lord Byron's unpublished *Autobiography*, the original of which was burned after his death, may turn up and be the literary find of our generation.

If your specialty is American literary autographs, you should be familiar with the fact that Herman Melville's library was sold soon after his death to a dealer who quickly dispersed it. As Melville was then almost forgotten, the books went forth anonymously, many without his signature, and today may be recognized only by the marginal notations in his hand. Melville's annotated copy of Thomas Beale's *Natural History of the Sperm Whale* was sold at auction in 1945 for $1,050. You can imagine the value of the unidentified volumes from his library, many of which await the keen eye of the informed searcher for sleepers.

If you are interested in Melville, you should know the names of the vessels on which he served, and keep a sharp eye out for ship's papers or other documents concerning them. It was from New Bedford in 1841 that the whaler *Acushnet* sailed, later to be transformed into a cosmic myth by the pen of seaman Herman Melville.

In going through the autograph files of a New York dealer, my wife ran across an unsigned fragment of about fifteen or twenty lines in Washington's handwriting, apparently cut from a letter. It was priced at fifty dollars, rather high for an unsigned and disconnected fragment.

"It is about four by eight inches," Doris explained, "and is written on both sides of the sheet."

"It is too expensive," I commented. Then, as an afterthought, I added: "Does it by any chance have the words 'Washington's handwriting' written diagonally in the left margin, signed 'J. S.' or 'Jared Sparks'?"

"Why, yes," answered my wife, puzzled. "How did you know?"

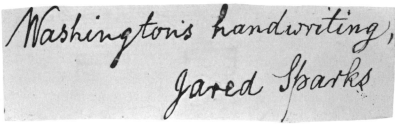

Jared Sparks's authentication of a Washington document.

"It is a part of Washington's undelivered first inaugural. Washington prepared it, then changed his mind and made an entirely different speech. In the 1830's the historian Jared Sparks cut the manuscript up and distributed the pieces to autograph collectors. It is unpublished, and much of it has never been recovered. By all means, buy it."

The value of the discovery was enhanced by the historical importance of the fragment, an unrecorded portion relating to the Constitution. It was sold to a collector for $750.

*When searching for finds, your best prospects are the big dealers.* Not long after I started in business, I called on most of the important rare book and autograph dealers in New York. I scarcely expected to find much material which I could handle at a profit and had little expectation of discovering any sleepers. I did not know then that the smaller dealer tends to overprice any really fine items, whereas the big dealer, who sees and handles rarities constantly, is not awed by them. Because of the huge volume of material which passes through his hands he frequently prices letters and documents without detailed research. He may overlook the very point which gives a document unique value. The small dealer, on the other hand, often "researches his material to death" before he offers it for sale. Nothing is left for the purchaser to discover.

At one of New York's largest dealers in rare books and manuscripts I discovered a document signed by Henry Hamilton, identified as "Governor of Bermuda" in a penciled note at the top of the page. The price was seventy-five cents and the dealer shook his head when I selected it, asking: "What on earth are you going to do with this junky autograph?"

I had recognized the writing of the famous "Hair Buyer," the notorious British officer who was known as a purchaser of scalps. Dated from Detroit during the Indian Wars, the document referred to payments, possibly for scalps. I turned it over that afternoon to another dealer at the reasonable price of seventy-five dollars.

For six weeks I canvassed the shops of New York's largest dealers. It was the most profitable period of my life. To list all the finds I made would require a chapter by itself. From a visit to the distinguished dealer, John Fleming, Rosenbach's successor, I learned the truth of what my friend Dr. Frank Siebert, collector of Indian autographs, has often told me: "The best buys I ever made were from Dr. Rosenbach!"

*Learn to "sharpshoot" catalogs!* The catalogs which reach my desk daily are a perennial source of finds. They receive top priority. One prominent dealer listed for fifty cents a letter about "the Old State House." Suspecting that it related to Independence Hall, I bought it. My surmise was correct, and I sold it for one hundred dollars. A document of James O'Hara, founder of Pittsburgh, was offered by an expert at one dollar and cataloged three times before I ordered it. A few months later, it fetched eighty-five dollars when I put it up for sale at auction.

*Finally, read every auction catalog you receive with great care.* Although auction prices are apt to be higher than those of the average dealer,

A rare Aztec manuscript on maguey paper. About 1590.

the catalogs are turned out under great pressure, often hurriedly prepared, and errors are frequent. Such mistakes may benefit the alert collector. In the spring of 1954 I received an English auction catalog listing some books and manuscripts from the library of the Earl of Derby. While casually reading it, I ran across the following description:

> Mexican Indians. Pictorial Native Manuscript on rough native cloth containing 32 crude coloured drawings of Mexican Indians with descriptions in a Mexican Indian dialect, folio, unbound, Mexico, circa 1760–1800.

This was extremely interesting. The date was relatively late for the use of "native cloth," since Spanish paper was readily available. I suspected that what the cataloger termed "rough native cloth" was actually very early paper made from the maguey plant. If so, the manuscript might be of Aztec origin, and the "Mexican Indian dialect" might be Nahuatl, perhaps a translation into Spanish characters of the pictographs in the document. I recalled a similar manuscript which was once on display in the New York Public Library. I dashed off a letter to my London agent, requesting a detailed report. His reply convinced me that the cataloger had misdated the document by at least two centuries. For the first time in twenty years, an original, priceless Aztec codex was on the auction block!

I cabled the highest bid which my exchequer could stand and great was my delight when I acquired the manuscript for a paltry forty-six pounds. Finally it reached me, a magnificent, superbly preserved Aztec codex, the finest of its type in existence. The delicate, pastel colors of the Indian artist portrayed various figures, one of them a knight in armor kneeling before a priest—perhaps Cortez himself! There were scenes of mountains and animals and birds and native Indians. The manuscript was a pictorial record of the Indian domains from the lands of the panther and eagle to the cultivated fields of the Toluca valley.

That afternoon a Boston dealer dropped in to see me.

"I just bought this original Aztec manuscript for $120," I told him. "You may have it for only $620. It's worth much more."

The Boston dealer shook his head, amused at my proposition.

Later he was present when my manuscript—Codex Techialoyan W—magnificently bound and expertly translated—was sold at the Parke-Bernet Galleries for $5,500 to a California dealer!

As you read these lines, I venture to say that there are, within *your* easy reach, scores of as-yet-undiscovered finds. Remember that in the eternal battle of wits between buyer and seller, the autograph collector with knowledge and courage must inevitably triumph.

# 3 THE CASE
## OF THE PURLOINED LETTERS

He was a massive young man with a shock of dark hair and a swarthy face. Among the documents which he handed to me was a magnificent letter in which Benjamin Franklin urged a spelling reform in our language. There was a series of letters from Thomas Jefferson to James Monroe, intimate glimpses into the mind and ideals of the author of the Declaration of Independence.

Swiveling my chair to face the sunlight I looked quickly at the old papers for any traces of a library or institutional stamp. There were none, and no signs of erasures.

"Would you mind telling me where these letters came from?" I casually asked the young man, whom my secretary had introduced as Martin R. Strich.

"They are the property of a gentleman who inherited them ten years ago. At the time he had little interest in them, and placed them in a safe deposit box. Recently he suffered financial reverses. He wants me to dispose of the old letters, and has promised me a percentage. I might add that these letters are only a very small part of the collection."

As he spoke, I was re-reading the Franklin letter. Addressed to Noah Webster, it was a unique fragment of Americana!

"The Jefferson letters are long and detailed," I explained, "and will need further study. But I'll buy the Franklin right now. I can give you one thousand dollars cash for it."

Strich stared at me, bewildered. My offer had paralyzed him; but I did not know whether it struck him as absurdly high or absurdly low. It was, in fact, a high offer, for I had sold many letters of Franklin for five hundred dollars or less.

Finally Strich whispered: "I'll have to consult my principal. Is it okay if I use your phone?

"Yes, yes!" I heard him say. "I'm here in Mr. Hamilton's office right now. Yes, I guess so. Well, he tells me that he has to read the Jeffersons carefully before he can make an offer. Oh, I see. He has made an offer of one thousand for the Franklin letter. Yes, that's cash. Well, I don't know whether we could or not. I think it's a fair offer, but it's up to you. Yes. Okay, then, I'll do that. Goodbye."

Strich turned to me: "He accepts your offer, but he wants a certified check. He also said you may keep the Jefferson papers overnight."

It was too late in the afternoon to get a certified check, so Strich contented himself with a phone call to my bank, verifying the fact that the check could be cashed in the morning.

That night I read the Jefferson letters. They were important for their political observations, and I was eager to buy them, but I had a vague feeling of uneasiness. Even now I am not sure how or why my suspicions were aroused. I asked my wife to check in the New York Public Library for a record of their previous ownership.

At eleven o'clock the next morning, Strich walked into my office. No word had come from Doris and, laboring under the philosophic error that "no news is good news," I made an offer of $864 for the letters of Jefferson. Strich accepted.

"What would this be worth to you?" He held out a clerical copy of a letter from John Jay to James Monroe.

"About two dollars," I answered, reaching for it.

Suddenly Strich pulled the letter away and stuffed it in his coat pocket. "It has the owner's name on it," he said, "and I am pledged to keep his identity confidential."

Explaining that he was leaving on vacation, and that he would come back in a few weeks with more Franklin letters, Strich left me, heading for the bank. A few minutes later my banker called, verified Strich's identity, and cashed my two checks, which totaled $1,864.

At noon my wife met me for lunch. She had learned nothing, as yet, about the ownership of the letters. "Why not telephone the Library of Congress?" I suggested.

"Are you sitting down?" It was the manuscript librarian, David C. Mearns, on the phone. "Well, our records show that the letters you describe are the property of the New York Public Library."

I had invested $1,864 in stolen letters!

Events moved fast. I called the library first, telling them of the theft. It required an hour for them to find and check the penciled slips on which was recorded their only evidence of ownership of these historic documents. Then I phoned my collection agent, Eddie O'Rourke. At 1:30 P.M. Eddie visited the Park Avenue address given us by Strich. He learned that although Strich lived in the apartment he was not at home. By 2:30 P.M. I was in the library with a photostatic copy of the check endorsements. It compared exactly with Strich's handwriting in the visitor's book of the library. The manuscript librarian, Edward Morrison, nervously explained that Strich had visited the manuscript room on several occasions. I turned the stolen documents over to him.

Morrison was so shaken that he found it hard to talk. "Relax," I said, "you aren't responsible. Besides, I'm the one who's lost the money!"

At 3:30 P.M. a detective arrived, and the library security officer, John McKearnin, entered the case. After a briefing, the detective posted himself in front of Strich's apartment.

When the detective went off duty at 6:00 P.M., McKearnin voluntarily took his place, watching Strich's apartment from a parked car. At 8:00 P.M. Eddie and I relieved McKearnin, using an automobile for our observation post. The doorman told us that Strich had a rifle in his room and, since none of us was armed, we decided to call in the police rather than to attempt the arrest without help.

At 9:00 P.M., McKearnin again resumed his watch, determined to stay until midnight if necessary, for we knew that Strich would soon leave on vacation.

Shortly after Eddie and I left, we got a phone call from McKearnin, saying that the police had just arrested Strich.

At the police station, I was kept out of Strich's sight and identified him through a small aperture in the wall. He was held without charge awaiting the arrival of the detective assigned to the case.

For a while Strich laughed and joked, chatting informally with the arresting officers while I waited in an adjoining room with Eddie and McKearnin. There the officers joined us, leaving Strich alone. Suddenly, at about 11:00 P.M., we heard gasping and outcries. Strich was in the throes of what seemed to be an epileptic fit. He writhed on the floor, foaming at the mouth and making weird noises.

From Bellevue an ambulance arrived and took Strich away.

Three minutes later over the police radio came the news that an ambulance had crashed into a truck. The police plotted the probable course of the vehicle carrying Strich. It was, they affirmed, the same ambulance.

"Are you positive of your identification," asked one of the officers. "We don't want to be sued for false arrest, and this man lives in a swanky apartment on Park Avenue. If he dies while under detention we might be in serious trouble."

"I'll identify him dead or alive," I said.

The police were relieved when we learned that it was a different ambulance which had crashed. Strich was safe in the hospital, under a sedative.

When the detective arrived at 1:00 A.M., he drove to the hospital and picked up Strich, now fully recovered from his attack. He confessed at once.

The first words Strich said to me were, "I'm sorry, Mr. Hamilton. I needed money desperately."

To the detective, McKearnin, O'Rourke, and myself he unfolded the story of one of the most incredible library thefts in history.

"Several weeks ago," Strich began, "I was in the library. I got to chatting with a man I never saw before and have never seen since. 'Do you know,' he told me, 'it would be easy to steal anything out of this library.'

"That remark set me to thinking. I needed money and I thought this was a good way to get it. I told the library authorities that I was a writer and was doing an article on the library. They opened all doors to me.

"The first autographs I stole—well, it took me several days to work up my nerve. Finally I asked for a file and the attendant brought it to me. I suppose I should have concealed the autographs I stole in my coat, but I was so unnerved that I scarcely knew what I was doing. I just stuffed them in a folder I was carrying. I was really terrified. I had never stolen anything before. When I left, the guard glanced into the folder and waved me on. The autographs I took on that day I sold to another dealer.

"A few days later I went back. This time I took the Jefferson and Franklin letters."

"How did you know that Franklin's autograph was so valuable?" I asked him.

"I didn't. As a matter of fact, the attendant brought the Franklin file to me by mistake. Since I had the file, I thought I might as well take the letter out of it."

"Did you know that you left the address-leaf of the Franklin letter in the file?" I said. "And did you know that the address-leaf had a library stamp on it?"

"No; I didn't know that. I wouldn't have taken the letter if I knew there was a library marking on it. I took only the unmarked letters. I guess I didn't see the markings on the other part of the Franklin letter because I was so nervous. I thought the address-leaf, as you call it, was some other document. It wasn't signed so I didn't take it."

"Would you have stolen any documents if they had been marked with a library stamp?" I asked him.

"No, I wouldn't. I know better than that. The document I grabbed away from you had a library stamp on the back. I saw it just as I started to hand it to you and it gave me an awful fright."

"Where is that document now?" asked McKearnin.

"I crumpled it up and threw it in a trash disposal box as soon as I got out on the street. I was afraid to keep it for fear it would get me into trouble."

"Just one last question," I said. "Who was it you telephoned when you were in my office?"

"Oh, that! Well, I was so startled by your high offer that I needed time to think. So I called my own number, knowing there wasn't anyone at home. I was talking to myself."

It was 3:00 in the morning by the time Eddie and I left the police station. I still had a foreboding that the case was not closed.

The library security officer, John McKearnin, whose alertness and determination led to Strich's capture, was reprimanded by the library officials for not leaving the matter to the police! He resigned several months later.

The rare-manuscript librarian, Edward Morrison, a gentle old man who was entirely innocent, took the thefts very much to heart. A few weeks later, he shot and killed himself with a revolver.

As for Strich, he pleaded guilty and received a suspended sentence. Most of my money was later returned to me.

Thefts of autographs are nothing new. Even the Appian Way, I imagine, had its manuscript heisters, for autographs were treasured by the ancient Romans. But not until the French Revolution did thieving begin on a massive scale. The archives of the French government were seized by the revolutionists and used for wrapping fish and for other purposes less refined.

The sudden appearance of so many choice documents signed by early kings of France started a renaissance of autograph collecting. Later, as Napoleon's armies swept across Europe, the pillaging continued. The Vatican archives were borne away by the French soldiers. Oxcarts, creaking overland, carried whole loads of papal bulls and ecclesiastical documents to France. Today more ancient papal documents turn up in France than in Italy!

Napoleon himself had a passion for old letters and treasured a few rare autographs in his personal collection. The great Spanish archives at Simancas, begun by Charles V and continued by Philip II, were looted by Napoleon's orders when the French took Simancas in 1809. Marshal Kellerman supervised the removal of the historical letters to the imperial library in Paris. In two years he dispatched to France more than two hundred wagon-loads, containing 7,861 bundles of valuable documents dating from the fourteenth to the eighteenth centuries. When the French retreated from Simancas in 1811, peasant marauders fell upon the archives and seized many of the remaining treasures. After the fall of Napoleon the Spanish ambassador at Paris demanded the return of the stolen manuscripts; but Louis XVIII, although he violently abhorred Napoleon's politics, approved his taste as a connoisseur of autographs, and returned only the less important papers.

The Nazi armies, as the shadow of the swastika fell over Europe, seized many rare manuscripts and documents. Much of this loot will never be recovered, and some was destroyed in the subsequent allied bombing of Germany.

But our American officials have, over the years, far surpassed the manuscript destruction of the Nazis!

Sometimes whole archives have disappeared, to reappear mysteriously on the autograph market. Such are the hundreds of Sangamon County legal briefs bearing Lincoln's signature and the Civil War files of the Adjutant General's office—thousands of orders written by Lincoln as President! Some years ago the government pitched out as wastepaper a huge file of Presidential documents, official authorizations to affix the government seal, and these were salvaged by an alert connoisseur. Today they are found in hundreds of private collections. Among them is Lincoln's signed authorization to affix the United States seal to the Emancipation Proclamation!

Nearly three decades ago the noted dealer, Walter R. Benjamin, wrote: "Some fifty years ago a man in Harrisburg made frequent trips to New York carrying a large carpet bag bulging with old state papers. These he sold to C. D. Burns, Simon Gratz, Dr. T. A. Emmett, and other collectors. The files of North Carolina were treated in the same way; also the Virginia files at Richmond, and those of Sangamon County, Ill. Officials and others in whose custody these papers rested did not consider them of any importance—nor that they were doing wrong in getting rid of them. The files at Albany—and of Charleston, S. C.—were also ransacked."

In New York, there were tons of documents sent to the paper mills by officials who decreed that the old custom house files must be discarded. Energetic dealers and collectors rescued many historical treasures. In Philadelphia, as recently as the 1930's, more than three tons of documents were ruthlessly pulped as wastepaper. These documents had been

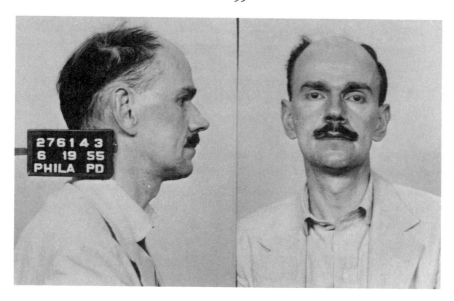

Carl M. Williams. Expert on early American silver and furniture, Williams is the author of a volume on early silversmiths of New Jersey. Although arrested several times on various charges, he was never convicted until he confessed to the theft of Rebecca Gratz's will from the basement of the Philadelphia City Hall.

stored in the basement of the old courthouse and were tossed out with little regard to their importance.

Better known, perhaps, is the story of Carl M. Williams who, for a period of more than twenty years, off and on, peddled "questionable" autographs to unsuspecting dealers in New York, New Jersey, and Pennsylvania. Although arrested several times on charges varying from fraudulent conversion to the illegal altering of markings on historic American silver, Williams was never convicted until 1959, when I identified the will of Rebecca Gratz, subsequently discovered to be the property of the Philadelphia City Hall, as a document which he had sold to me. After a long pursuit, he was captured and sentenced to two and one-half to five years imprisonment in Eastern State Penitentiary. Action was taken to protect the Philadelphia City Hall Archives from further looting. Valuable documents which had been rotting in cardboard cartons in the basement were properly filed and restrictions placed upon their use.

When will this orgy of destruction and thievery end?

It will end when librarians, historians, archivists, and all those charged with the responsibility of preserving public records take the proper steps to prevent theft and ill-advised pulping and burning of records.

*The archivist or librarian who fails to mark valuable papers with an indelible stamp is inviting, even encouraging, thieves to help themselves to his files!*

In addition to marking his valuable documents, every archivist should exercise care in screening visitors or users of important autographs and rare books. Obviously, it is impossible to prevent thefts. Yet who but a very rash thief would wish to steal marked documents?

*No official papers of any kind, whether the property of local, state, or federal government, should be pulped or burned without the written approval of a qualified historian.* Even on the local level, town and county records should be saved and cared for unless pulping is authorized by the county historian or archivist.

So frequent have been the thefts and the wholesale discarding of obsolete documents that it is no longer possible to distinguish what has been discarded from what has been stolen or given away!

# 4 FORGERIES—
## AND HOW TO UNMASK THEM

"WHAT'LL YOU HAVE?" asked the little man at the bar, taking from his coat pocket a fountain pen loaded with Waterman's brown ink. "Napoleon's signature? How's this one? The Emperor himself couldn't tell this from his own scrawl. Isn't that worth a drink, my friend? No? Well, just buy me a shot and I guarantee to deliver a satisfactory product—Lincoln, Washington, Franklin—you name it, I'll write it!"

Like a poet who trades ballads for beer, the genial Joseph Cosey, most notorious forger of modern times, was always ready to swap a forgery for a drink. Sometimes he sold his fabrications for cash, and his imposing list of victims includes the Library of Congress and the New York Public Library.

Cosey was only one of an ignoble line of forgers who have for two centuries bedevilled the scholarly world. The Italian, Tobia Nicotra, specialized in composers, pouring out spurious Mozarts and Handels; "Antique" Smith, expert in Robert Burns, created forgeries which are often found in some of the world's great libraries; "Major" Byron was adroit in fabricating Keats, Shelley, and his alleged father, Lord Byron; Robert Spring turned out "Washingtons" which still plague the unwary; and the specialty of Charles Weisberg was Lincoln.

Then there was William Henry Ireland, a seventeen-year-old whose Shakespeare forgeries (originally devised to humor his aging father, an admirer of the bard) beguiled James Boswell into an unaccustomed reverence as he knelt before the manuscripts of "Hamlet" and "Lear," on which the ink was scarcely dry. Young Ireland might have gone on for years fooling the academic world—his forgeries were placed on exhibition by the British Museum—had he not essayed "an original and hitherto

Shakespeare's signature, forged by William Henry Ireland.

unknown" drama of Shakespeare. *Vortigern* was produced from Ireland's manuscript at Drury Lane Theatre, and although it starred John Philip Kemble, the crowd hissed and booed, and its failure exposed Ireland's other impostures. When Kemble learned that Ireland was a forger, he exclaimed angrily: "Damn the fellow! I believe his face is a forgery!"

There was Vrain Lucas, the Frenchman, who gave a classical touch to his forgeries by creating letters of Julius Caesar, Cleopatra, and Alexander the Great—all penned in modern French.

Not one of these forgers was able to elude detection. Each refused to accept the fact that *no handwriting can be imitated without ultimate exposure,* for somewhere in every fabrication there is a clue to its real nature.

Of all relics associated with great men and women, very few are susceptible of positive identification. An autograph is, in a sense, self-proving. Other relics are easy to fabricate. Of hats "worn by Napoleon" there are enough to equip a regiment. The six-shooters allegedly owned by Jesse James would fill an arsenal. Of "Lincoln's pens," the abundance would suffice to outfit a stationer's. I once saw in an auction catalog an item described as "a lock of hair from the head of Charles the Bald."

Most forgeries are as conspicuous as a purple cow. They have a beggarly air about them. They come cringing on scraps of paper, blurred and torn, and sometimes crudely stained with coffee. Generally offered at bargain prices, they seem aware of their lack of pedigree. "A nice old gentleman came to see me," is the familiar story, "and he offered me this Lincoln legal document for only ten dollars." Whereupon we are treated to the sight of a "Lincoln" brief by Joseph Cosey.

"A man wrote to me," explained a book dealer, one of Weisberg's victims, "saying that he had discovered a cache of Lincoln endorsements on Civil War letters. I told him to send the Lincolns on to me. He offered them for a few dollars each—much too cheap to pass up. I bought the lot."

"What happened then?" I asked.

"Well, almost immediately I got another letter from the man, and he said he had an even bigger supply of Lincolns, and would I like to buy a couple of hundred dollars worth. The price was so attractive that I told him, 'Yes, send the whole bunch.'"

"Why," I inquired, "didn't you go to an autograph dealer and make sure that you weren't buying fakes?"

"I was afraid to let anyone else in on it. It seemed like such a good thing, and the price was so cheap; I figured I would make a small fortune

The author examining a rare document on the Alabama Claims.

on the deal, provided I kept the source to myself. After I had laid in a big supply, I offered a couple in one of my book catalogs. An autograph dealer hurried in to my shop. He took one look and said, 'Oh! oh! These are fakes.' Then I showed him the whole group, and the dealer pronounced them all forgeries."

It was Weisberg's usual approach—and Cosey's, also—to offer at low prices rare documents "just discovered in an attic trunk."

Nicknamed "the Baron" because he had a dapper goatee, Weisberg was an outstanding student at the University of Pennsylvania. He made his mark on the world, but not in the way which his professors predicted! Discovering that he had a facility for "creating" historical documents, "the Baron" launched enthusiastically into a career which was to disrupt American historical scholarship and net Weisberg several prison terms, during the last of which he died at Lewisburg on May 4, 1945.

A high school classmate recalls: "I used to see him stop on the street and dust a letter or document to give it the appearance of age. He composed a diary of an imaginary silversmith, one Elfreth, who worked in early Philadelphia. It was so perfectly contrived that any craftsman could make silverware after reading it!"

It is said that the University of Pittsburgh bought many Stephen Collins Foster forgeries by Weisberg, but I was unable to confirm this, as my inquiry to the librarian was not answered. Weisberg's "original surveys" of Mount Vernon were skillfully drawn. Examples found their way into the Morgan Library and the Library of Congress. Constantly evading the law, Weisberg wrote, on September 10, 1940, to Samuel Moyerman, a Philadelphia collector who threatened to expose him: "Anytime you feel like 'taking a swat' at me, I am ready; ready with 225 lbs. of pretty desperate strength, seasoned for five years in as muscle-wracking an existence as a man ever led. I would not only never back away from a worn-out crow like yourself, but never for that matter from anybody. My career has taught me how to fight . . . . I have never had one business deal with you and you have never been provided with one active, direct excuse to charge me either with forgery or with hypothecation: the two themes which seem to occupy your castigations."

Weisberg's specialty was tacking a Lincoln endorsement or notation on an authentic letter addressed to Lincoln. But neither Weisberg nor Cosey was aware of Lincoln's peculiar custom of writing his comments or instructions directly under the clerical docket on the verso of a document. Both forgers had an eye for the dramatic, creating Lincoln autographs "suitable for display." Any Lincoln endorsement which can be shown conveniently is suspect, for our great Civil War President was much too

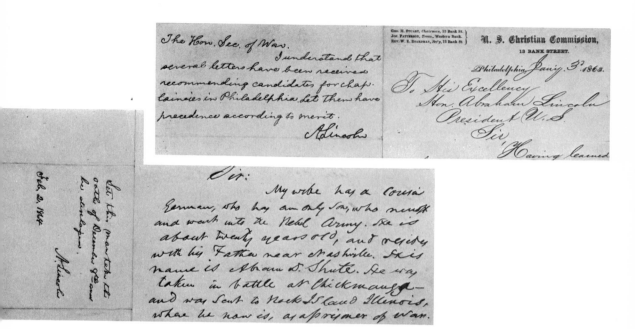

Genuine and forged notes on actual letters to Lincoln. *Left.* Authentic holograph note signed by Lincoln. *Right.* Lincoln note forged by Joseph Cosey on a genuine letter to Lincoln. Notice the different positions of the notes.

involved with the problems of war to devote any thought to placing his signature in a convenient spot for framing or exhibit. Characteristic of both Weisberg and Cosey is a tautology alien to the simple, terse expression of Lincoln.

Sometimes a forger, carried away by his imagination, will place historic names in astonishing juxtaposition. I recall a forged document of Cotton Mather in which the Boston divine condemned a witch to death. It was also signed by King Philip, the noted Indian leader. The forger had bungled, for Mather was not a judge and had no authority to pass sentence, and King Philip could neither read nor write. Even more amazing is a similar forgery, now in my personal collection, which orders the execution of a suspected witch and bears the signatures of both Cotton Mather and Robert Calef, noted opponent of the witchcraft craze!

Perhaps because of fear of a lawsuit, the forger seldom imitates the writing of his contemporaries. An exception is a series of letters and documents addressed to, or inscribed to, Henry A. Woodhouse. Sold by a warehouse to a reputable book dealer, these curious documents have recently glutted the market. Among the forgeries are inscribed photographs of Richard E. Byrd, Roald Amundsen, Robert E. Peary, and other distinguished Arctic explorers. One letter, referring to aviation, is an example of the anachronisms which trap the unwary forger, for it is signed by both Alexander Graham Bell and Amelia Earhart, who was an unknown girl of nineteen at the time! Among other fakes in this warehouse collection were first-day stamp covers bearing a shaky fabrication of the signature of Woodrow Wilson.

The most prolific of all American forgers were Robert Spring and Joseph Cosey. The favorites of Spring were holograph checks of Washington, dated during the last five years of his life, each bearing a perforation cancel at which Spring was so adept that he could have qualified as a bank clerk. Cosey's "mainstays" are Lincoln legal briefs, generally penned on blue paper similar to that which Lincoln used, and pay warrants bearing the forged signature of Franklin, often with their corners artistically rounded. If Franklin had signed all the pay warrants forged by Cosey, the sums involved would have bankrupted the State of Pennsylvania!

Speaking of Franklin recalls my quest for an original manuscript, "The Rules and Regulations of the Philadelphia Chess Club," signed by Franklin as President of the Society. Gusto was added since William E. Lingelbach of the American Philosophical Society had never heard of the Philadelphia Chess Club! The document turned up in the collection of a wealthy doctor in Paris, where Franklin had spent much of his time during the Revolutionary War. My brother, then in Paris, persuaded the doctor to send me the document.

From a photostat, the document had appeared genuine, although the signature of the secretary of the Philadelphia Chess Club, Stephen Gorham, puzzled me. Gorham is not a well-known Philadelphia name, and Franklin had made no mention of such a person in his *Autobiography*. However, the chess rules were similar, with a few variations, to the regulations laid down in Franklin's essay on the playing of chess. When the document reached me, I found myself the owner of an excellent forgery. No more than a second was needed to determine its spurious nature. The ink, the parchment, the writing, the signature—indeed, the whole of the document revealed its true character. The French doctor refunded my money upon the return of the forgery!

A few years ago, lured by a Poe letter, I visited a dilapidated house in Brooklyn. As I entered, I spotted a framed letter hanging on the wall. Even at a distance I felt certain that it was one of Cosey's productions.

Washington and his forgers. *Top.* Authentic holograph note signed by Washington. *Center.* Forgery of Washington document by Joseph Cosey (about 1930). *Bottom.* Forgery of a Washington check by Robert Spring (about 1865).

*Right.* Joseph Cosey, most notorious of American forgers. *Below.* A Franklin pay warrant forged by Cosey. Notice the dockets written diagonally across the warrant to give it an appearance of authenticity. The rounded corners and Palmer penmanship are also characteristic of many of Cosey's forgeries.

When I picked it up, my expectations were confirmed. Both the paper and ink betrayed the modern origin of a remarkable (were it genuine!) letter of Poe about "The Cask of Amontillado."

My disappointment was tempered by the discovery of several hundred authentic letters of Whittier and William Dean Howells tucked away in an old file in this strange house. After paying the owner for the authentic material, I gathered my purchases in several cartons, leaving behind the Cosey forgery.

About three weeks later an antique dealer burst into my office: "I've made a great discovery!" he exclaimed. "A letter of Poe!"

I shared his enthusiasm and eagerly we unwrapped the package under his arm. "Alas," I said sadly, "this letter is an 'old friend.' I saw it only three weeks ago in Brooklyn. It's one of Cosey's products."

Although I offered the dealer ten dollars for it, so that it could be taken out of circulation, he refused, saying that he had paid a great deal more.

Six weeks passed. One afternoon I received a most urgent telephone call from a curio dealer.

"I've made a tremendous find," he declared, his voice trembling with excitement. It's an unpublished letter of Edgar Allan Poe."

I asked whether it was about "The Cask of Amontillado," and was in an old walnut frame.

"Good heavens! How did you know?"

"Because," I explained, "I've seen it twice before and have no desire to see it again."

Early in 1960 the Government issued the first of a new series of "Credo" stamps. It bore a quotation from Washington's writings, beneath which was a crude copy of the signature of our first Chief Executive. Because I felt that it detracted from Washington's dignity to publicize an inept imitation of his graceful and beautiful signature, I complained to the Post Office. Authentic signatures were promised on the balance of the Credo series.

When large numbers of a salable autograph suddenly glut the market, it suggests the possibility of forgery. For example, the auction seasons of 1944–48 record the sale of ninety presentation copies of books by Lewis Carroll, the shy author of *Alice in Wonderland*. Assuming that a portion of the ninety represent copies which appeared several times at auction during the period, this prolific record has never, to my knowledge, been equaled by any other author. Perhaps all of these presentation copies were authentic (although I have seen several Carroll forgeries recently), but I am reminded of what an art critic said of Corot: "He produced a total

*Top.* Altered signature of Washington on U. S. stamp. *Bottom.* Authentic signature of Washington.

of eight hundred paintings during his lifetime, of which more than sixteen hundred are in the United States!"

The German and Italian forgers of the last century were astonishingly successful in imitating the color of ancient ink. They fabricated letters of the leading Renaissance figures. A letter of Melanchthon was offered at a Swiss auction several years ago and, as I was the successful mail bidder, the letter was dispatched to me. Penned in Latin, it bore every characteristic of an original, yet the more I studied it, the more certain I felt that it was a forgery, even though it had been authenticated by several European experts. The paper was heavier than the usual Renaissance foolscap, and the ink lay on the surface, rather than knifing through by the aging process of oxidization. Many Renaissance documents, written on the smooth-surfaced paper of the period, are so affected by the old ink that when held up to the light they seem like lace filigree. I sent the letter to Herr Gunther Mecklenburg, of J. A. Stargardt, in Germany for examination. After a thorough study by Latin experts it was pronounced a forgery, for it contained grammatical errors of which Melanchthon would not have been guilty.

Because of the ease with which a name may be written in a volume, forgers are tempted to create an *ex libris* of some author or statesman whose autograph is in demand. Some years ago there appeared quite a few volumes bearing the forged signature of Eugene Field; and the collector should be wary of any volume purportedly from the library of the "poet of childhood." In my collection of forgeries is a copy of Bret Harte's poems bearing forged signatures of Bret Harte, Mark Twain, and Eugene Field! At the time when the signatures were supposedly signed, Mark Twain and Bret Harte were not on speaking terms! In this volume, as in other similar forgeries, is a notarized statement by Eugene Field II that the book came from the library of his father.

Several years ago, a scout located a book from Washington's library, bearing a presentation inscription from Cornwallis to Washington! A more desirable association volume could not be conceived. It had been authenticated by a noted librarian. Reasonably valued by the owner at ten thousand dollars, this gift from the defeated to the victor lured me as had no other inscribed volume!

Although I am a man of sedentary habits, I made a journey to Philadelphia to examine and buy the book. With me I carried a cashier's check to bind the deal. As I entered the owner's office—a pretentious Victorian room—I had a premonition that my quest would be fruitless. On the wall was a photo of Lincoln, bearing a forged signature. The owner took from his safe a luxurious morocco case, out of which he ceremoniously extracted a battered volume. A glance convinced me that it contained a crude forgery of Washington's signature and an even cruder forged inscription of Cornwallis. It is hard to believe that so naïve a fake could deceive anyone, but the owner had paid a large sum for this fraudulent volume. It was one of forty or fifty books, all allegedly from the libraries of our Presidents. Nearly half of the volumes contained forged signatures, some of them obviously executed in the same ink and in the same handwriting by the same forger on the same day—even though they purported to be signed by Presidents who lived as much as fifty years apart!

It adds piquancy to the chase when you reflect that the forger is never idle. Recently a World War II colonel offered me a group of quavery signatures of the Nazi war criminals. Included were Goering and Keitel. "Just before the Nazi criminals were executed," he explained, "I purchased these signatures, perhaps the last they ever signed, from one of the few Americans allowed admittance to the condemned men." The colonel was so enthusiastic about his collection that it was with regret that I told him the reason for the shakiness was that the signatures were forgeries. I pointed out to him that the handwriting, although in some cases a fairly accurate imitation, did not reveal the characteristics of German chirography.

Here are the basic rules to follow in detecting forgeries:

Rule 1. *Watch out for bargains!* The man who offers you an autograph of importance "for whatever you think it's worth" may have just manufactured it with Waterman's brown ink. If you buy a "Lincoln" from him, he will be back the next day with a nice "Washington" and a "Franklin" or two. Several years ago an English dealer sent me a "Byron" manuscript for "whatever you think it's worth." It consisted of several pages of adolescent doggerel, penned in a sloppy hand not unlike Byron's, accompanied by an affidavit of John Murray III, son of Byron's publisher, testifying to its authenticity. Even if Murray could not tell infantile rhymes from poetry, he could have held the manuscript up to the light and read the watermark "1834"—ten years after Byron's death!

Rule 2. *Ignore affidavits by people who are not recognized as authorities on autographs.* An authentication of a Lincoln autograph by Robert T. Lincoln or John Hay, for instance, is of little value because these distinguished statesmen were not experts on handwriting.

Rule 3. *Make sure the address-leaf is correctly written, sealed, and folded.* Before the days of envelopes (which were not widely used before 1845) letters were generally folded to a small size, sealed with wax, and addressed on the outside leaf. When the letter was opened, it left a small tear and remnants of wax, as well as traces of the original folds. Crude forgeries lack not only the proper folds, but even the seal and postmark. Only one forger executed postmarks and seals to perfection. That was "Major" Byron, whose Byron fakes are among the most expertly contrived forgeries. They may be recognized by the peculiar stains near the bottom of each page, and by the fact that "Major" Byron never took in-

### Authentic Signatures Showing Variations

A script may vary greatly because of the writer's age, mood, haste or leisure, illness, or other factors. In checking a "suspect" document against an example of known authenticity, pay special attention to the general character of the handwriting. In his excellent monograph on autographs, written for *The Concise Encyclopaedia of Antiques* (Volume IV), P. J. Croft points out:

"It is advisable first of all to take in the general appearance of the handwriting to be examined—its size, slope, spacing, its degree of clarity and neatness. Having thus acquired the 'feel' of the hand . . . the following points will be found particularly useful for comparison: the writing of *th, ing, of,* and other common combinations; links between letters and (in some hands) between words; the ascenders and descenders, their length in proportion to the bodies of the letters, how far and in what way they are looped, etc.; the crossing of *t*; abbreviations, particularly the formation of the ampersand; deletions and additions; punctuation; capital letters and numerals; the writing of *n* and *u* which are sometimes virtually indistinguishable, and any other features which may tend to make the hand difficult to read."

Two signatures of U. S. Grant, both actual size. The lower signature was evidently penned in a mood of exuberance.

Two signatures of Aaron Burr, exhibiting the effect of maturity on handwriting. *Left,* in 1795; *right,* in 1776.

Two signatures of Reverdy Johnson. The bottom signature was hurriedly scrawled.

Two signatures of John Hay, showing his upright and slanting styles of handwriting.

Two signatures of John Hancock, showing the effect of age upon handwriting. *Top,* 1777; *bottom,* 1792.

to account the changes in Byron's handwriting, using the style of Byron's youth.

Rule 4. *Check doubtful handwriting against a genuine example of the same period.* Washington and Aaron Burr altered their handwriting markedly during their careers. Others, like Lincoln, changed very little. Still, every man tends to vary his script, even in the same document. Sometimes he will make a *g* with a curled tail, sometimes with the tail straight down. Sometimes his capital *R* will be florid, sometimes plain. The inexperienced forger often betrays himself by his consistency. Several years ago I was investigating a suspect Mary Baker Eddy letter which I believed was the work of Cosey. I took it to a large library and showed it to a young man in the manuscript room. "Oh," said he, "it is probably a forgery. Notice that the capital *M* is made in three different ways." For an answer, I showed him a bill just submitted to me by my printer. The printer had made his capital *T* in three different ways—and I left behind a very astonished young man!

Rule 5. *Beware of a signature which differs in any marked way from the usual signature of the writer.* It was Lincoln's custom, for example, to sign his letters "A. Lincoln" and his official Presidential documents, as required by law, with his full signature. Not more than three or four *let-ters* exist which were signed in full. Probably these were signed at the same time as a group of official documents, and Lincoln inadvertently wrote out his full name. Washington always signed "Go: Washington." He never signed his name in full except in the text of a legal or similar document. Patrick Henry abbreviated his first name to *P*, and not long ago I saw a forgery which was instantly apparent, as it was signed with a full "Patrick Henry."

Authentic signature of Patrick Henry.

Rule 6. *Examine the paper carefully.* Many forgers blunder in the selection of paper. I was once offered a spurious Washington autograph on parchment! It purported to be a receipt for the sale of a slave, but it looked more like an abortive lampshade. Except for legal or official documents, parchment was seldom used in the eighteenth and nineteenth centuries; and only a very clumsy forger would use parchment for a letter or a receipt.

The size of the sheet may be a clue to authenticity. In the eighteenth century and earlier the folio (very large) sheet was popular; in the second half of the nineteenth century, the octavo (very small) held sway. Today we use predominantly the quarto, about eight and one-half by eleven inches, a size also popular in the late eighteenth and early nineteenth centuries. One can make a pretty good guess as to the approximate age of a document from its size. Forgers, as a rule, use scraps of paper, seldom the full folio or quarto sheet with the blank integral leaf. In his quest for paper the forger loots the fly-leaves from old volumes. Such leaves may bear faint type offsets or evidence of a once-sewed margin.

The physical composition of the paper may be significant. Recently I identified a document as a forgery because, although plainly dated "1793," it was on wood pulp paper, not widely used until about 1845–55. Many forgers use paper watermarked ten or twenty or more years after the death of the supposed writer. If you doubt the authenticity of a document, hold it up to the light and inspect the watermark.

*Rule 7. Exercise caution when handwriting is noticeably small.* One of the most striking marks of a spurious document is the forger's unconscious tendency to shrink the size of the subject's handwriting—probably because of a psychological desire to conceal his fraud by making it less easy to read. Robert Spring often used a diminutive handwriting in his Washington fakes. In my personal collection of forgeries is a Spring forged signature which measures exactly one and three-fourths inches. The average length of Washington's signature was about three inches, but sometimes it ran to three and one-half inches, exactly twice the size of the puny, shaky fake by Spring. Several years ago I was offered a Robert Burns manuscript in which the handwriting was smaller than usual. Despite the distinguished provenance of the manuscript, I pronounced it a forgery. My opinion was later confirmed.

*Rule 8. Do not be misled by dealer markings on a document, or by repairs or evidences of prior framing.* Such details are frequently rigged by the forger, who beguiles his victim into a false sense of security by creating the impression that the document has already passed under critical eyes.

*Rule 9. Compare the ink with that of a genuine document of the period.* You may imagine that the study of inks is very complicated and is the province of a few specialists. Yet it is not difficult to recognize the ink that is "wrong." Earlier inks usually bite into the paper. An almost imperceptible brownness is sometimes visible at the edge of the writing. Ink used before 1875 may show evidence of corrosion due to iron gall. Forgeries, on the other hand, have a washed-out brown or blackish purple cast quite unlike genuine old ink. Even the faint brown of pokeberry ink or the watery black of gunpowder ink does not look like the products of recent forgers. The Lincoln fakes of Cosey, often in ink mixed from iron rust, an improvement on his earlier Waterman's brown ink, are unlike the rich brown or almost jet black ink used by our Civil War president.

Recent forgery of Abraham Lincoln. *Top.* Facsimile of an original letter of Abraham Lincoln. *Bottom.* Freehand forgery of the same letter, sent to me from Santa Monica, California, together with masterfully executed forgeries of Mark Twain, Eugene Field, and Oscar Wilde. My efforts to obtain the co-operation of the United States Post Office in indicting the vendor were unsuccessful.

Rule 10. *Any autograph of exceptional rarity, or with remarkably fine contents, merits careful investigation.* Forgers attempt to fabricate valuable items, and one often finds "Button Gwinnett" or "Thomas Lynch, Jr." signatures in old books. Such fakes may be detected because of the slight fuzziness of the ink, for modern ink blurs when applied to old paper.

Rule 11. *Check the contents of the document against known facts.* In the case of remarkably well-done forgeries, the primary suspicion may depend upon internal evidence. Little errors of date or place, tiny facts which fail to dovetail with our other knowledge, premature mention of books and ideas were the evidences on which "Major" Byron's adroit forgeries of Shelley and Byron were first condemned. Of equal significance are blunders in language and syntax. If the letter of an eighteenth century notable were to conclude with the words, "Cordially yours" instead of "I am, Sir, Your humble Servant," or a similar extravagant phrase, the deviation would justify a careful examination of the letter.

Rule 12. *Be suspicious of shaky handwriting, or any evidence of erasures or tracing.* The forger may first "draw" or trace his imitation in pencil, later going over it in ink. But a tracing does not always mean forgery. Occasionally the recipient of a penciled letter from a noted person will trace it in ink for better preservation. Recently I sold a letter of Mark Twain which some misguided admirer had treated in this outlandish fashion.

To understand in practice the typical marks of a forgery, let us examine one of the most famous of American facsimiles, the Bixby letter, which purports to be an exact copy of a letter from Lincoln to Mrs. Bixby. The original of the Bixby letter has never been discovered—if, indeed, it ever existed—but the familiar lithographed reproduction is a superb example of a transparent forgery, since it reveals (even without an examination of the original paper and ink) nearly every blunder to which the forger is prone:

1. The writing in the Bixby forgery is uniform, showing none of the variation which exists in Lincoln's handwriting.

2. The script in the Bixby forgery tends to be diminutive, a typical characteristic of forgeries.

3. The individual words in the forgery weave up and down, showing that the forger was concentrating on the formation of the letters in each word, rather than upon writing the word itself.

4. Nearly every word in the forgery is penned with exaggerated legibility. Lincoln never wrote a letter as legible as the Bixby forgery.

5. The individual letters of each word are incorrectly formed in the

The Bixby forgery exposed. *Top*. Authentic holograph letter, signed, of Lincoln, reproduced by courtesy of the Brown University McLellan Collection. *Bottom*. The Bixby forgery, often regarded as a facsimile of the nonexistent original.

Executive Mansion,

Washington, April 30, 1862.

Adjutant Genl. Thomas
My dear Sir:

My personal friend, Dr. T. A. Perkins, who will hand you this, at my own instance, was appointed a Surgeon some time ago, and has since been in the service — I fear he has committed a blunder — He was at Charleston Va. & ordered to his transfer New when his family, and, as a mode of effecting it, has tendered his resignation, hoping to get another appointment — If this can be done, all right — Please see him, & try to fix some way so that he may not be thrown out altogether. Yours tuly, A. Lincoln

To Mrs Bixby, Boston

Dear Madam:

of the War Department
General of Massachusetts
five sons who have die
I feel how weak and
mine which should
grief of a loss so overw
from tendering you th
in the thanks of the r
pray that our Heavenly Father may assuage the anguish
of your bereavement, and leave you only the cherished
memory of the loved and lost, and the solemn pride
that must be yours to have laid so costly a sacrifice
upon the altar of freedom

Yours very sincerely and respectfully,

A. Lincoln.

Bixby forgery. Notice especially the *d*'s, final *e*'s, the *t*'s,—in fact, not a single letter in the forgery bears more than a slight similarity to Lincoln's writing.

6. In the forgery, the nib of the pen produces a very even, regular mark; but in genuine autographs, written with Lincoln's wide-nibbed pen, the flow of ink is very uneven, varying from letter to letter within each word.

7. In the Bixby fake, the handwriting is perceptibly shaky, but Lincoln's handwriting, although irregular, was always firm and strong.

Were the original of the Bixby fabrication lying before us, we would find it not wanting in the other marks of the forger's handicraft. The paper would probably not be of the variety customarily used by Lincoln; the ink would be of modern or relatively modern vintage; the folds in the letter (if any) would not be the correct ones to accommodate the letter to an envelope of the period; there would no doubt be evidence of erasures; and likely a magnifying glass would disclose that the forger had first drawn his words in pencil, afterwards tracing them in ink.

With an amateurish fake, such as the Bixby letter, it is not necessary to examine the original document to pass upon the imposture. Most forgeries—and we can be thankful for this!—are very easy to identify! You need not be at all hesitant about purchasing autographs from a reliable dealer. Inexpensive autographs are not worth the forger's time or trouble to create, and valuable autographs are examined by the autograph dealer with great care, so that there is no chance of a forgery slipping past his critical eye.

# 5 TO SIGN OR NOT TO SIGN: SIGNATURES BY PROXY

ON THE BRIDGE OF HIS FLAGSHIP, the admiral was urgently trying to make contact with a rear admiral commanding his largest battleship. It was during World War II, and a storm was lashing the fleet, then riding at anchor.

There came the reply: "The rear admiral is on shore leave!"

Angrily, the admiral summoned his chief yeoman. Unknown to the admiral (so the yeoman told me later), he had as usual signed the rear admiral's request for shore leave with the admiral's name.

"Who authorized the shore leave?" demanded the admiral.

"Why, you did, sir!" declared the chief yeoman without blanching. "I brought the request in, placed it on your desk, and you approved it."

The admiral was not convinced. His fury mounted with the storm, reaching a climax when the rear admiral's battleship was driven aground, a catastrophe widely publicized at the time.

When the rear admiral was at last located, the admiral asked to look at his shore leave. Examining the signature carefully, but not recognizing the yeoman's fabrication, he said apologetically, "Well, it is my signature, all right, but I can't imagine what I was thinking about when I signed it, for I didn't intend to let you go ashore!"

Doubtless such proxy signatures, signed by clerks, have more than once changed the course of history!

Three hundred years ago the French kings resorted to *secrétaires de main*, clerks empowered to sign the monarch's name. The number of routine letters, military commissions, and grants of privileges signed by the French royal clerks is staggering. They are the most abundant of lawful forgeries. Sometimes it is not easy to identify these proxy signatures.

You must be guided by the nature of the document as well as by the signature. Often a secretary, in signing for the monarch, would write his own signature beneath, drawing a crude arrow upward to the king's name.

In old chronicles we read that the French kings were barely able to sign their names and passed the task on to a secretary. Samuel Pegge tells us that Louis XIV, in writing his signature, put down six diagonal lines and a wriggling snake, //////S, and filled in the strokes to form his name. This is not true, for I have seen letters signed personally by the Sun King at the age of six, and his handwriting was clear and bold, a credit to his writing master.

The later rulers of England and Germany personally signed all letters and documents. So zealous was Kaiser Wilhelm II that, as the German army expanded to gratify his martial ambitions, he continued to place his gigantic signature at the bottom of every military appointment, even those for the Prussian equivalent of the lowly shavetail. Like his predecessor Frederick the Great, he preferred to examine and sign every document calling for his approval.

Napoleon, the most prodigious letter-writer in history, left nearly a quarter of a million letters and documents bearing his illegible scrawl. His motto that "time is everything" was applied at the desk as on the battlefield, for he employed a secretary to sign his signature to brevets and other routine documents. Although commissions for officers of brigadier-general or higher were personally signed by Bonaparte as First Consul, most of the brevets for lesser officers were signed for him by his secretary of state, Hugues Maret. Many such proxy documents are on the market, often framed with portraits or medals of the great Corsican. They can be identified because the signature lacks the familiar slashing paraph, that

Napoleon Bonaparte and his proxy signers. *Top*. Two authentic signatures of Bonaparte as First Consul. *Bottom*. Two proxy signatures from the consular period.

Jefferson Davis and his proxy signer, Varina Davis. *Top.* Holograph
letter written and signed for Jefferson Davis by his wife, Varina. Note
the period after the signature. *Center.* Signature and complimentary
close from a letter of Varina Davis.
*Bottom.* Holograph quotation signed by Jefferson Davis. Note the absence of the period after the signature. When examined closely, the
two handwritings reveal many dif-
ferences, Davis' being more compact and legible than that of his
wife.

final dramatic stroke which so often spread-eagled the quill's nib and splattered ink over the page.

During the American Revolution, and especially during the Civil War, every headquarters was a documentary beehive, swarming with written directives, orders, and instructions, many of which were copied a dozen or more times to be dispatched to lower echelons. There exist many "clerical" copies of important letters and telegrams, authentic in every respect, except that they were not personally written or signed.

After the fall of the Confederacy, Jefferson Davis was constantly badgered by strangers who sought written information or opinions. Sometimes he turned over such inquiries to his wife Varina. Writing in the name of her husband, Varina was able to express precisely the ideas and beliefs of the man whom she venerated. So remarkably well did she imitate Davis' handwriting, even to the signature, that scholars often affirm that letters written for Davis by Varina are in the hand of Davis himself. "I succeeded in writing so much like Mr. Davis," Varina wrote, "that he could not tell which of us had written a letter and no one could distinguish my signature of his name from his own." Generally more crabbed, Varina's imitation lacks the verve of Davis' own script. The distinguishing mark is the period which she placed at the end of the signature, for Davis never put a period after his name.[1]

The story of the proxy signatures turned out for our Presidents is extremely interesting. When President Washington looked at the daily mountain of documents requiring his signature he must have winced. He was required by law to sign the ship's papers for every vessel, even if no larger than a yawl, sailing from any American port. All army commissions,

[1] The discovery of Varina Davis' use of the period was made by Mary A. Benjamin.

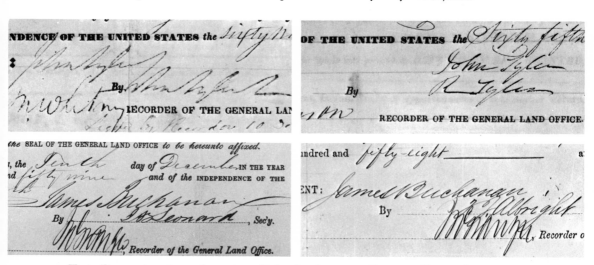

*Top.* Proxy signatures from two Tyler land grants. *Bottom.* Proxy signatures from two Buchanan land grants.

political appointments, and land grants bore his graceful signature. He must have put his name to well over one hundred thousand documents during his official career.

The Louisiana Purchase set Madison and Monroe to driving the quill, signing tens of thousands of land grants for veterans who wished to settle in the new regions. Finally, Andrew Jackson rebelled and put a stop to the Presidential stint of signing several hundred papers daily. Jackson continued to place his signature on ship's papers and commissions, but after 1834, there exist only a half-dozen land grants which bear the personal signature of the President.

In Lincoln's day, the pressure on the President was so great that many of the documents which had previously required his signature were signed by minor officials, but commissions and appointments continued to be signed by the President. During his Presidential campaign, James A. Garfield poured out thousands of letters to his admirers and supporters, answering every question put to him, declining or accepting every invitation. He employed a secretary to whom he dictated many of his letters, all of which Garfield personally signed. So skilled was his amanuensis that he imitated not only Garfield's habit of running words together, but also the fluency and spirit of his chirography.

One of the most elusive cases of handwriting imitation is that of Franklin D. Roosevelt and his secretaries. At various times in his career, Roosevelt had seven or more secretaries who signed letters or documents for him.

Suspecting that Dwight D. Eisenhower had, during his first campaign for President, employed secretaries to put his signature to correspondence and to sign photographs, I was amazed to run across a letter of

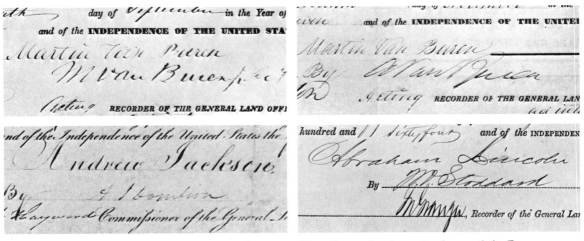

*Top.* Proxy signatures from two Van Buren land grants. *Lower left.* Proxy signature from a Jackson land grant. *Lower right.* Proxy signature from a Lincoln land grant.

his secretary Ann C. Whitman to a collector: "I want to tell you that although I was not with the President at the time your photograph was signed, I am confident that it is authentic. No one else is, or has been, authorized to sign his name."

Intrigued, I wrote to Miss Whitman, asking her to comment on two proxy signatures of Eisenhower which I enclosed with my letter. After checking, Miss Whitman replied: "During the 1952 campaign, I understand, there were several persons authorized to sign the candidate's name. Since he has been President, no one is or has been so authorized." Miss Whitman's statement tallies with my experience; nor have I seen any proxy signatures of Eisenhower dated during his army years.

Probably the autograph collector of the twenty-first century will find the problem of proxy signatures difficult to solve, for the growing responsibilities of executives leave less and less time for the old-fashioned custom of putting a personal signature to official letters and documents.

In the summer of 1960 the New York columnist, Hy Gardner, printed

Coolidge and his proxy signer. *Top*. Authentic signature of Coolidge (1921). *Bottom*. Proxy signature of Coolidge (1920). There also exist proxy signatures of Harding and Truman, dating from their Senatorial periods.

a remark that "Washington's handwriting looks like he wrote with a little hatchet." In publishing a letter of rebuttal from me, Mr. Gardner added: "Hamilton, incidentally, has a beautiful signature." I might have felt more flattered had not my letter to Mr. Gardner been signed for me by my assistant!

The rubber or steel stamp signature, actually a facsimile, presents a problem similar to that of the proxy signature, for it is always affixed to an authentic document. The Spanish kings (unlike the French kings who employed a *secrétaire de main*) often signed routine letters with a steel stamp, as did some of the Holy Roman emperors, and a few early English sovereigns.

The first President to have a facsimile of his signature printed on documents was Andrew Johnson, who injured his right hand shortly after taking office. At least ninety per cent of the commissions, pardons, and ship's papers of his administration—the bulk of the official papers requiring his signature—

*continued on page 64*

Proxy signatures slightly reduced

Seven proxy signatures of Franklin D. Roosevelt. *Top*. Authentic signature of Franklin D. Roosevelt (1932), followed by six proxy signatures, all by different secretaries (1928–32). *Bottom*. Check filled out and signed for Roosevelt by Missy LeHand, with signature of Missy LeHand from the letter which accompanied the check.

Sincerely,

*Dwight D Eisenhower*

I know you feel as strongly as I do that we must work day
and night and personally sacrifice far beyond the normal
call to duty to succeed in this crusade. We must put party
lines and all personal prejudice behind us, and go forward
to victory.

Sincerely yours,

*Dwight D Eisenhower*

I know you feel as strongly as I do that we must work day
and night and personally sacrifice far beyond the normal
call to duty to succeed in this crusade. We must put party
lines and all personal prejudice behind us, and go forward
to victory.

Sincerely yours,

*Dwight D Eisenhower*

Eisenhower and his proxy signers. *Top.* Authentic signature of Dwight D.
Eisenhower (1951). *Center.* Conclusion of the "go forward to victory" letter,
October 17, 1952, signed for Eisenhower by a secretary. *Bottom.* Conclusion of
an identical letter, also dated October 17, 1952, but signed by a different secretary. There exist many first-day covers and photographs which were signed by
proxy for Eisenhower during his first Presidential campaign.

*Not One of These Men Signed*
*The Declaration of Independence!*

Although they were all living in 1776, these men were only "namesakes" of the famous patriots who signed the Declaration. There were, for example, dozens of John Adamses residing in Massachusetts at the same period as the noted Signer of the Declaration.

The autograph of a noted person's namesake usually possesses only trifling value. Here are a few of the famous individuals who had contemporary "name doubles": Oliver Cromwell, Horace Walpole, Sarah Siddons, Charles Dickens, Alfred Tennyson, John Paul Jones, John Howard Payne, Nathanael Greene, Benjamin West, Gunning Bedford, James Buchanan, Thomas Lynch, and Alexander Hamilton. Many of these names represent father and son combinations, with only the father's autograph being of value.

Autographs of namesakes, or "mistaken identities," pose a problem very similar to that of proxy signatures. They are genuine in every respect, except that they were not penned by a noted person. You should learn how to spot them as imposters.

The obvious method is to compare the suspect specimen with an example of unquestioned authenticity. If no authenticated writing is available for comparison, however, it is possible to recognize the mistaken identity by the following tests:

1. *Internal evidence.* Do the date, place of origin, and contents of the document or letter check with the known facts regarding the alleged writer? Obviously, a man would not write a mature letter at the age of eight or nine, nor would he write a letter dated after his death. He would not send the cordial regards of his wife, if he happened not to be married. Nor would he, under ordinary circumstances, write a friendly letter to a man known to be his bitter enemy. By such discrepancies mistaken identities are often exposed.

2. *External evidence.* If the letter is undated, is the stationery of the type ordinarily used during the lifetime of the alleged writer? How about the ink? Does it match or compare favorably with the ink on other letters of the period? Even if you had never seen the handwriting of Chief Justice John Jay, it would be difficult to confuse his letters, penned in rich brown ink on chain-lined folios and quartos of the late eighteenth century, with the letters of his noted descendant, the diplomat of the same name, who wrote in aniline ink on the glossy octavos and duodecimos of the Victorian era.

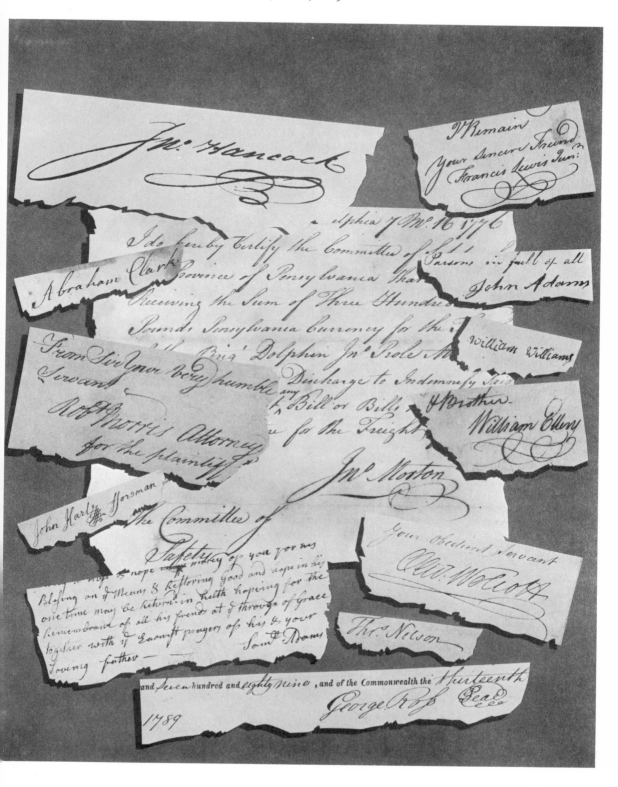

bear his printed signature. Since collectors insist upon a personal signature, such documents are of small
value.

Not many Presidents have used rubber stamps to
sign their letters. But both Roosevelts, while governor of New York and at no other time, resorted to
rubber stamp signatures. The same may be said of
Woodrow Wilson, the first President to use a typewriter personally. As governor of New Jersey, Wilson signed many of his letters with a rubber stamp,
even those to his intimate friends. When President,
he gave up this practice and took full responsibility
for all his communications by placing his personal
signature on them. He continued to type his own
letters, and the clatter of the typewriter late at night
was a familiar sound in the President's study during
his two administrations.

Strangely enough, an original document may
sometimes have the appearance of a facsimile. Both
Franklin D. Roosevelt and Harry S. Truman signed
official documents in very black ink, and Roosevelt
humorously referred to such papers (on which the
ink took several minutes to dry) as his "laundry."
Visitors recall his office in which recently signed
documents were often spread out on almost every
article of furniture!

Authentic and proxy signatures of
President Kennedy. *Above.* Authentic
signature of Kennedy (1959). *Below.*
Secretarial signature of Kennedy on
a campaign letter (1960). Kennedy's
own signature is less legible.

Occasionally, an unscrupulous person may alter a facsimile so that it
appears to be an original. The usual technique is to place a blot on some
part of the reproduction. Recently I was offered a facsimile signature of
Eisenhower as President, printed on an engraved White House card. The
card had been split to remove the printed statement on the verso, "This
is a facsimile reproduction," and the vendor had cleverly added a smudge
on the signature to give it an authentic appearance.

Another problem is the ball-point pen, which leaves an ink trail very
much like that of a facsimile. Under a magnifying glass, however, the
writing reveals the same characteristics as all pens, with overlapping
strokes and variations in pressure.

There are thousands upon thousands of facsimiles! Those which turn
up most often are Jefferson's letter to Craven Peyton dated from Washington, November 27, 1803; Byron's letter to Galignani, denying the
authorship of *The Vampire*; Robert E. Lee's General Order No. 9, issued

Thank you so much

for your kind message.

It gave me much

pleasure.

Winston S. Churchill

April 49 55

Facsimile holograph letters of Harry S. Truman and Sir Winston S. Churchill. Very deceptive in their appearance of authenticity, these facsimiles are characteristic of the lithographed letters sent out by many leading statesmen of today. They may often be recognized because they lack a formal salutation to the recipient, and because they are mailed in typewritten, rather than personally handwritten envelopes, as would be the case if they were actually penned by the sender.

RRY S. TRUMAN
L RESERVE BANK BUILDING
SAS CITY 6, MISSOURI

February 10, 1953.

Your good letter congratulating me on the past national administration's work for all the people, and wishing Mrs. Truman, Margaret and myself happiness and prosperity for the future is highly appreciated.

Thank you very much.

Sincerely,

Harry Truman

by the Lakeside Press on lined blue paper; Stonewall Jackson's letter thanking a little girl for breakfast; George V's letter welcoming the American soldiers in April, 1918; Hitler's Christmas and New Year's greeting cards; and a form letter of Eisenhower from Columbia University, dated February 3, 1949.

How can you identify a facsimile? If the ink on the letter can be removed by eradicator, the letter is probably genuine. In testing, use a tiny drop of eradicator on a toothpick and apply to an inconspicuous part of the letter, not the signature. Genuine documents reveal obvious shading in the intensity of the ink flow, with overlapping strokes, but facsimiles show only a variation in the thickness of the strokes. Finally, under a magnifying glass, authentic writing appears to be an uninterrupted flow, but printer's ink shows tiny breaks or ink bubbles.

With a little practice, you will have no difficulty in spotting a facsimile.

# 6 GO WEST, YOUNG COLLECTOR, GO WEST

TAKE A WAR PARTY OF INDIANS, add flying arrows and bullets, mix with a few buckskinned pioneers and a covered wagon train, and season well with adventure. There you have it—the recipe for a frontiersman's biography! From such exciting ingredients were created the lives of Daniel Boone, Davy Crockett, Buffalo Bill, and other almost legendary figures of the Old West.

Like most men of action, the frontiersman handled a musket more adroitly than a pen. It is said that Jim Bridger, the famous trapper and guide who led the Mormons to Great Salt Lake, did not know how to write. Nevertheless, he must have placed his X on at least a few documents, perhaps receipts for skins or pay. What a prize would be any spot marked by such an X!

Most noted of all Indian fighters is Daniel Boone. His handwriting was as unpretentious as the man himself, with phonetic spelling and a halting but very legible script. Once in a while, for variety, he wrote his name "Boon." Only a score of full autograph letters signed by Boone are known, but his autograph is occasionally available in the form of signed receipts, promissory notes, and documents signed as surveyor for Lincoln County, Kentucky. Modest relics, perhaps, when one considers Boone's life of adventure, but they sell for prices high in the hundreds.

Signature of Daniel Boone.

Scarcer still is the autograph of Boone's friend, Simon Kenton, whose knowledge of the three r's, especially 'ritin,' was extremely limited. The renegade Simon Girty, whose tart brushes with Boone

Signature of Simon Kenton.

add interest to frontier history, was unable to write more than his initials.

Letters and documents about the Lewis and Clark expedition are not often encountered, for most of them have already gone into institutions. A lucky collector in Los Angeles recently bought from the descendant of an Indian chief a certificate of the chief's friendship to

Signature of Meriwether Lewis.

the United States, signed by both Lewis and Clark during their epochal journey. More spectacular was a letter of Jefferson which I acquired in 1959. Writing to Robert Patterson in Philadelphia on March 2, 1803, Jefferson outlined his plans for the expedition:

"We are at length likely to get the Missouri explored, & whatever river heading with that, leads into the Western ocean. Congress by a secret act has authorised me to do it. I propose to send immediately a party of about ten men with Capt. Lewis, my secretary, at their head . . . .

"I shall be particularly obliged to you for any advice or instruction you can give him . . . nothing should be said of this till he shall have got beyond the reach of any obstacles which might be prepared for him by those who would not like the enterprise."

Of all frontiersmen, the most picturesque was David Crockett, whose classic *Autobiography* is one of the most amusing books ever penned by an American. The disputed authorship of this volume can be settled by a letter in which Crockett asked his publishers, Carey and Hart, not to advertise the book as *by* him, but rather as *based on notes furnished by him*. Certainly the whimsical expressions are Crockett's, for the same kind of delectable humor is found in his letters. Like Boone, Crockett wrote a brand of English at variance with the spelling books. Until he was appointed magistrate at Shoal Creek, he did not know how to write. During his first month in office, while making the acquaintance of pen and ink, all his warrants, so he tells us, were in "verbal writing."

Signature of Colonel David Crockett.

Crockett was slain when the Alamo fell in 1836. He was one of the last survivors in the fort and surrendered to the Mexicans only after resistance was useless. Colonel Crockett was taken before General Santa Anna, who shouted angrily: "Shoot him!" Furious, Crockett leaped for Santa Anna's throat, but before he could reach him, a Mexican saber

Signature of General Santa Anna.

Signature of Colonel James Bowie.

pierced his heart. Because of his romantic career, Crockett's autograph appeals to collectors and is very expensive.

Crockett was only one of the great frontiersmen who perished at the Alamo. There was Colonel Jim Bowie who, although he lay desperately ill at the time of the assault, accounted for two Mexicans with his pistols. A third attacker was found sprawled over his bed. Hilt-deep in the Mexican's belly the dying Bowie had thrust one of the dreaded knives which bear his name. Bowie's autograph is of great rarity, occurring mainly (when it can be found at all!) on legal documents. The brilliant young lawyer William B. Travis was the third colonel, and the commanding officer, at the Alamo. Nearly all of his few surviving autographs are routine and colorless documents on legal matters.

The delaying action fought by the Alamo enabled Sam Houston to prepare his little army for battle. A few weeks later he won a decisive victory over the Mexicans at San Jacinto. Compared with the autographs of Bowie and Travis, Houston's letters seem very common, yet they seldom appear for sale. A man of force and vigor, Houston signed his name boldly, with an ornate flourish beneath. The "Sam" in his signature looked not unlike "I am," and Houston's political enemies seized upon his chirographic eccentricity to label the Texan hero, "The Great 'I am' Houston."

One of the most appealing of Western heroes was General George A. Custer, who was killed at the age of thirty-six when he recklessly attacked a large encampment of Sioux. A few years ago it was my good fortune to purchase a collection of fourteen youthful letters of Custer to Mollie J. Holland, his first sweetheart. The most ardent were dated during his boyhood days in Ohio, and a few, less passionate and more deliberate in tone, were written not long after his arrival at West Point. Custer's earliest outpourings of love, including a proposal of marriage, were indited in now-faded frontier ink of pokeberry

Signature of Colonel William Barret Travis

Signature of Texas patriot, Stephen F. Austin

Signature of General Sam Houston.

Signature of General George A. Custer.

juice. Occasionally he signed himself "Bachelor Boy." It is strange to think that this brilliant soldier once planned to study law, but that is one of the many facts disclosed by these early letters.

Another colorful figure of the Old West was Kit Carson, a scout who held the rank of Brigadier General in the United States Army. Carson seldom put anything on paper. Many years ago, a small cache of Kit Carson documents—all dated from Taos, New Mexico, in the late 1850's—was discovered. They were quickly absorbed by eager collectors.

In the collection of Lucius S. Ruder of Clearwater, Florida, is a letter of Carson—the only one I have ever seen. It is addressed to Antonio Joseph, a young friend at school in St. Louis: "You desired I would write to you, as the boys at the College would not believe you that I lived here," wrote Carson. "I have lived here a number of years and it is my intention to remain in this place as long as I live . . . . All I have to say to you is,

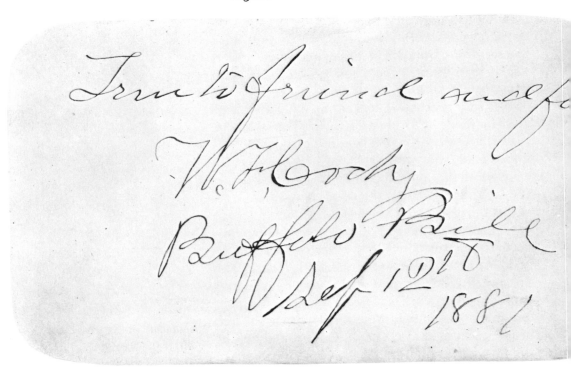

Signature of Kit Carson.

Holograph sentiment, signed, of Buffalo Bill.

Antonio, Be a good boy, attentive to your studies, obedient to your teachers and kind to your comrades."

The idol of several generations of Americans, Buffalo Bill was delighted to hand out his signature to all who requested it, signing in sprawling, bold letters, "W. F. Cody, 'Buffalo Bill.'" His favorite sentiment, which he wrote out hundreds of times, was "True to friend and foe." Letters of the great scout are rather scarce, for he was not a facile writer. Most of them are on picturesque stationery of his Wild West show and deal with circus matters.

Recently I obtained one of the earliest known letters of Buffalo Bill, a recital of his activities written from Ft. McPherson, Nebraska in 1872 to the man who was to make him famous, Ned Buntline. Cody wrote: "I have been quite buisy [*sic*] scouting for the last month. When cold weather comes I will send . . . a variety of the choisest game we have on the plains. I am packing a good deal this summer with pack mules, and have been thinking about the mess kit . . . it might be adopted in the army for prairie campaigning where we use pack mules or when transportation is scarce."

Two of Buffalo Bill's associates are firmly ensconced in the gallery of American frontier heroes: Wild Bill Hickok, who was not very wild and whose name was not Bill, and Annie Oakley. In thirty years I have seen nothing from Hickok's pen except a signature, "J. B. Hickok," signed for an autograph collector during his brief acting career. Wild Bill's real name was James Butler Hickok, and apparently he disliked fighting as much as he did writing, for modern historians regard him as a paranoid who preferred to shoot his victims in the back. More appealing is the pretty Pennsylvania girl—"Little Miss Sure Shot," as Sitting Bull called her. Annie Oakley's letters are seldom encountered and the few which have turned up were eagerly pounced upon by avid collectors.

Frequently I am asked for autographs of the great sheriffs and outlaws: Wyatt Earp, Bat Masterson, Pat Garrett, the Daltons, Jesse James, and Billy the Kid. One would suppose that Masterson signed many letters in his later years as a sports writer. If so, they must be hidden away in some obscure corner of the land! Billy the Kid enjoyed reading and occasionally gave away the books he had

Signature of outlaw leader, Emmett Dalton

finished, with his signature, "William H. Bonney." In 1881 Billy's slayer and biographer, Sheriff Pat Garrett, copied this autograph note from the

Signature of Annie Oakley, wife of marksman Frank E. Butler.

Letter of Jesse James. Signed "Thomas Howard," the name he used while in hiding, this letter was written only a month before his murder.

unpainted pine door of The Kid's prison cell in Lincoln: "William Bonney was incarcerated first time, December 22, 1878; Second time, March 21, 1879, and I hope I never will be again. W. H. Bonney."

What is probably the only surviving letter of Jesse James came my way recently and is now in the collection of Warren A. Reeder. In it, the outlaw indicated his intention to give up banditry. Signing with his alias, "Thos. Howard," later made famous by the ballad, "That dirty little coward that shot Mr. Howard," Jesse replied to an ad offering a farm in Lincoln, Nebraska: "I will not buy a farm unless the soil is No. 1. . . . I suppose your land can be made a good farm for stock and grain . . . ." The letter was dated March 2, 1882. A month later Jesse was dead, treacherously shot by Robert Ford.

The interest in Western autographs extends to stagecoach operators, like Henry Wells and William G. Fargo, gun inventors like Samuel Colt, and even artists! The prices paid today for sketches by Frederic Remington and Charles M. Russell would astonish their creators!

On January 24, 1848 a big man with a heavy black beard and a sharp eye caught the glitter of metal in a creek near Sutter's Mill. His name was James W. Marshall, and news that the glitter was gold quickly travelled back East. Men eager to prospect voyaged around the Horn to San Francisco. Others made the trip overland. Standard equipment included a Conestoga wagon, heavy boots, a horse and a cow or two, a good musket, a hunting knife, several cooking utensils—and a diary! Yes, a diary, for these intrepid adventurers who faced hostile Indians, burning heat, deadly cholera, freezing cold, terrible thirst, and awful hunger to reach El Dorado were making history—and they knew it. A few of the diaries are pedestrian, recounting only the number of miles traversed each day, but most of them tell of adventures and high hopes. A mention of Indian smoke-signals can move the value up, and any diary which describes an Indian attack is apt to be very costly.

They were a picturesque lot, these builders of a new frontier. Their letters to the folks at home are chock-full of news and statistics. They write in Eng-

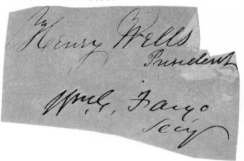

Signatures of Henry G. Wells and William G. Fargo.

Signature of Samuel Colt.

Signature of California colonizer, Father Junipero Serra.

Signatures of Frederic Remington and Charles M. Russell.

lish that stumbles and limps. They tell of street fights and tavern brawls, steamboat explosions, towns that were born fast and died fast, the tough problems of panning for gold, tall tales of those who struck it rich and sad tales of those who died of the cholera. Once in a while you may run across a letter-writer who is more poet than prospector and who foregoes news and succumbs to nostalgia. He longs for his wife or sweetheart; he deplores the absence of Aunt Fanny's cookies; he oozes sentiment at the thought of a Christmas Eve in the old homestead. The value of such letters is negligible. It is facts—interesting facts, recounted in detail—which ravish the collector of Western Americana!

Hundreds of gold seekers got rich, but Marshall lived and died in the ironic tradition which is the lot of discoverers and adventurers. Near the end of his long life he printed a few cards, picturing Sutter's mill, with a note about his discovery of gold. These he signed personally and sold for a modest sum, perhaps fifty cents or one dollar. It was a poor livelihood at best. Sometimes a kindly bartender would help him out with an introduction: "This here is Jim Marshall, who discovered gold in Californee. He never got none of it himself, and now he's selling a little picture of Sutter's mill personally signed. It's a great souvenir—only a dollar."

These modest relics—mere signatures, if you please—are today worth as much or more than an ounce of that precious metal Marshall discovered!

From the autographs of Western heroes it is but a step backward to the pictographs of the American Indians. Painted on birch bark or animal skins or beaded into wampum belts, the curious drawings called pictographs represent an ancient form of writing used by the Indians long before their first contact with the white men. Often pictographs were just aids to memory, used in preserving religious or tribal records. They held no significance except to the writer himself or to some person instructed by the writer.

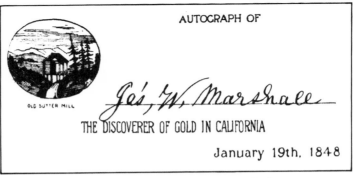

Card signed by James W. Marshall.

Among the Ojibways and other tribes whose civilization was more advanced, pictographs were standardized and many symbols had a recognizable meaning. "Life" was a plain circle; "death," a black circle; "spirit," a circle with a dot in the center; "evil spirit," a snake; "to see," a man's face with dots issuing from the eyes; "to speak," a face with dots coming from the mouth; "war," a man carrying a bow and arrows. There were more than two hundred such symbols, enabling the Indians to send written messages.

Eventually the Indians would have worked out an alphabet, but the coming of the white man forced them to take up the tomahawk to defend their lands. One of the first to "take the white man's road" was James Printer, an Indian who helped to set type for the Indian *Bible* (1661), translated into Natick by John Eliot. Printer was able to write his name with fluency and some elegance. But most Indians deliberately refused to learn how to write. The celebrated King Philip, who led the Indians in a desperate all-out attack on the early settlers of Massachusetts Bay, was able to write only his initial *P*, which he used in "touching the goosequill" to treaties. Documents signed by Philip occur for sale at long intervals; one offered at auction in 1958 fetched $1,850.

Many of the early Indian chiefs signed their names with an X-mark, but a few learned to trace their initials. Henry Montour, the half-blood translator of the Pennsylvanian frontier, was able to sign only "H. M." Other Indians used "totem" signatures, crude drawings of animals representing the clan to which the signer belonged. A member of the turtle clan, for example, would sign with a small sketch of a turtle. Thus the early treaties, when signed by many chieftains, present a picturesque sight with their quaint totem signatures. Once in a while an Indian leader would devise his own peculiar mark. Pontiac had a unique signature, a series of spiraling circles. It is of great rarity, and if an example were offered for sale it would certainly bring a colossal price.

In the middle of the eighteenth century came a great burst of Indian learning. Through the efforts

Signature of James Printer.

The mark of King Philip.

Totem signatures of Cayuga chiefs (eighteenth century).

of Eleazar Wheelock, founder of Dartmouth College, many Indians were taught to read and write English and Latin. Most of the Redmen were indifferent scholars. Wheelock's two outstanding pupils were Joseph Brant, the great Mohawk chieftain who fought with the British during the Revolution and who became Sir William Johnson's private secretary, and the Mohegan leader, Samson Occom, who raised the money to found Dartmouth. Brant was painted by Reynolds and lionized by English society. His letters are very scarce, but even scarcer are letters of Samson Occom.

Signature of the Mohawk chief, Joseph Brant.

With the nineteenth century, Indian autographs became comparatively plentiful. You will occasionally find Indian signatures on annuity receipts. Little Turtle, Red Jacket, Cornplanter, Young King, and other noted chiefs of the time are usually represented in autograph collections with X marks by which they acknowledged payment of their government pensions.

It became the custom among Indians to select a promising youth and send him to school to study the white man's "talking leaves," so that on his return he would be able to write letters for the tribe and act as interpreter. By 1850 many Indians had mastered English.

A most unusual personality among educated Indians was Eleazer Williams, claimant to the throne of France. Williams flogged himself with bramble bushes, then rubbed his wounds with tartar emetic to produce scars similar to those left by chains. Alleging that the scars were caused by a ruthless French jailer, he put forward the claim that he was the "Lost Dauphin" (Louis XVII), generally believed to have died in prison during the French Revolution. Williams found many supporters, and not until it was proved that he was a pathological liar did his adherents fall away. His letters are very scarce and usually concern missionary affairs.

Of all American Indians, the most celebrated is the great Sioux medicine man, Sitting Bull, who spent most of his life defending the hunting grounds of his people against the advancing whites.

Sitting Bull's early signature was a pictograph of a buffalo bull, seated

Signature of Eleazer Williams.

Signature of Sitting Bull.

on its haunches. Later, in Canada after the Custer battle, he learned to write his name in the white man's way. Years later, he joined Buffalo Bill's Wild West Show, where he signed autographs upon payment of a small fee. His signature, which he generally wrote in pencil without understanding the significance of the individual letters, was once rather plentiful. It is now very rare and you may have to wait years to obtain an example.

Even rarer than Sitting Bull's autograph is that of the famed Apache chief, Geronimo, who went on the warpath when a group of Mexican soldiers butchered his mother, wife, and three children. The Mexican government had offered a bounty of fifty dollars for a squaw's scalp and twenty-five dollars for a child's scalp, and although Geronimo's band was at peace with the whites, the soldiers were eager to collect the reward and attacked the village while the warriors were absent. The total bounty from the slaughter of Geronimo's family was only $175, but before Geronimo was captured he had repaid the debt many times over in Mexican blood. As an old man in 1904, he visited the World's Fair at St. Louis, where in the Indian Building he signed his signature in pencil for fifty cents or one dollar. A woman who met Geronimo at the Fair wrote to me recently: "It made me sad to see him confined behind fences in view of the public . . . his eyes were penetrating and crafty, too, but I remember he smiled at me, evidently not resenting children or young people . . . it was quite an effort for him to write his name and we talked with the guard while he wrote." Another eyewitness recorded that Geronimo printed his signature vertically (with each letter sideways), proceeding from top to bottom. To see his signature as Geronimo originally penciled it, turn this book sideways, with the letter G at the top.

Signature of Geronimo.

Relatively modern is one of the most bizarre varieties of Indian signatures—the thumb print. Among those who used it are Flying Hawk, distinguished Sioux chief, and Iron Tail, one of the Sioux who posed for the Buffalo nickel.

Shortly before the death of James Earle Frazer, who designed the buffalo nickel, I wrote to him, asking which Indians had posed for this noted coin. He replied:

"I did not make a portrait of any particular Indian. I had made several Indian portraits in the round. These I used to produce the Buffalo Nickel. As to the feathers they were the feathers attached to the scalp lock and sometimes stood upright but more often hung at the side head. I felt the latter was better as far as design was concerned.

"Iron Tail came to my studio to pose when he was in New York with a group of Indians. He had one of the most magnificent heads I had ever

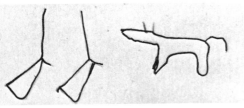

*Signature of Chief Two Guns White Calf.*

seen. He arranged the scalp lock feathers in several ways. I recall quite vividly his sign language story of following a panther for two days over the hills with the sunrise and sunset and finally treeing the animal and shooting it." Although Frazer did not mention the fact, Chief Two Guns White Calf also posed for the composite portrait on the nickel. The autograph of this distinguished Blackfoot chief is among the most fascinating of Indian signatures, a pictograph of two crudely drawn rifles followed by a calf!

If you delight in Americana you will find Indian and Western autographs of great interest, but you should remember that there are many collectors and few autographs.

*Smithsonian Institution*

Original drawing by Sitting Bull depicting his capture of an enemy horse. The Sioux leader drew a line from his mouth to his pictographic signature of a seated buffalo, upper right.

# 7 THE EXCITING QUEST FOR THE PRESIDENTS

My quarry was a rare Washington letter!

Tales of it had reached me from a historic suburb of London. I cabled my brother Bruce, then my agent in Paris, to go to Richmond and try to persuade the owner to sell his treasure.

"It was late in the afternoon when I arrived at a handsome Tudor residence," my brother told me later. "My host greeted me cordially, but the first words he said were, 'I'm not at all sure that I wish to sell any autographs.'

"After a delicious dinner, we drew up our chairs in front of a genial fireplace and my host brought in his collection. He was a pleasant fellow, but as he chatted of his affection for these old documents I felt certain he would never part with any of them. 'Of course, I can't dispose of this,' he would say, tantalizing me with a glimpse of a Queen Elizabeth or Henry VIII letter. Or, 'This one must remain in the family,' and he would tenderly show me a beautiful document of the ill-fated Charles I.

"Presently we found the letter of Washington. I saw with pleasure and relief—for I feared my chase might end with a forgery or a facsimile —that the letter was not only authentic but of very early date.

"I noticed that my host was lavishing his praise entirely upon his superb collection of British royalty and that his brow clouded slightly when he spoke of Washington. Obviously he felt—although he was too much of a gentleman to say so—that Washington was an interloper. I dropped a few subtle remarks to encourage this belief, and to my delight, he burst out, 'I have decided to dispose of the Washington.' "

A few weeks later this great letter was in my hands—one of Washington's earliest letters, unknown to biographers, and written to Governor

Hon^ble Sir

If the Vessel your Honour hir'd of
Col^o Eyre was not left York, or M^r Carlyle's Norfolk
and Hampton We should be glad to have as many
Tents sent up as can be spar'd, for there is no proper
Linnen to make them of here and would be difficult
to get done if there was We also are much in want
of Cutlasses, Halbards, Officer's half Pikes, Drum's &c.
which I am inform'd are in the Magazine That
Drum which was sent up with the Artillery being very
bad is scarcely worth the trouble of carrying

The generality of those Men, who have enlisted
for this Expedition are much in want of, and press
greatly for Cloathings They all desire so earnestly
to be put into a Uniform Dress that they would gladly
do it at their own Expence to be deducted out of their
Pay it was the greatest objection to enlisting and many
have refus'd solely on that account after coming purposely
to do it with Expectation of getting a Regimental Sute
and if I may be so bold to offer my Opinion I can't
think

First page and signature from Washington's letter written at age twenty-
two to Governor Dinwiddie, March 7, 1754.

Dinwiddie on March 7, 1754, when the future President was only twenty-two years old. As I read the faded lines, I felt that exhilaration which comes in opening a fresh page of history! Urging that the militia be given red uniforms, the young frontiersman had written: "It is the Nature of Indians to be struck with, and taken by show and this will give them a much higher conception of our Power and greatness and I verily believe fix in our Interests many that are wavering . . . if it was only a Coat of the Coarsest Red which may be had in these parts it would incur their Attention. Red with them is compared to Blood and is look'd upon as the distinguishing marks of Warriours and great Men. The shabby and ragged appearance the French common Soldiers make affords great material for ridicule amongst the Indians . . . it is my acquaintance with these Indians and a Study of their tempers that has in some measure let me into their Confidence and dispositions . . . ."

Washington's autograph exists in many forms. Years ago I acquired a few fragments from an exercise notebook kept when he was a lad of twelve. Authenticated by the historian Jared Sparks, these early notes revealed a meticulous handwriting and an acute grasp of mathematics. In his youth, Washington was a surveyor and there are still in existence many manuscript surveys executed in his eighteenth or nineteenth years, signed with a tall, aristocratic signature. Every decade these surveys become rarer and the time is coming when they will be unobtainable at any price.

During the Revolutionary War, Washington dictated most of his letters, for his correspondence was enormous. The number of his war letters runs high into the thousands. To this staggering total must be added the immense amount of letters which he penned as President and during his years of retirement at Mount Vernon.

Considering all varieties of Washington's autograph, such as those on the early Potomac Company

George Washington

John Adams

Thomas Jefferson

James Madison

James Monroe

John Quincy Adams

Andrew Jackson

Martin Van Buren

William Henry Harrison

John Tyler

*James Knox Polk*

*Zachary Taylor*

*Millard Fillmore*

*Franklin Pierce*

*Abraham Lincoln*

*James Buchanan*

*Andrew Johnson*

documents, the Mountain Road lottery tickets, ship's papers, military appointments, and certificates of the Society of the Cincinnati, his is one of the most plentiful of the Presidential autographs.

I do not recall reading any letter of Washington which did not, in some way, add to his stature. Is it not the measure of the man that he found no duty, however onerous, beneath his dignity? When the time came, in the summer of 1783, to release the soldiers who had won independence for the United States, Washington began to sign personally the thousands of honorable discharges, including those for privates.

"That is not necessary, general," explained an officer. "The division or brigade commanders can sign the discharges for their men."

Washington shook his head. "No," he said, "these soldiers have fought long and hard. I wish to sign the discharge for each man, so that he will leave the army knowing that I appreciate his work and that I have personally looked upon his name and testified to his honorable conduct."

Washington discharges often turn up badly worn and creased. Folded carefully in the family Bible or grandfather's clock, they were taken out from time to time and reverently displayed. In many states, a military tract was set aside for Revolutionary veterans, with about six hundred acres available upon presentation of a signed discharge. Some discharges were sold to speculators, others were shuttled from one court of claims to another. But today only necessity will bring an owner to part with the Revolutionary War discharge of a patriotic ancestor!

Take a vote among American collectors and you will find that of all autographs the most zealously sought are those of the Presidents. This is as it should be, for a complete collection of Presidential letters serves as a sort of history-in-the-rough of our country.

The autographs of the Chief Executives vary in price from modest sums for routine documents to

1757, age twenty-five.

1780, as General-in-chief.

Washington's handwriting during the Presidency.

1751, age nineteen.

1749, age seventeen.

1768, age thirty-six.

1796, as President.

The development of Washington's handwriting.

U. S. Grant

Rutherford B. Hayes

James A. Garfield

Chester A. Arthur

Grover Cleveland

Benjamin Harrison

William McKinley

Theodore Roosevelt

William Howard Taft

Woodrow Wilson

astronomical amounts for important letters about great historical events. Land grants signed by Madison may be picked up for a few dollars, but a significant letter of Madison about the writing of the Constitution might easily command several thousands. Postwar letters of Grant are available for modest amounts, but when he writes, "I propose to fight it out on this line if it takes all summer," the price mounts like a space rocket!

The American collector is fortunate because the Presidents are fairly common in autographs. The series has its scarcer names, but even these are plentiful compared with such rarities as Henry VII or Louis XI, the kings with whom the British or French collector generally begins his national series.

To add zest to the chase, you may deliberately handicap yourself by searching for Presidents' letters on a special subject or of Presidential date. Letters with medical or dental references, about Indians, concerning financial or political matters—all have their ardent devotees. Not long ago I sold a letter of Washington to his dentist, Dr. Baker of Philadelphia, and the price was a great deal more than Washington paid for his false teeth!

Madison's autographs are not scarce, but the following letter, now in the University of Virginia's Alderman Library, fetched a good price:

It being intimated that an autographic specimen from me, as from some others of my countrymen, would be acceptable for a collection which the Princess Victoria is making; these few lines, with signature, though written at a very advanced age, and with Rheumatic fingers, are offered for the occasion. They will be an expression at least, of the respect due to the young Princess, who is understood to be developing, under the wise counsels of her august Parent, the endowments and virtues which give beauty and value to personal character, and are auspicious to the high station to which she is destined.

JAMES MADISON
February 1, 1834.

As queen, Victoria continued to collect autographs. I recall a letter to an American friend in which she pleaded for a scrap of Washington's handwriting to complete her Presidential set.

Rarest of the Presidents in autographs written while in office is William Henry Harrison, who died exactly one month after his inauguration. I know of only three full autograph letters of Harrison as President. Documents signed by Harrison at this period are also of great scarcity and generally turn up in the form of ships' papers. Not more than a dozen or two exist. Second in rarity as President is James A. Garfield, whose autograph is one of the commonest when dated during other periods of his career. Scarce, too, are Presidential letters of Johnson (almost unobtainable in holographs as President), Zachary Taylor, Chester A. Arthur, and William McKinley.

The autographs of the earlier Presidents are much easier to come by than those of the recent Chief Executives. A President's autograph always becomes more abundant after his death. The friends and acquaintances who received letters from him, and who hesitated to sell them while he was alive, hasten to the nearest autograph dealer with their prizes. Harding was once the rarest of Presidents in full autograph letters (of any date during his career), until the spot was taken by Coolidge, then by Hoover. Today it is almost impossible to obtain full handwritten letters of Hoover, Truman, or Eisenhower. Our future Presidents will conform to this pattern of rarity, and you can always anticipate that the full handwritten letters of living Presidents will be unobtainable.

Some Presidential autographs may be rare in one generation and common in another. Holograph letters of Jefferson were once extremely abundant and sold for modest prices. At the same period, letters of William Henry Harrison and John Adams were rarities, fetching five or ten times as much as comparable Jefferson letters. Today letters of Jefferson are

Warren G. Harding

Calvin Coolidge

Herbert Hoover

Franklin D. Roosevelt

Harry S. Truman

Dwight D. Eisenhower

John F. Kennedy

Lyndon B. Johnson

Richard M. Nixon

not too plentiful and have moved up sharply in value. Adams and Harrison are much commoner. A few years ago, when I bought a huge portion of the papers of Elbridge Gerry, Signer of the Declaration of Independence from Massachusetts, I found more than two dozen letters of Adams, some of them eight or ten pages in length and of great historic importance. Such bonanzas do much to relieve the scarcity of an autograph. About twenty years ago a dealer in up-state New York discovered a folio volume filled with hundreds of short documents and letters of Harrison, penned while an officer in the Old Northwest.

"Harrison was terribly scarce at the time," he told me, "so I offered the first documents at twenty-five dollars each. They sold readily. When the market was saturated, I cut the price to ten dollars."

"And of course you sold many more."

"Yes, I did. But the supply was greater than the demand, so I reduced the price to five dollars. When there were no more takers at this low price —who could have guessed that Harrison would ever sell so cheaply?—I offered the inferior documents at one dollar each, and dealers bought them in batches."

By a turn of events that any farsighted collector could foresee, these documents are now selling for fifteen to twenty-five dollars. Undoubtedly they will increase in value as the available supply is absorbed by new collectors.

It is no exaggeration to say that Lincoln's is the most universally desired of all autographs. There survive many of the early legal briefs prepared by the brilliant young attorney, most of them dated from Sangamon County and signed by Lincoln with one of his firm names, such as "Lincoln and Herndon" or "Lincoln and Logan."

There is not much difference between the script of Lincoln's early—and very rare—quarto letters, generally on legal matters, and the short letters he penned as President. But his Presidential letters are so hurriedly penned that the author of "The Gettysburg Address" sometimes omits a word or makes a grammatical error! There is a marvellous impetuosity to his chirography, a sort of shooting the rapids in pen-and-ink!

Of the many distinguished Lincoln collections, there come to mind those of the Illinois State Historical Library, under the direction of Clyde C. Walton, Jr., the private collection of Justin G. Turner,

The development of Lincoln's signature.

1833, when in New Salem.

1848, U. S. Congressman.

1862, President.

and the huge assemblage of Lincoln photographs gathered by Lloyd Ostendorf, of Dayton, Ohio. There is even a shop in Chicago which specializes in books and autographs relating to the Civil War President—the Abraham Lincoln Bookshop of Ralph G. Newman.

An accident which happened to me not long ago would have delighted Lincoln himself. A friend unexpectedly dropped by my apartment. In one hand I had a Manhattan and in the other a trio of Lincoln documents. I put the documents and my drink on the coffee table as I greeted my visitor. My Labrador retriever greeted him, too, enthusiastically wagging her tail. She knocked over the Manhattan, spilling liquor over the Lincoln documents. Quickly I rushed them to a basin and plunged them in lukewarm water, the best treatment for fresh stains. But the water intensified the ugly blotches! A sudden inspiration hit me, and I asked my wife to mix another Manhattan. Gently and carefully I bathed the old documents in the liquor. The stains disappeared. When I dried the documents out, they were perfect, with no discoloration or odor of alcohol.

When Daguerre invented the first practical camera he paved the way for a new phase of collecting. The earliest President to sign photographs was Millard Fillmore. Not more than a dozen or two exist. Almost as rare are signed photographs of Franklin Pierce and James Buchanan. The photographs they signed were the familiar *carte-de-visite*, measuring

Robot signatures of John F. Kennedy, Lyndon B. Johnson, and Richard M. Nixon. Written in pen-and-ink by the Autopen 50, a device which can scribble 3,000 signatures in a working day, these mechanical autographs are frequently signed on routine letters, photographs, and souvenir items.

about two and one-half by four inches, and printed in gold or brown wash. By the time of Lincoln's inauguration, the collecting of signed *carte-de-visite* photographs was a popular hobby. Unsigned photographs could be purchased by collectors for about ten cents each. Lincoln's signed photos are very rare and in great demand. His successor, Johnson, did not learn to write until he reached manhood, and his signed photographs are extremely uncommon. Generally he signed in a cramped hand beneath his photograph, then more boldly on the blank verso.

Grant and Hayes are fairly common in signed photographs. Most of the photographs of Hayes are of cabinet size (about five by seven inches), as were those of his successors until the period of Wilson, when the modern quarto photograph was introduced. Of the Presidents who followed Johnson, only Chester A. Arthur is really scarce.

Assembling volumes owned by, or presented by, the Presidents is a challenging and difficult pursuit. Volumes from the library of Washington generally bear his armorial bookplate and his signature at the top of the title page. Although he left 884 volumes at his death, many of them were incorporated in the Boston Athenaeum. Most of the books signed by Lincoln are legal tomes, frequently stamped with the firm name of "Lincoln and Herndon." Volumes from the libraries of Jefferson and John Adams are very desirable; and almost unprocurable are books which belonged to James Monroe, William Henry Harrison, Zachary Taylor, and Warren G. Harding.

If you like to pursue the elusive, start a collection of Presidential checks! You will quickly get the impression that our Presidents were very remiss in paying their bills. Checks of Washington and Lincoln are especially difficult to find. For every authentic Washington check there turn up twenty-five forgeries by Robert Spring; but Spring never used the printed forms which are preferred by collectors. Authentic Washington checks are generally filled out on a printed form issued by the Bank of Alexandria. Lincoln's are usually drawn on printed forms of Riggs and Company, or the First National Bank in Washington.

Among the scarcest in bank checks are those of John Adams, Jefferson, Fillmore, Buchanan, Johnson, Grant, both Roosevelts, Wilson, and living ex-Presidents. Hayes and Garfield are also rare, generally represented in collections by salary drafts addressed to the sergeant-at-arms of the House of Representatives. Of extreme rarity are checks of Grover Cleveland, Franklin Pierce, and John Tyler. Distinguished for their profusion are checks of Calvin Coolidge, James Madison, and William McKinley.

As a fillip, some collectors include in their Presidential collection a letter or document of David R. Atchison who was, according to his own

To the Bank of Alexandria.

No. M.ᵗ Vernon ⸺, Nov. 18ᵗʰ ⸺ 1797
11
Pay to Mr. Ja.ˢ Anderson or bearer,
Five hundred ⸺ Dollars, ⸺ Cents.
500
100 DOLLARS.
G Washington

Bank of the United States, July 6. 1793.

PAY to Henry Pepper ⸺ „ ⸺ or Bearer,
twenty seven dollars and sixty seven cents of Dollars.

27. DOLLARS 67 cents
Th Jefferson

No. 26 WASHINGTON, D.C. Feb. 18 1865
Riggs & Co.
Pay to Self ⸺ or bearer
Seven hundred & sixty one ⸺ Dollars
$761.00
A Lincoln

Guaranty Trust Company of New York 1-107
Fifth Avenue Office
New York May 30 1925
No. 1000
Pay to the order of Waldo C. Moore ⸺
One Cent ⸺ Dollars
Payable through the New York Clearing House
$ 01/100
Franklin D Roosevelt

Presidential checks. Personal checks filled out and signed by Washington, Jefferson, Lincoln, and Franklin D. Roosevelt. Note the amount on the Roosevelt check. Never cashed, it is today worth twenty-five thousand times its face value!

*From the collection of Nat Stein*

statement, the most popular of America's Chief Executives during his term of one day. Facetiously he recorded in his diary that he had appointed a full cabinet. He served as President between the end of Polk's term on Sunday, March 4, 1849, and Zachary Taylor's inaugural on Monday, the following day, by reason of his official position as President pro tempore of the Senate!

Since it is fashionable to make nominations for various honors, here are a few candidates:

For the most legible handwriting—Woodrow Wilson.
For the most virile handwriting—Abraham Lincoln (first place); Andrew Jackson (second place).
For the most beautiful and graceful script—George Washington.
For the most interesting letters—John Adams.
For the dullest letters—Calvin Coolidge.
For the funniest letters—Warren G. Harding.
For the secretary who best imitated a President's handwriting—James A. Garfield's secretary who wrote the body of Garfield's letters during the Presidential campaign of 1880–81.
For the boldest signature—John Adams (when President).
For the spideriest signature—John Adams (when aged).
For signing the most land grants—James Monroe.
For signing the most ships' papers—James Madison and James Monroe (jointly).
For the pepperiest letters—Andrew Jackson.

The development of Franklin D. Roosevelt's signature.

1912, New York State Senator.

1916, Assistant Secretary of the Navy.

1933, Governor of New York.

1939, President.

# 8 GOOSEQUILLS THAT SERVED LIBERTY

OUT OF AN OLD LADY'S SEWING BASKET came one of the most spectacular documents discovered in the last decade—Washington's holograph order of battle by which he hoped to annihilate the entire British Army in 1780! One afternoon a young man entered my office with a small folder under his arm. "These papers are probably not of any value," he remarked casually, placing the folder on my desk, "but I didn't want to throw them out before checking with you." As I opened the folder, half a dozen yellowed sheets of paper fluttered out and I recognized the familiar handwriting of Washington. I saw that they were a portion of the lost Jared Sparks papers, a series of important Washington documents described in Sparks' work on the first President.

"Where did these papers come from?" I asked.

"Out of my grandmother's sewing basket."

"Were your grandparents friends of the historian Jared Sparks?"

"Why, yes! Sparks was a good friend of the family."

Is it not strange that after more than a century and a half such great and moving relics from our country's past should still turn up in unexpected places? Even as I write these lines, I cannot help

*John Cadwalader*

John Cadwalader

*Ethan Allen*

Ethan Allen

*Charles T. Armand*

Charles T. Armand

*John Armstrong*

John Armstrong

*Benedict Arnold*

Benedict Arnold

*Prudhomme De Borre*

Prudhomme De Borre

*Geo. Rogers Clark*

Geo. Rogers Clark

George Clinton

James Clinton

Thomas Conway

William Davidson

Philippe Du Coudray

Christopher Gadsden

Moses Hazen

Nathanael Greene

wondering how many other great American documents await discovery!

The Revolutionary War is one of the supreme dramas in history, and you will find it an exciting pursuit to assemble the letters and documents of Washington and his generals. The more important or famous a general, the more abundant his letters. You will find it easy to obtain letters or documents of General Henry Knox, commander of the Artillery; Daniel Morgan, buckskinned leader of the famous "Riflemen"; Philip Schuyler; "Lighthorse Harry" Lee; and the Marquis de Lafayette. For more than fifty years after playing a dominant role in the American Revolution, Lafayette carried on a vast correspondence from his ancestral home at La Grange. His letters, penned in English or French, reflect his urbanity and charm.

The obscure French and German officers who fought for American liberty left the sparsest supply of autographs. Rarest is Rochefermoy, the one "un-

The Chevalier Duportail

Horatio Gates

John Glover

Mordecai Gist

William Heath

Edward Hand

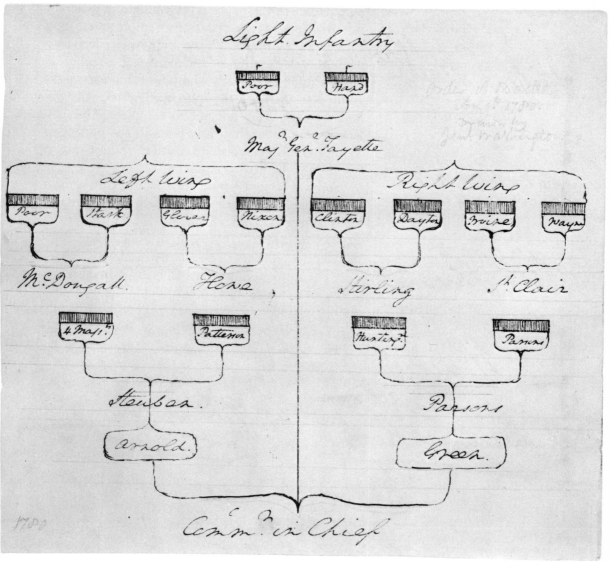

*From the collection of Elsie O. and Philip D. Sang*

Original order of battle in Washington's handwriting. An important historical document (August, 1780). Notice that Washington misspells the names of three of his generals—Lafayette, Paterson, and Greene!

*John E. Howard*

John E. Howard

*Robert Howe*

Robert Howe

*Isaac Huger*

Isaac Huger

*Wm. Irvine*

William Irvine

*HKnox*

Henry Knox

*The Baron de Kalb*

Baron de Kalb

*T. Kosciuszko*

T. Kosciuszko

*Lafayette*

Lafayette

*Charles Lee*

Charles Lee

*Henry Lee*

Henry Lee

*Andrew Lewis*

Andrew Lewis

*Wm. Maxwell*

William Maxwell

*Benjamin Lincoln*

Benjamin Lincoln

*Francis Marion*

Francis Marion

obtainable" in the roster of Washington's generals. But with persistence you can assemble interesting autographs of nearly all the military leaders who made the Declaration of Independence a reality. If you include the generals who bore the brevet ranks granted to them by the individual states, you will find the series very difficult to complete. One collector spent more than fifty years in the pursuit of Washington's generals and finished the set only a few months before his death.[1]

Some years ago I purchased in England a most remarkable Revolutionary War letter, a long report of General Burgoyne on Bunker Hill. Writing from Boston on June 25, 1775, Burgoyne, who had commanded the artillery in the battle, declared:

"The British empire in America is overturned. If the confederacy of this continent is general as I am inclined now to believe, & you determine to subdue it by arms, such a pittance of troops as great

[1] A complete list of Revolutionary War generals may be found in the Appendix.

Britain & Ireland can supply will only serve to pro-
tract the war . . . . [The Battle of Bunker Hill] is
glorious to the troops & important to the nation in
as much as the disgrace of the 19th of April is erased,
& the superiority of the Kings' troops confirmed. It
is certain we had the odds of 3 or 4 to 1 to contend
with. [The Americans are] inspired (I may so call
it) with the fanaticism of a favorite demagogue
[Warren] . . . but our victory has been bought by an
uncommon loss of officers, some of them irreparable,
& I fear the consequences. It not having been my lot
to be personally engaged farther than in the super-
intendence of a cannonade, I had leisure to observe
& a complication of horrors rendered it the greatest
scene the imagination can conceive . . . ."

This great letter, the property of Richard Maass,
is the stellar piece in his collection of Bunker Hill
autographs.

Many times the written accounts of ordinary soldiers would excite the most blasé historian. Although

Alexander McDougall

Lachlan McIntosh

Hugh Mercer

Thomas Mifflin

Richard Montgomery

James Moore

Daniel Morgan

William Moultrie

Peter Muhlenberg

Lewis Nicola

John Nixon

Samuel H. Parsons

John Paterson

Andrew Pickens

Charles Cotesworth Pinckney

Enoch Poor

Count Pulaski

Israel Putnam

Joseph Reed

Arthur St. Clair

Philip Schuyler

Charles Scott

he did not fight at Bunker Hill because he was on detached service, Samuel Emerson wrote a dramatic account of it to his son sixty-five years later. Now in the collection of Justin G. Turner of Los Angeles, his letter brings vividly alive the days when powder and shot were midwives to liberty:

"Genl Warren was the first man that fell on the memorable 17th of June 1775; he showed a good disposition & a brave heart, but was cut down before he began to fight. I have wished a thousand times that I had been in that tremendous conflict; to [have] seen Colo: Prescot stand undaunted, as the British column moved up: 'don't pull a trigger 'till I give the word, then level your guns below the waist-band of their breeches!' The word *fire* was pronounced & the whole front plattoon bit the dust: the second fared the same fate on the second fire; they broke & ran down the hill, while the yankees were decking the ground with red-coats & dotting the splendid carpet with plumed helmets! Scarce a sin-

Elisha Sheldon

William Smallwood

John Stark

Adam Stephen

gle man of our Regiment, was wounded 'till after the last bullet was shot, & the intrepid Commander was forced to order the retreat for want of ammunition. I have heard Colo: P[rescott] relate a curious anecdote which happened just at the time when he ordered the retreat, or more properly, flight. A little fellow, whose nose was bleeding, sat down under the breast work, with his last charge in his gun; a British officer jumped upon the wall right over his head, swung his sword & exclaimed, in triumph, by G. we've won it; the little fellow pointed his gun to his breast & poured its contents thro' his heart! As the officer fell, the boy exclaimed—by G. you've lost it! But George, I am growing young: I must stop this career or run off on foot, like an old soldier of the Revolution. Adieu, my son, may you live long to enjoy the blessings purchased by the blood of true Patriots of the last Century."

A few years ago, a scout offered me a manual on the cover of which was written "Camp at New

John Sullivan

Jethro Sumner

Thomas Sumter

James Varnum

Baron von Steuben

Lord Stirling

Artemas Ward

Joseph Warren

George Washington

Anthony Wayne

*[signature]*

James Wilkinson

*[signature]*

O. H. Williams

York," and the date. The writing appeared very much like that of Nathan Hale, whose autograph is so rare that I had seen only a facsimile. Gambling on the accuracy of my memory, I paid the scout a high price. On investigation I was delighted to find that this was the very manual which Hale had used in his study of military tactics!

The history of the American navy starts with John Paul Jones. Generally his letters are gratifyingly peppery. If Jones could not come to blows personally, he had recourse to his pen. Once, after he had scornfully refused a British bribe, Jones commented in a letter to Jonathan Williams: "They are not rich enough to buy 'the pirate Paul Jones.'"

*[signatures]*

Variant signatures of John Paul Jones.

It was Jones' custom to affix a bold signature to his letters, giving the impression that the body of the letter was written by a secretary. Most of his letters are signed "Paul Jones," but on rare occasions, he used the signature "Jno. P. Jones." Of all American naval autographs, Jones' are the most desirable and the most costly.

An intimate friend of Jones and one of the most influential patriots in the development of the early navy was Joseph Hewes of North Carolina. Hewes' autograph is of great scarcity. Of the Fifty-six Immortals who signed the Declaration of Independence, only a few are harder to obtain.

The engrossed Declaration of Independence was not completed until August 2, 1776. On that day most of the members of Congress appended their signatures. Some who were supposed to sign—Clinton, Alsop, R. R. Livingston, Wisner, Will-

*[signature]*

William Woodford

*[signature]*

David Wooster

ings, Humphreys and Rogers—did not. Others, like Thomas Lynch, Jr., who was a temporary member of Congress, substituting for his father, were not expected to sign, but did. Some members did not affix their names until later in the fall; and Thomas McKean of Delaware added his signature in 1781. The last to sign was John Hay, secretary of state under Theodore Roosevelt, who early in the twentieth century, affixed his name in certifying to the Declaration's authenticity.

By far the rarest of the Signers are Button Gwinnett of Georgia and Thomas Lynch, Jr., of South Carolina. Lynch's autograph is usually represented in collections by tiny cut signatures, removed by his sister from books in his library and presented to pioneer American collectors. Gwinnett was killed in a duel with Lachlan McIntosh less than a year after he signed the Declaration. His signature holds the record price among signers. In 1927, a letter signed by him was retrieved from an outhouse and put up at auction where it fetched the startling price of $51,000. One full handwritten letter of Gwinnett is known to exist and the only full handwritten letter of Lynch, addressed to Washington, is one of the treasures of the New York Public Library.

You may never own a full letter of Gwinnett or Lynch, but you may still have a great deal of pleasure in assembling the autographs of Signers. If you wish to handicap yourself, try collecting only documents and letters which bear the magic date of 1776. Just as intriguing would be a collection of letters and documents of the Signers from your own state, provided you do not live in Georgia or South Carolina! Even a miscellaneous group of Signers, gathered without the hope of completion, is of interest. It is my opinion that an important war letter of Robert Morris, commonest of the Signers, is far more significant than a mere signature of Thomas Lynch, Jr., even though the Lynch signature would be ten times as costly. A sense of proportion is necessary, and in a collection of Signers this is especially true!

Sir Banastre Tarleton

John Burgoyne

Sir Guy Carleton

Cornwallis

Sir Henry Clinton

Sir Thomas Gage

Richard, Earl Howe

Sir William Howe

Signatures of the fifty-six Signers of the Declaration of Independence.

Francis Lightfoot Lee
Carter Braxton    Benj Harrison
Casar Rodney    Tho Nelson jr
Geo: Read    Matthew Thornton
Tho M: Kean    Step Hopkins
Edward Rutledge  William Ellery
Roger Sherman
Tho Hayward Junr
Thomas Lynch Junr
Arthur Middleton    Charles Carroll of Carrollton
Geo Clymer
George Wythe    Jas Smith
Sama Huntington
Richard Henry Lee  Wm Williams
Josiah Bartlett    Oliver Wolcott
Wm Whipple    John Adams
Saml Adams    Rob Treat Paine
Th Jefferson    Elbridge Gerry

Here are some verses I wrote many years ago as a guide to rarity:

*Collectors often wonder why*
*Some Signers of the D. of I.*
*Chose such an awkward time to die.*
*Gwinnett and Lynch, immortal pair,*
*Are most unconscionably rare*
*Gwinnett dueled unsuccessfully*
*And Thomas Lynch was lost at sea.*
*R. Morris on the other hand*
*Left I. O. U.'s throughout the land.*
*Not even prison and its fetters*
*Could stem his tidal wave of letters.*
*C. Carroll's work was never done.*
*He lived to more than ninety-one,*
*Scribbling epistles by the ton.*
*John Hancock's flourish, known to all*
*Is common as pumpkins in the fall.*
*B. Franklin's letters cost a lot,*
*But as for being rare they're not.*
*Collectors often get the blues*
*Because they lack a Joseph Hewes;*
*And, hard as this may be to bear,*
*A. Middleton is also rare.*
*Hooper and Taylor, Wythe and Penn*
*Were also leary of the pen;*
*And those who seek them oft confess*
*They'll settle for a poor D. S.*[2]
*(As for G. Washington, you'll find,*
*The D. of I. he never signed.)*

Some of the Signers of the Declaration also signed the Constitution. Of these the autograph of Franklin is the most costly. Because he was serving in the army, Washington was unable to sign the Declaration of Independence, but he served as President of the Constitutional Convention and was the first to sign the Constitution. The outstanding rarity among Constitution signers is Abraham Baldwin of Georgia. Since it is not difficult to form a complete set, you may wish to include members of the Convention who attended but did not sign.[3] Such a handicap adds zest to the chase and will give your collection an unusual historic interest.

[2] Document Signed.
[3] A complete list of Constitutional Convention members appears in the Appendix.

# 9
## THE INTRIGUING FIELD OF AMERICAN JUDAICA

I RECALL ONE OF THE MOST STARTLING QUESTIONS ever put to me: "Did you know that Columbus may have been a Jew?

"Just consider," my instructor continued, "that nothing is known about Columbus' ancestry. Jacob Wasserman says that Columbus had a Jewish bent in his character. Experts in portraiture claim that he had a Semitic cast in his features. Why, even Columbus' signature is the Jewish triangle, a symbol used on religious vessels. The name Colon, by which Columbus was known, was a Jewish as well as a Christian name . . . ."

"That's very interesting," I interrupted, "but . . ."

"Furthermore, in the letters written to his son, the explorer put a monogram at the top left corner which is actually two Hebrew characters, *Beth* and *Hai*, the second and fifth letters of the Hebrew alphabet and the abbreviation of the Hebrew expression *Baruch Hashem* (Praise Be the Lord).

"And in his will Columbus left half a mark in silver to a Jewish friend 'who lives at the entrance to the ghetto in Lisbon.' "

As my friend paused for breath, I said: "That is a most unusual theory, but I doubt if you will find positive proof for it."

"Maybe not, but there is one thing we do know for certain. It was Abraham Zacuto, the distinguished Jewish astronomer, who urged that Columbus undertake his voyage and whose astronomical calculations were used by Columbus."

If you are a collector of Judaica, I hope that you will not ask that I supply you with a letter of Columbus or Abraham Zacuto as the cornerstone of your collection! The earliest Jewish autographs dated from America which you can hope to obtain would postdate Columbus by two hundred years.

One of the most colorful of the early Jews was Asser Levy, who insisted that he and other Jews be allowed to join the military guard of New Amsterdam. When Peter Stuyvesant refused them this privilege, even putting a tax on them, Levy bought a uniform for himself and his friends and proceeded to stand guard all the same! No autographs of this doughty man have come my way, but I never look at a document dated from New Amsterdam without a hopeful glance for the signature of Asser Levy.

About six hundred Jews fought in the War of Independence, and the autograph letters and documents of all of them are treasured today. Especially desirable are the letters of Colonel David S. Franks, who was killed in a fight with the Indians. Eagerly sought, too, are the autographs of two members of Washington's staff, Major Benjamin Nones and Colonel Isaac Franks.

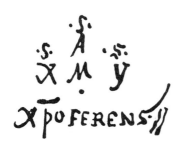

Signature of Christopher Columbus.

Signature of Rebecca Gratz.

Signature of Barnard Gratz.

Signature of Aaron Lopez.

No less appreciated are letters of the Philadelphia merchant, Michael Gratz, whose daughter Rebecca was an intimate of Washington Irving and the reputed prototype of Rebecca in Scott's *Ivanhoe*.

Some years ago a New York dealer offered for $7.50 a Revolutionary War loan certificate made out to the noted Rhode Island merchant Aaron Lopez. I telephoned my order at once and on receiving the document, which bore the signature of the Signer of the Declaration of Independence, Francis Hopkinson, I was delighted to find that it was endorsed with a bold signature of the noted Jewish leader. Here was clear evidence that Lopez had supported the Revolution!

Of all Revolutionary autographs, none is more keenly sought than that of Haym Salomon. One of the few who backed the war effort with hard cash, Salomon had the misfortune to die at the early age of forty-five.

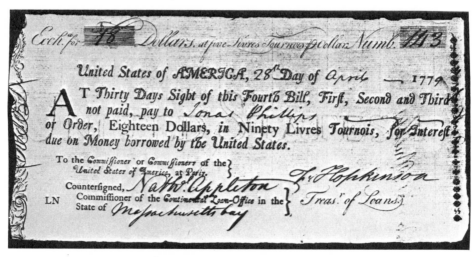

Signature of Haym Salomon.

His autograph is of great rarity. The last example I saw was an endorsement on a loan certificate of Francis Hopkinson, knocked down at auction for $550.

Recently I bought a large collection of loan certificates signed by Hopkinson. Among them I discovered one made out to, and endorsed by, the famous Philadelphia patriot, Jonas Phillips.

The wisdom of the early Jews is apparent in a letter of advice by the Philadelphia merchant Isaac Moses, one of the richest men in America. To his son, Salomon, embarking on a business journey to India, Moses wrote on January 15, 1798: "Remember to do as you would wish others to do unto you, and you need not fear. Avoid disputes. Never meddle

Loan interest certificate issued to Jonas Phillips.

with Religion or Politicks. Enjoy your own Opinion and let everyone do the same. If the Company you are in will enter upon those Topicks, be the hearer. Weigh all your words before you speak & you will find the advantage. Hear every man with patience, without interruption."

Among American naval figures, Commodore Uriah P. Levy, credited with abolishing corporal punishment in the navy, is of special interest to collectors. A letter from his pen might bring several times the amount of a comparable letter by the more famous Oliver H. Perry.

Few realize that Uriah P. Levy had a brother whose career was far more dramatic—Captain Jonas P. Levy. My introduction to this remarkable man came one afternoon when his grandniece entered my office with a bulky manuscript under her arm. That night I read the autobiography of Jonas P. Levy, one of the most amazing men in the annals of American history! With the manuscript were letters of commendation from General Winfield Scott and other Mexican War officers under whom Jonas had served—letters which attested to the truth of his astonishing tale. Like his brother Uriah, he became a sailor as a youth. He had been an engineer on the Mississippi, fought Indians, suppressed mutiny, been attacked by pirates, played an important role in the Mexican War and then, in his old age, penned this lively autobiography as a present to his children. I was eager to buy this undiscovered fragment of history. When it finally became mine, I read it a second time, relishing each page.

Of the Jews who served in the Civil War, there were no less than nine generals and twenty-one colonels! The most brilliant Jewish figure was undoubtedly Judah P. Benjamin, Confederate secretary of state and secretary of war. While his letters are rare and desirable, most of his surviving autographs date from his later years of voluntary exile in England. An

Signature of Uriah P. Levy.

Signature of Judah P. Benjamin.

immense cache of Benjamin letters was recently discovered by Dr. Maury A. Bromsen of Boston. They were included with the Samuel L. Barlow papers, a huge collection of family documents acquired by the Huntington Library for one hundred thousand dollars in 1960.

The most appealing branch of American Judaica is not the historical, but the cultural. If you collect rare books, you may be interested in the autographs of Benjamin Gomez, the first Jewish bookseller in New York City. His distinguished career included publishing. In many respects, he was the precursor of the great publisher Abraham Hart, partner of Carey, whose notable publications include the *Autobiography* of Davy Crockett. The distinguished autograph collector Simon Gratz, author of a volume on the hobby, and Dr. A. S. W. Rosenbach, the outstanding American rare-book dealer, represent the culmination of Jewish bookselling and publishing. Dr. R. would doubtless be amused and delighted to know that his letters are now valued by collectors. Carrying on the literary tradition of Dr. R. is his former employee, Edwin Wolf, II, librarian of the Library Company of Philadelphia and coauthor of *The Jews of Philadelphia*.

Much prized are the letters of scientists. Albert Einstein's letters have a universal appeal. Now and then a page of original manuscript from his Unified Field Theory comes on the market. While a Princeton professor, Einstein carried on a colossal correspondence, and typewritten letters bearing his tiny signature are extremely abundant. Many of his letters were devoted to a subject close to his heart—the establishment of a Jewish nation in Israel. A strong Zionist, Einstein held views very different from those of Sigmund Freud. In a letter which I recently acquired, Freud wrote in response to a request that he support a Jewish settlement in Palestine:

"I should like to ask you not to treat me like 'a leader in Israel.' I

Notes by Einstein for his Unified Field Theory.

should like to be considered only as a modest scientist. Although a good Jew, who has never denied his Judaism, I nevertheless cannot overlook the fact that my absolutely negative attitude to every religion, including the Jewish, separates me from the majority of our fellow Jews and makes me unsuited for the role that you would assign to me."

Signature of Sigmund Freud.

This letter of the great psychoanalyst is now in the collection of Dr. Bernard L. Pacella.

There are three towering figures in American jurisprudence who appeal to collectors, all of them at one time members of the Supreme Court —Louis D. Brandeis, Benjamin N. Cardozo, and Felix Frankfurter. While they are readily obtainable in the form of typewritten letters signed, all are scarce in full handwritten letters. If you search for holograph letters of Brandeis, you will have many competitors.

Of the many distinguished American Jewish artists, one of the most popular was Frederick B. Opper, illustrator of books by Mark Twain and creator of "Happy Hooligan." His cartoon strips delighted several generations of Americans, and some years ago, when the files of the old "Puck" were broken up, scores of his cartoons became available to collectors. More serious are the oil paintings of the eccentric artist, Louis M. Eilshemius. His letters, rambling and pathetic, are often signed with a boldly written "Mahatma."

The Jews have given our country many of its outstanding dramatists and actors, none of whom is more intriguing than Adah Isaacs Menken. An intimate friend of Alexander Dumas, Adah was photographed on his knee, a pose which still causes discerning Frenchmen to look knowingly and wink. Her divorce from the prizefighter Heenan caused a great stir, as did her performance in *Mazeppa*. A most interesting letter by this remarkable woman now lies before me. Writing to her agent, whom she addresses as "brother Ed," Adah describes her triumph in Baltimore: "Houses crowded every night . . . . I had $1,500 worth of diamonds presented me by the citizens, and all for 'Mazeppa.' It was the greatest present ever got up in Baltimore, and no humbug about it either. Someday, Ed, I am going to be the greatest artiste in the world, and you will be proud to have me for your affectionate sister, Adah."

The first important Jewish literary figure in America was Mordecai M. Noah, lawyer, statesman, journalist, patriot, and author. In 1820, Noah tried to establish a Jewish colony at Grand Island on the Niagara River, even erecting a monument inscribed, "Ararat, a City of Refuge for the Jews, founded by Mordecai M. Noah in the Month of Tishri, 5586 [Sep-

*Signature of Mordecai M. Noah.*

tember, 1825] and in the Fiftieth Year of American Independence." Noah's autograph is very scarce, and an interesting letter would fetch a large sum. His signature is readily obtainable only in the form of certificates signed as New York Customs inspector; but you should be on guard against certificates bearing his stamped signature.

Not many autographs are so desirable as that of Emma Lazarus, author of the lines, "Give me your tired, your poor," which are inscribed on the base of the Statue of Liberty. Emma Lazarus died at thirty-seven and her autograph is extremely rare. Relatively common are the letters of Bret Harte, whose grandfather was a soldier in the War of 1812. You will have no difficulty in obtaining a letter of Harte, for few authors were more prolific than the creator of "The Outcasts of Poker Flat."

*Signature of Emma Lazarus.*

Of modern writers, none is more colorful than the spectacular, eccentric poet with the flowing tie who took Greenwich Village by storm in

*Signature of Maxwell Bodenheim.*

the 1920's—Maxwell Bodenheim. Bodenheim's autograph is scarce, and you will find it too late to obtain, as others often did, a holograph sonnet in exchange for a drink.

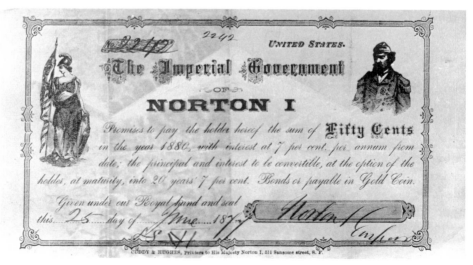

*Society of California Pioneers, San Francisco*

Bank note issued by Norton I.

The most picturesque of American Jews lived in early California. Arriving in San Francisco in 1849, the merchant Joshua Abraham Norton had by 1853 amassed half a million dollars. A fire wiped him out, unhinging his mind. Five years later he came out of obscurity to issue a proclamation as Norton I, Emperor of the United States. For twenty-three years he reigned. His courtly bearing was in striking contrast to his ludicrous uniform, with its gold braid and epaulets, a gigantic sword (a present from a local ironmonger) and shoes which revealed their owner's toes. He deluged San Francisco with remarkable proclamations, sought today by collectors.

The most intriguing facet of the Emperor's activities was his issuance of currency, signed and dated with the imperial signature. These ornate bank notes, often for so modest a sum as fifty cents, were good-naturedly accepted by the San Francisco banks, and are today reckoned at many times their "face" value! A note for fifty cents would easily bring one hundred times the amount set upon it by the "Imperial Government" of Norton I. If there is an Elysium for uncrowned monarchs, Norton I must contemplate with satisfaction the fact that his currency has proved a sounder investment than similar fractional currency issued by the United States of America!

# 10

*Joel Barlow*

*Chas. Brockden Brown*

*J. Fenimore Cooper*

*Stephen Crane*

*Richard H. Dana, Jr.*

*Theodore Dreiser*

WHEN CAPTAIN JOHN SMITH laid down his arquebus and took up a quill to relate a few whoppers about his life among the Indians, he unwittingly launched one of the great literatures of the world. The first important writer to draw his inspiration from America and a great campaigner for the New World, Smith must have penned hundreds of fascinating letters, which his correspondents read avidly, then used for starting their fires. Hardly a letter of Smith's survives!

The successors of Smith were pen-shy. There are few autographs of Michael Wigglesworth, Anne Bradstreet, and Thomas Morton. Some relief from scarcity is provided by Cotton Mather, whose unsigned sermons occasionally occur for sale. Mather penned his notes in minuscule, printlike handwriting on slips of paper which he concealed in his palm during a sermon which might last two hours! Another prolific Colonial author was the diarist Samuel Sewall, a witchcraft judge who recanted. His autograph generally turns up in the form of routine legal documents.

In the times that tried men's souls one of the most sorely tried was Thomas Paine. Elected a member of the National Assembly during the French Revolution, he refused to vote for the execution of

*W. C. Bryant*

Louis XVI and was imprisoned. He barely escaped the guillotine. Many of his letters are mere business notes, but occasionally a really fascinating letter makes its appearance. Paine was an amateur inventor, and not long ago I sold a letter in which Paine described in detail his plans for a rapid-firing cannon! Written to his friend, Jefferson, this letter is now in the collection of Colonel Richard Gimbel of Philadelphia.

The first professional American author was Charles Brockden Brown, whose quaint Gothic novels, much admired by Shelley, are still read by scholars. If honors were awarded for autographic rarity, Brown would be a claimant, for his letters are excessively scarce. Some time ago I obtained three long, youthful letters in which the novelist philosophized darkly on the meaning of life. Adolescent outbursts, strangely introspective and of a graveyardish turn, they strongly suggested Brown's later writings. The price fetched by these letters, now in the collection of C. Waller Barrett, far exceeded Brown's largest yearly income from his literary work!

In the quarter of a century after the American Revolution, New England poetry was dominated—one would almost say ruled—by the Hartford Wits. Their effort to create a native school of poetry fizzled out because there was not a single bona fide poet among them. You may recall Timothy and Theodore Dwight, Joel Barlow, Lemuel Hopkins. With the exception of John Trumbull, the wittiest of the wits, their autographs are not hard to obtain. Whatever their merit as poets, they are a vitriolic group of writers and offer a splendid opportunity for the collector of limited means. Some time ago I acquired a letter of Theodore Dwight in which he commented on his political enemy Jefferson: "Mr. Jefferson has lost a nail from one of his fingers, & wears a *sling*. He has been engaged for some time in a philosophical calculation of the period it will take for the new one to grow. Was ever a country blessed with such a useful sovereign?"

Alexander Hamilton

Timothy Dwight

T. S. Eliot

R. W. Emerson

William Faulkner

Eugene Field

Philip Freneau

Robert Frost

Hamlin Garland

Bret Harte

Nathaniel Hawthorne

Lafcadio Hearn

Ernest Hemingway

W. D. Howells

Henry James

John P. Kennedy

Washington Irving

Oliver Wendell Holmes

After two hundred years of doggerel, American poetry flowered in 1817 with Bryant's "Thanatopsis," written when the poet was only sixteen. Occasionally you may run across a signed excerpt from "Thanatopsis"—such poetic fragments come high! —but Bryant was partial to his lesser known verses when asked for "an autographed quotation." His favorite was the stanza beginning, "Truth, crushed to earth, shall rise again," and he must have copied it out hundreds of times.

Many a poor goose, shorn of its quills, went shivering in the barnyard, and many an ink pot was drained to the bare pewter—all because of the energy of the New England poets! Picture them, if you please, hunched over their desks day and night, scratching out odes, sonnets, and epigrams, and then, for good measure, tossing off a few dozen letters and a mountain of signatures for autograph hounds. In his *Journal* (January 9, 1857), Longfellow noted: "Yesterday I wrote, sealed, and directed seventy autographs." And the amiable Oliver Wendell Holmes complained, in his jocular manner: "I am what my friends and autograph hunters call a 'noted person,' sometimes perhaps 'notorious,' but I am not quite sure of this. They also remind me that I am advanced in life and not likely to be good for autographs much longer, so that it would be the civil thing in me to hurry up my signature before it is too late."

Signed quotations from Holmes's more famous poems, with the exception of "Old Ironsides," are easy to come by. Holmes often wrote out the final stanza from "The Last Leaf," Lincoln's favorite, which begins:

*"And if I should live to be*
*The last leaf upon the tree . . ."*

He was also partial to excerpts from "The Chambered Nautilus," usually the first stanza; and during the Civil War he customarily furnished admirers

*Julia Ward Howe*

with the stanza commencing, "Lord of the Universe, shield us and guide us . . ."

The autographs of Whittier and Lowell are abundant. Whittier seldom quoted his famous "Snowbound," and an excerpt in his hand from that great poem would bring a high price. While the letters of Emerson are numerous, it is hard to find a letter with fine contents. Much of his career was spent in lecturing and, judging from the letters available, it appears that when Emerson was not delivering a lecture he was writing *about* lecture engagements. Such communications are inexpensive; but important letters are far more costly.

*Francis Scott Key*

*Sidney Lanier*

Emerson did not often transcribe his poems, but in the past two years I have acquired complete manuscripts of his famous "Concord Hymn" and "Rhodora." Both were written out in the 1850's, before Emerson developed the aversion to transcribing famous lines which is an occupational hazard of celebrated poets.

*J. R. Lowell*

A man of unbounded generosity and good nature, Henry W. Longfellow never refused a request for his autograph. "If I didn't send it," he explained, "some little boy or girl might watch for the postman day after day and be disappointed." The gentleness and warmth of Longfellow's personality is reflected in his correspondence. His early quarto letters are scarce and expensive, but the letters he penned during the last thirty years of his life are available for modest sums. Longfellow was addicted to lengthy letters and most of them run to three or four pages. His calligraphy was very distinctive. He often broke the individual letters of a word into separate strokes, sometimes such minute strokes that they appear to be a series of tiny dots. He sometimes used ink of a washed-out brown and his letters seem faded, even when perfectly preserved. Longfellow's favorite quotations, often penned for collectors, were the first stanza of "Excelsior," and the quatrains beginning, "The night shall be filled with music," and "Lives of great men all remind us."

*Edgar Lee Masters*

*Cotton Mather*

*Herman Melville*

*George Jean Nathan*

*Henry W. Longfellow*

*Edna St. Vincent Millay*

Eugene O'Neill

Thomas Paine

J. K. Paulding

Sydney Porter (O. Henry)

Carl Sandburg

Samuel Sewall

There is now much interest in the great Southern writers—Simms, Poe, Lanier, Cooke, Timrod, and Hayne. Poe used two styles of handwriting, a fluent script in his letters to intimate friends, and a painstakingly legible hand in his formal letters and

Variant signatures of Edgar Allan Poe.

the manuscripts he prepared for publication. Poe's is the most avidly sought of American literary autographs. Anything in his hand, signed or unsigned, commands an awe-inspiring price.

Few autographs have increased in value so rapidly as Walt Whitman's, possibly because Charles E. Feinberg of Detroit has gathered up so many of them. Mention of Whitman reminds me that not long ago an elderly man entered my office and placed a bulky envelope on my desk. "Original letters," he announced, "original letters of—" he paused dramatically, "—of Ella Wheeler Wilcox!"

Remembered as the versifier who wrote "Poems of Passion," a volume containing neither poetry nor passion, Ella Wheeler Wilcox is an "uncollected" author.

"In these barbaric times," I said, letting my visitor down as gently as possible, "sentimental verse is not esteemed, and these letters would be worth more to you than to me."

The old man then told me that his grandmother had been an intimate friend of Miss Wilcox and had also, early in life, known Walt Whitman.

At this exciting turn in the conversation, I leaned forward eagerly. "Ah!" I exclaimed. "And do you have any letters or manuscripts or books of Whitman?"

"My grandmother," said my visitor, folding his hands piously, "was disgusted by Whitman's vulgarity. He sent her a copy of the first edition of *Leaves of Grass*, with a long presentation inscription. She sat down at the hearth to read it, but she

John Howard Payne

W. H. Prescott

had not looked at more than half a dozen pages before she saw the sort of book it was, and she pitched it into the fire."

Such disappointments do not discourage me. I never know when an unprepossessing figure enters my shop what will be in the envelope in his pocket or in the dilapidated folder under his arm. From a plumber in Brooklyn I bought the original manuscripts of James G. Huneker's *Painted Veils* and *Steeplejack!*

No autograph vanishes more speedily from a dealer's files than a letter of Mark Twain, for the interest in him waneth not, and the ranks of his admirers waxeth year by year. I have owned remarkable Twain items, including the original manuscript of his oft-quoted statement that "the report of my death is greatly exaggerated," and the last penciled words which he scribbled as he lay dying. "Clara," he wrote, addressing the daughter at his bedside, and his pencil wandered over the page as he sought to put in writing the words he could not speak. Perhaps he was asking for a drink of water or, perhaps—who knows?—he was trying to set down his last gibe at a world which had tried him sorely and left him an old and bitter and tired man.

Zealously pursued are the letters of Nathaniel Hawthorne, Henry David Thoreau, and Herman Melville. Hawthorne's full letters are scarce, but the documents he signed as surveyor of Salem Port (often in red ink!) or as United States consul at Liverpool, are very easy to obtain. Thoreau is hard to find in any form, but unsigned pages from his journal are

Signature of Samuel L. Clemens at age eighteen.

Henry D. Thoreau

W. Gilmore Simms

Captain John Smith

Gertrude Stein

Harriet Beecher Stowe

John Trumbull

Daniel Webster

Noah Webster

John G. Whittier

Thomas Wolfe

The great question of the day does not disturb me; for I believe there will be no eternal punishment, except for the man who invented steel pens.

S L Clemens
Mark Twain.

Dec<sup>r</sup> 77

The earth is rude, silent incomprehensible at first — Nature is rude & incomprehensible at first; Be not discouraged — Keep on — There are Divine things well envelopt — I swear to you there are divine things more beautiful than words can tell.

Leaves of Grass — page 125

Walt Whitman

Handwriting of two great American authors. *Top.* Holograph jest signed by Mark Twain. *Bottom.* Holograph excerpt signed from *Leaves of Grass* by Walt Whitman.

occasionally offered. As for the wonderful letters he wrote to his friend Emerson—just try to get one today! A few years ago they could be had for a modest outlay. Herman Melville's autograph is of great rarity. It was his custom to throw out, as soon as answered, all the letters he received, and apparently his correspondents followed the same policy. One explanation for the scarcity of Melville's autograph is that during the last years of his life and in the thirty years following his death in 1891, he was almost forgotten. Few bothered to preserve his letters. But with the publication of Weaver's critical work in 1921, Melville was recognized as a great creative writer and there was a scramble for first editions and autographs, a scramble in which many collectors were doomed to disappointment.

Seldom will you find a letter of Emily Dickinson. She lived and died unknown, only five of her poems being published during her lifetime. Most of her manuscripts, penciled on slips of paper, are in the Harvard library. Emily Dickinson's autograph is the rarest of all major American authors. Her handwriting is delicate and beautiful. Cursive and printlike, it reveals the originality and genius so apparent in her literary work.

One afternoon a debonair young man with a cultivated accent walked into my office. He took from his pocket a slender envelope. "These," he said, removing three scraps of paper on which verses were penciled, "came to me direct from descendants of a friend of Emily Dickinson."

They were forgeries. I felt certain that the young man had fabricated them, but I could not, of course, make any accusation.

"I'm sorry to tell you," I said, "that these are not in the poet's hand writing. They may be copies made by some friend."

The distinctive handwriting of Emily Dickinson.

"I was told by those who ought to know that they were written by Emily Dickinson."

The fellow's brash assurance annoyed me. I walked to a shelf and took down a volume of facsimiles.

"Look," I observed. "Here you see a facsimile of Emily Dickinson's handwriting. Compare it with the manuscripts you have handed me. True; the two handwritings look alike. But notice the sensitivity of Emily Dickinson's hand. Compare it with the ugly, unimaginative scribbling in your examples. Whoever wrote these"—and I picked up the papers he had brought—"is a dull, heavy-witted person, prosaic and without talent."

Later I learned that the young man had visited other dealers, seeking a buyer for his aprochryphal wares.

Half a century ago, in a little New York hotel, O. Henry jokingly quoted a popular song as he lay dying. "Turn up the lights," he whispered, "I don't want to go home in the dark." The lights still burn brightly for O. Henry. His stories, which critics once frowned upon for their "surprise endings," are now regarded as superb portrayals of American life. Few autographs are more appreciated than O. Henry's. I once had a first edition of *Strictly Business* in which the humorist had added an alliterative adornment. "In the name of the Seven Saddle-blankets of Saggitarius," wrote O. Henry, "I swear I will not swerve from sincerity." This fragment of wit from the genial North Carolinian fetched a handsome price!

If you were a friend of William Sydney Porter, alias O. Henry, and your name were William and you were a Colonel, you were in luck, because the noted writer would address you as "Dear Bill," or "Dear Colonel." But if your name were Jack and you had never been in the army, chances are that O. Henry would still greet you as "Dear Bill" or "Dear

Holograph quotation, signed, of O. Henry.

Colonel." His custom of using the same salutation for nearly all of his friends makes it difficult to identify his correspondents. Beautifully written in a bold, flowing hand, his letters reveal the delectable humor of their begetter. Unlike the almost forgotten Joseph Hergesheimer, who treasured the drafts of his novels in a safe, O. Henry never looked upon himself as a great writer. His manuscripts, scribbled in pencil on cheap yellow paper, are now brittle, often crumbling at the touch.

Stephen Crane was one of the first authors to use a typewriter. His letters, even when typed, are hard to find. Scarcer still are the letters of Frank Norris, one of the most brilliant of the turn-of-the-century writers. Except for unsigned pages from *McTeague*, Norris' autograph is practically unobtainable.

Many letters of Henry James survive, mainly acceptances or declinations of dinner invitations. Amazingly, James often turned out a four-page letter which, when the verbose message is boiled down, reduces itself to, "I'm sorry I can [can't] come." On the other hand, Theodore Dreiser's letters are pungent and pithy. You may be astonished to learn that the lyrics to "On the Banks of the Wabash Far Away" were written by Dreiser. I once had a manuscript of this song in Dreiser's hand, with his comment, "I suppose you will put this down as a piece of youthful folly!"

Some of the most eagerly—I might say frantically—collected of modern literary autographs are those of William Faulkner, Eugene O'Neill, Willa Cather, Ernest Hemingway, and Thomas Wolfe. All are scarce and costly. The output of Wolfe was tremendous. He wrote a pound of manuscript for every ounce which was published, but very few of his letters and manuscripts are available to collectors.

Among poets, the letters of Ezra Pound, T. S. Eliot, Robert Frost, and Hart Crane are especially sought. Several colossal correspondences of the eccentric Pound have come my way. His letters are distinguished for their obscurity, odd abbreviations, and obscenity. He delights in oblique communication, and his thoughts are submerged in a bog of abbreviated words. Of Hart Crane I have handled but one letter. When a student in college, early in 1933, I ran across a copy of *The Bridge*. It dazzled me with its symbolism and high-galloping imagery. Except for Shelley, no poet had so immediately overwhelmed me with his power and beauty. I wanted desperately to meet Crane, then a little-known writer. I wrote to him saying that I would hitchhike or ride the rails anywhere to see him. When I searched for an address to which to send my letter, I learned that Crane was beyond handshaking, for he had just committed suicide. It is no exaggeration to say that Crane's letters are rarer than those of Edgar Allan Poe!

Speaking of modern American poets recalls a strange story which I heard many years ago in a little bookstore in Los Angeles. One afternoon I was chatting with my favorite bookman when a tall stranger wandered into the shop. Uninvited, he joined our conversation. Presently he sat on the floor, folding up his long frame like an accordion and clasping his hands over his knees. Somewhat adroitly, I thought, he veered our talk into American literature and after a few random comments, he related this tale:

"Back in 1914, there lived in Chicago a lawyer named Edgar Lee Masters. He was just an attorney, and nothing more, although he aspired to be a poet. He had published several volumes—perhaps you know them? —of trite, imitative, tenth-rate verse. As he paid for the publication himself, it was a harmless vanity, but Masters remained as unknown as before the books were printed.

"One day a college student came to him, an impoverished young man, and asked Masters' help in getting a poetry manuscript published." Our narrator paused, and a wistful look came into his eyes. For a moment I had an unaccountable feeling that he was the college student. "Masters agreed to read it. Although without talent himself, he could spot genius when he saw it—and he certainly saw it in this remarkable book of lyrics which the student had called *Spoon River Anthology*.

"Masters had a daring idea. Why shouldn't he *buy* the volume outright, and publish it as his own? He offered the student five hundred dollars in cash. To the youth it was an immense sum, more than he had ever possessed at one time, and he accepted, giving up the manuscript and also, as it were, the very birthright of his genius.

"Since the lyrics in *Spoon River* were different from any of the anemic verse in his own volumes—in fact, Petit the poet, with his ballads and rondeaux was modeled on Masters himself—the lawyer decided it would be best to publish the collection one poem at a time, and give the impression that he was dashing them off in odd moments of inspiration.

"They were printed one after another, as you know, by William Marion Reedy. As they appeared, their effect was cumulative. They dazzled the critics. Overnight Masters was recognized as a great American poet." Our visitor's voice took on a tone of bitterness.

"Never before or after *Spoon River*," he continued, "did Masters publish a single line of what may be called poetry. His later volumes are feeble, uninspired imitations of *Spoon River*. Either of you could write as well and maybe better.

"Whenever Masters is asked about the original manuscript of *Spoon River* he gets furious. 'There never was an original manuscript,' he roars. 'I wrote the poems on scraps of paper and threw the originals away as soon as I made a fair copy.' [This part of the mysterious stranger's tale is true, for I have since seen letters in which Masters vehemently denied the existence of an original manuscript.]

"Masters and I know the truth about that book," concluded our guest. "You can believe what you wish, but I have just told you the facts behind some of the greatest poetry of this century."

My friend and I were silent, half-stunned by this incredible yarn. Was it possible that here, seated on the floor across from us, was the genius who had created those magnificent poems? For a moment I almost believed his story. Then the thought struck me that he was a sort of Ancient Mariner, seeking an audience for his marvelous tale. Even after he left—and we never saw him again—my friend and I continued to sit in silence. Of course, his tale was fabrication, a pure invention, and yet . . .

*Jos. Addison*

Joseph Addison

*J. Austen*

Jane Austen

*W. Blackstone*

William Blackstone

*W Blake*

William Blake

*B ronte*

Charlotte Brontë

*Robert Browning*

Robert Browning

"THIS TRAITOR," SAID THE AIDE OF CHARLES II, placing before the King a death warrant for John Milton, "was a notorious pamphleteer who vilified His Late Majesty, your father, and who was rewarded for his evil writings by an appointment as Latin Secretary to Cromwell."

The king dipped his quill to sign the warrant.

"He is now blind," said the aide.

Charles paused. "Blind, you say?" He pushed the death warrant away and put down his pen. "Well, then, let him suffer!"

Thus a sardonic monarch preserved the life of the great poet who had yet to write *Paradise Lost*.

The giant figure of Milton dominates his age. His handwriting, always legible, varied considerably throughout his lifetime, becoming shaky only after his blindness. His autograph is of great rarity, obtainable only on deeds or in the body of letters signed by Cromwell.

Even rarer is the autograph of his predecessor, William Shakespeare, of whom only five or six signatures are known. If a full letter of Shakespeare were to turn up, it would sell for around one million dollars!

Of Christopher Marlowe, he of the mighty line, not a pen scratch remains! In my lifelong quest for

*Elizabeth Barrett Browning*

Elizabeth Barrett Browning

*James Boswell*

James Boswell

*John Milton*

Milton's signature in 1649, age forty-one.

Milton's signature in 1663 when blind, age fifty-five.

*Robert Burns*

Lord Byron

Thomas Carlyle

G. K. Chesterton

S. T. Coleridge

Abraham Cowley

Daniel DeFoe

the autographs of Marlowe and Shakespeare, it is my practice to scan the signatures on all documents of their period. How many thousands of old indentures and deeds, mildewed or clean, vellum or paper, crinkled or fresh, faded or bright, in courthand or chancery, my eye has ricocheted over! Always hopeful, I probe each old document for the signature of Shakespeare or Shaxpur or Shaksper, and for Marlowe or Marlow or Marley or Marlin, all the romantic ways in which the great dramatists spelled their names.

Many of Shakespeare's contemporaries, such as Thomas Sackville and Francis Bacon, are occasionally available in autographic form. Available, but very costly! Bacon's signature is more expensive when signed "Fr: Bacon" instead of the usual "Verulam." Once in a decade there turns up an example of Sir Philip Sidney, the cavalier-poet, or of Elizabeth's favorite, Sir Walter Raleigh.

Shakespeare's friend and drinking companion, the dramatist and soldier Ben Jonson, had a large library, and books containing his small, gracefully written signature often occur for sale. I am not very partial to signatures in books. They are the forger's delight.

Thomas DeQuincey

Lewis Carroll and

C. L. Dodgson

Conan Doyle

John Dryden

John Evelyn

Henry Fielding

John Gay

Edward Gibbon

Oliver Goldsmith

Signature of Francis Bacon.

Signature of Bacon as Lord Verulam.

Not long ago I was chatting with an expert on Izaak Walton. The question of presentation books by the great angler came up. Nearly all of the inscribed books by Walton are signed "Iz: Wa:," but my acquaintance told me of a volume, now treasured in a great library, which the Contemplative Man had presented to a lady and in which he had written his name *in full!*

"Surely," I said, "Walton mentioned *The Compleat Angler* in his inscription."

"Why, yes," replied the expert, "but how did you know?"

"Well," I explained, "no enterprising forger would be content with improving upon Walton's signature. He would also want to pitch in a mention of *The Compleat Angler*."

"But I assure you, this is absolutely and definitely NOT a forgery."

I made no answer. I have not looked at the book, so I cannot speak with authority on it. But with such a volume I should require a complete provenance stretching back to the very day—nay, to the very hour—that it was inscribed!

As we move into the seventeenth century, there

Thomas Gray          Robert Herrick          Leigh Hunt

is little relief from rarity. Donne, Suckling, Lovelace, Herrick, Burton, Fuller, Browne, Bunyan—all are of great scarcity, even in ordinary signed documents. In the eighteenth century, we encounter the first plenitude among English literary autographs. John Dryden's letters are of exceptional rarity, although signed receipts for his salary as poet laureate turn up once in a great while. Of the prose writers of the first half of the eighteenth century, the autographs of Defoe, Swift, and Fielding are the rarest. Sterne and Smollett are occasionally available, and letters of Samuel Richardson are fairly common. A few years ago I acquired a collection of documents by Jonathan Swift about the winding up of Sir William Temple's affairs. How eagerly I searched this mass of receipts, which included even the invoice for the black gloves Swift wore at Sir William's funeral, for a document signed by Stella! Alas! Every member of Temple's household had signed receipts except the spritely Esther Johnson.

Fifty years ago, an English dealer received a letter, offering him a collection of letters signed by a pope. The dealer asked to look at them, and was astonished and delighted to find that they were signed by A. *Pope*. Letters of the satirist, always chatty and humorous, are very desirable. Pope's autograph often turns up in the form of partly printed, signed receipts for subscriptions to his translations of Homer.

The diminutive, printlike hand of Thomas Gray has always appealed to collectors. Gray's autograph is most often encountered in the form of unsigned notes, or his tiny signature in volumes from his library. His letters (to the chagrin of collectors) are generally not signed or are signed merely with initials.

Occasionally an acquisitive collector can turn a common autograph into a rarity. Such is the case with Horace Walpole. If you should run across a letter signed O, you should not discard it, for it may be one of Walpole's later epistles, penned when Earl of Orford, and signed with his initial. All but van-

Rudyard Kipling

David Hume

Dr. Samuel Johnson

Ben Jonson

James Joyce

John Keats

Charles Lamb

D. H. Lawrence

John Locke

Tom Hood

*Walter Savage Landor*

Walter Savage Landor

*W. S. Maugham*

W. Somerset Maugham

*Thomas Moore.*

Thomas Moore

*Pepys.*

Samuel Pepys

*A. Pope.*

Alexander Pope

*Mat Prior*

Matthew Prior

*D. G. Rossetti*

D. G. Rossetti

*S. Richardson*

Samuel Richardson

*W Ruskin*

John Ruskin

*Walter Scott*

Sir Walter Scott

ished from the market are the letters of Dr. Samuel Johnson, the Grand Mogul of the Coffee Shops. Recently I discovered a collection of eight letters of Dr. Johnson to Mrs. Thrale, and, in less time than it takes to say "Rasselas," they disappeared into the collection of Donald and Mary Hyde.

Of the literary group which gathered around the scrofulous bulk of Dr. Johnson, the rarest—autographically speaking—is Oliver Goldsmith. If one of his letters were to show up today, it would command a price in four figures. Not too difficult to obtain are autographs of Boswell, Burke, Gibbon, Joshua Reynolds, and Mrs. Thrale.

Often we think of the great poets of the Romantic era as the embodiment of eternal youth. Keats died at twenty-five, Shelley at thirty, and Byron at thirty-six. In their early deaths we have the key to the rarity of their holographs. Keats is by far the rarest. Especially treasured are his love letters to Fanny Brawne. Some years after Keats died in obscurity, his friend, the artist Joseph Severn, handed out the original manuscripts which the poet had bequeathed to him. Eventually, with the supply almost gone, Severn was obliged to cut up pages from "Otho the Great," one of Keats' minor works. Two or three lines snipped from it are today of great value. Many of the poet's manuscripts are in the Harvard Library, collected by Amy Lowell, who believed herself to be the spiritual reincarnation of Keats.

Shelley's letters are more plentiful than those of Keats, yet important letters are very difficult to find and bring high prices. About forty years ago the dispersal of a large group of Shelley's checks made it possible for many admirers to obtain his signature. Like all checks of the period, they bear a criss-cross, four-line pen cancellation over the signature.

An indefatigable correspondent, Lord Byron spent long hours at his desk, transmitting gossip to his friends. His sloppily scrawled missives are invariably interesting, often exciting. The frankly expressed comments make his letters extremely desirable.

Wordsworth, Coleridge, and Southey are autographically common, with the letters of Coleridge the scarcest and those of Southey the most interesting. Robert Burns's autograph, most often found in the form of unsigned manuscripts, has increased in value during the past few years.

Walter Scott has his devotees, and so have the delightful Charles Lamb and his friend William Hazlitt. Of the three, Hazlitt is by far the rarest. Often his autograph is confused with that of a son who bore the same name.

It would not be proper to quit the Romantic period without a mention of two solitary personalities. William Blake, the mystic artist-poet, who lived to an advanced age, wrote very few letters; and his contemporary, Jane Austen, wrote even fewer, most of them being destroyed by her sister Cassandra. The discovery of an unknown letter by Jane Austen is always a literary event. Collectors do not share Mark Twain's opinion that "any library is a good library which does not contain Jane Austen." Also of great rarity are manuscripts penned in microscopic letters by the three Brontë sisters.

You may find it especially interesting to specialize in your favorite author and his circle. If you collect Shelley, for example, you may also draw into your autographic net the letters of Leigh Hunt, Edward John Trelawney, Thomas Love Peacock, Thomas Medwin, William Godwin, Edward E. Williams, and Mary Shelley.

The Victorian period, increasingly popular with collectors, furnishes an abundance of autographs. The letters of Tennyson, Matthew Arnold, William Morris, Dante Gabriel Rossetti, George Meredith, Thomas Hardy, and Robert Browning are so plentiful that the supply will last for many years.

The Armstrong-Browning Library at Baylor University in Waco, Texas marks the triumph of a literary enthusiasm. In a handsome building, lighted by stained glass windows adorned with scenes from *The Ring and the Book*, is enshrined a great collec-

Sir Walter Raleigh

William Shakespeare

George Bernard Shaw

Mary Shelley

Percy B. Shelley

R. B. Sheridan

Philip Sidney

Richard Steele

Jonathan Swift

Robert Southey

Robert Louis Stevenson

A. C. Swinburne

Alfred Tennyson

John Vanbrugh

Horace Walpole

John Wesley

William Wordsworth

Virginia Woolf

Oscar Wilde

W. B. Yeats

tion of letters and manuscripts of Robert and Elizabeth Barrett Browning.

One of the world's most zealous correspondents, Charles Dickens penned letters on the slightest occasion, often without an occasion. From his tireless pen came a flow of fascinating letters, reflecting his hatred of hypocrisy and the affection which he lavished on his friends. For more than thirty years after that great day in 1836 when Mr. Pickwick and Sam Weller burst upon a delighted world, their begetter was a Titan among letter-writers. Many a footsore postman must have sighed wearily as he carried bags of mail to or from the inexhaustible Dickens.

Before me lies a most illuminating letter of Dickens written to his friend David C. Colden during his trip to America in 1842:

"I went to the President's [John Tyler], too, this morning, in company with a namesake [Asbury Dickens] who is Secretary of the Senate. He has a good face (I mean the President) and his manners are very mild and gentlemanly. He expressed great surprise at my being so young. I would have returned the compliment; but he looked so jaded, that it stuck in my throat like Macbeth's amen.

"Some twenty gentlemen were sitting in a lower room, for audiences. There is no denying that they did expectorate considerably. They wrought a complete change in the pattern of the carpet, even while I was there."

Modern biographers speak of Dickens as irascible and egotistical, a hurler of inkpots at his wife, a merciless fellow who disdained to assist the needy members of his family. But how many letters have I seen in which he offers help to orphans or destitute women, or writes in gentle words his advice to beginning authors, or generously opens his purse to some unfortunate!

The handwriting of Dickens as a young man was bold, forceful, and clear, but as he aged rapidly from overwork, it became more and more crabbed. Even the signature shrank and the dashing paraph lost

Development of Charles Dickens' signature.

1831, age nineteen.

1832, age twenty.

1838, age twenty-six.

1859, age forty-seven.

1870, age fifty-eight.

much of its gusto. Yet it was always decorative! Dickens' later signature was reproduced upon the cover of his works, issued by Ticknor and Fields, a set known as the "Snarleow Edition " because of the resemblance of his signature to those words. Dickens wrote with a quill pen and, in his later years, used aniline blue ink. Since he had an aversion for pencils and blotting paper, he preferred the new type of ink which dried quickly.

I know of nothing more provocative than the first reading of an unknown Thackeray letter. He lavished much care on the epistolary art, sometimes illustrating his notes with delightful drawings (occasionally self-portraits), and signing with a great variety of nom de plumes, such as W. M. Tompkins, Chevalier de Titmarsh, or an ornate monogram. Occasionally he indited a letter in the form of an elaborate design or the initials of his correspondent; or he might turn out an invitation in handwriting so tiny that you would need a microscope to read it. Thackeray employed two styles of calligraphy—slanting and up-and-down. The slanting type was used with a quill pen and is the earlier. In later years, when he used a steel pen, Thackeray wrote in the more often encountered up-and-down hand.

The atrabilious Carlyle, whose letters are full of controversial remarks, had a two-word comment for collectors who asked him for a signature and a sentiment—"Autographs—don't!" Apparently Carlyle's plea had little effect, for most of the Victorian albums in which this injunction is pasted are replete with the signatures of other victims.

Whenever I see a letter of Robert Louis Stevenson, I recall the wonderful boyhood summer in which I "discovered" his books, and galloped excitedly through his complete writings. He captivated me, and I came to regard him as a personal friend. It never occurred to me then that I should

W. M. Thackeray's two styles of handwriting.

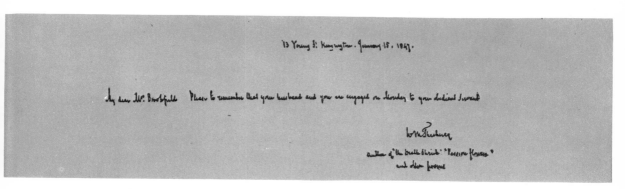

Two unusual Victorian signatures. *Top.* Signature of Dickens' illustrator, George Cruikshank, reproduced in actual size. *Bottom.* Autograph Letter Signed, of W. M. Thackeray, also actual size.

one day be rich enough to own any of his letters. Several years ago, an elderly man, a "picker," entered my office and introduced himself.

"I run a junkshop," he announced, "and I have here something which might interest you."

From a battered satchel he took a small packet of letters. Even before he passed them to me I recognized the distinctive writing of Stevenson. The letters were all addressed to his mother during his travels with Modestine. Every page was redolent with Stevensonian charm. I made a handsome offer, which my visitor accepted.

As I signed the check, I asked, "How did you happen to get these letters?"

"All my life I've been hoping for a real 'find,' and now I've made one at last! Right out of the colored section of Brooklyn these letters came. An old colored lady found them in her closet. She was going to throw them out, but decided to show them to a friend who knew how to read. Her friend said, 'Why, these are by that writer man Stevenson. Maybe they are worth money. You better get a junkman in right away.' So they called me in, and I took one look and I saw they were worth big money. So I bought the lot fast, before they changed their mind about selling."

The picker took the check from my hand and studied it thoughtfully. I could see what was passing in his mind. "Maybe," he suggested, "I'm selling these letters too cheap."

"Why, you bandit!" I exclaimed, laughing. "I'll bet you didn't pay more than twenty-five dollars for them!"

"Oh, yes I did!" he answered vehemently. Then, in a whisper, he added, "Almost."

Among modern British authors, the letters of A. E. Housman, Rupert Brooke, William Butler Yeats, Dylan Thomas, James Joyce, and Virginia Woolf are avidly sought; but there is little interest in Arnold Bennett, H. G. Wells, and John Galsworthy. Rudyard Kipling was constantly badgered by autograph hounds, one of whom finally wrote, in exasperation:

"Dear Mr. Kipling: I have solicited you half a dozen times for your signature, without success. You have not even replied. I understand that

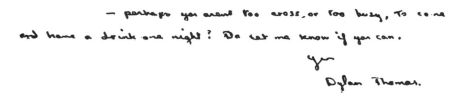

Autograph Note Signed, of Dylan Thomas.

Ayot Saint Lawrence. Herts.
31 July 1946

Try all the creeds, and believe as much of them as suits you: If you find the rituals agreeable, you can attend them and pray your way by putting sixpence (or what you can afford) into the collection. Do not expect any of them to explain the universe to you. None of them can. But all of them may be good for your soul, more or less.

I do not myself belong to any denomination but I find a cathedral a good place for contemplation. I can even endure the service if the music is good and the preacher has something to say and says it well ——

G. B. S

Characteristic Shavian advice from George Bernard Shaw.

you are paid five dollars per word for your poems. I am enclosing a five dollar bill. Please send me one word in your handwriting."

Back came his letter (minus the five dollars). At the bottom, Kipling had written one word, *Thanks*.

A most candid letter writer was D. H. Lawrence, whose prim script suggests the painstaking effort of a schoolboy. His expressions are always pungent and original. I once owned a letter in which he expounded his philosophy of love, offering suggestions to a woman who was infatuated with Katherine Mansfield's husband. More recently I had a letter brimming with nostalgia, penned during his long quest for a sanctuary from his illness: "I'm just longing for a nice amusing time with somebody simpatico. Ordinary people *are* so boring. It is a question of pulse-beat."

There is a great deal of interest in George Bernard Shaw, who wrote half a million letters and cards and never a dull one. His letters are brilliant, pithy, and pertinent. Recently I acquired a characteristic letter in which he discussed the difference between a character actor and a great actor:

"You must always remember that there are lots of people on the stage who seem to be quite charming & delightful players in the five minute turns they get in ordinary fashionable plays. The first ten minutes disposes of all curiosity about you personally, your good looks are exhausted, your dress is exhausted, your tricks have been repeated three times over, there is nothing left to go upon but the play and sheer acting."

# 12 A PAGEANT IN ERMINE

"FROM A PRIVATE GENTLEWOMAN," wrote Anne Boleyn to Henry VIII, after he had condemned her to death, "you have made me first a marchioness, then a queen, and as you can raise me no higher in the world, you are now sending me to be a saint in heaven."

This final epistle of the unfortunate queen is in stark contrast to the impassioned love letters which Henry had written to her only a few years before. Not many letters of Anne Boleyn survive, and the same is true of Henry's other queens. But you will have little difficulty in getting a document of Henry VIII.

However, if you collect the English monarchs, you will probably wish to begin with Henry VII. Earlier rulers were not liberal users of the pen and their autographs are exceedingly hard to get. Ten years ago the only extant signature of William the Conqueror—a mark, or "sign manual" in the form of a cross, for William could not write—was offered by an English dealer for about seven thousand dollars!

Of extreme rarity, too, are the autographs of Richard II and Richard III. Documents signed by the energetic humpback before he clawed and stabbed his way to the throne bear the signature,

/ 137

*Anne Boleyn*

Edward IV

Richard III
as Duke of Gloucester, 1476

Henry VII

Henry VIII

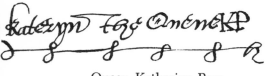
Queen Katherine Parr

Edward VI

MARIE R
Mary, Queen of Scots

Marye the quene
Mary I

"R. Glocestre," and are more plentiful than his kingly scrawl.

The sovereign, as the first man in the kingdom, usually signed documents at the top of the first page; but letters were sometimes signed at the end, after the complimentary close. Henry VII and Henry VIII often appended no more than their initial, followed by the word *Rex* [King]. The word *Rex* was sometimes abbreviated to *Rx*, and to those unfamiliar with the "secretary" or "court" hand[1] of the period the *x* may appear to be a flourish or paraph. Full holograph letters of either ruler are almost unobtainable.

The signature of Elizabeth I is as familiar to British collectors as the signature of John Hancock to Americans. With its ornate flourishes, it was a work of art. Documents signed by the Virgin Queen excite enthusiasm whenever they appear for sale. Like most of her contemporaries, Elizabeth employed two styles of handwriting—a beautifully indited Italian calligraphy, not unlike modern italics, and a rapidly flowing secretary hand.

Oliver Cromwell's signature also occurs in two varieties. Before he took the title of Protector, he signed his name in full or as "O. Cromwell." When

[1] The section entitled *Alphabets* in the Appendix illustrates both the "secretary" and the "court" hand.

James R
James I

Charles R
Charles I

Elizabeth I

Oliver Cromwell
Oliver Cromwell, as General

ANNE R
Queen Anne

Oliver Cromwell, as Lord Protector

dictator, he adopted a regal form of signature, "Oliver P." The earlier form is more desirable. The difficulty of obtaining an example of Cromwell's son, Richard, is more than compensated for by the ease with which you may pick up a document by his supplanter, the rollicking Charles II. Charles was a sloppy penman and his eccentric spelling is less noticeable to most collectors since his full handwritten letters are generally in French. Sometimes his official documents were also signed by the diarist, Samuel Pepys, who was secretary of the admiralty in the reigns of Charles II and James II.

The most colorful of the successors of Charles II is George III. If you collect American Revolutionary autographs, you might wish to include a letter or document of George III, "our last king." His readily available autograph is of unusual interest because in his later years he was insane and blind, and his signature became a weird overlapping of lines and blots.

So abundant are the autographs of George IV and William IV that if all of their letters and documents were laid end to end they would encircle the British empire. During his father's periods of insanity, George IV was prince regent, signing official documents, "George P. R."

Queen Victoria was a prodigious letter writer. Most of her official letters were penned in the third person: "The Queen requests that Lord Palmerston will pay a visit this evening." Her personal letters, of which she wrote vast numbers, are usually signed

James II

Richard, Lord Protector

Charles II

James II, in French

George III

George III, when blind

William IV, as Duke of Clarence

_Victoria_

_Albert, Prince Consort_

_Edward VII, as Prince_

_Edward VII_

_George V_

_Edward VIII_

_George VI_

with initials—V. R. I. Not long ago I had a letter in which the sedate monarch offered advice for an unmarried mother. "Let her wear a ring," wrote the queen, "and no one need be the wiser."

The autographs of the recent British rulers, like those of recent Presidents, are difficult to obtain because they have not yet appeared on the autograph market. Twenty years ago it was almost impossible to get a specimen of George V; but since his death a great many of his letters have turned up, and collectors of one hundred years hence will find his autograph as easy to obtain as that of Queen Victoria or Edward VII. The signature of Elizabeth II is far rarer than that of her Tudor namesake who reigned three centuries ago!

One of the most attractive features of the autographs of the French kings is that, considering their significance, they are priced inexpensively. A few exceptions only make the chase more exciting.

Occasionally you may run across an autograph of Louis XI, the "Spider King," credited with the creation of modern France, but it is with Francis I (crowned 1515) that the royal series usually begins. Documents of his predecessors are costly and hard to get. If you have sufficient funds, you can even obtain a specimen of John II, who came to the throne in 1350.

Once the opponent of Henry VIII in a jousting match, Francis I was a patron of the arts and a great letter writer. Indited on oblong strips of parchment

_Elizabeth II_

in old French script, his letters are fairly easy to obtain. Less plentiful, though no more expensive, are letters of his successor, Henry II, who was slain during a tournament. Francis II, husband of Mary Stuart, left only a few autographs. He is one of the exceptions for which you must expect to pay a high price.

Although he died at the age of twenty-four, Charles IX's autograph is not especially costly, since he reigned for fourteen years and signed vast numbers of documents. Charles was followed by a brace of Henrys—Henry III and Henry IV—both fascinating monarchs and prolific with pen and ink. The numerically consecutive Louis XIII, XIV, XV, and XVI were incessant wielders of the pen and their letters and documents are readily available.

Following Louis XVI, you will come upon another rarity—the Lost Dauphin. Louis XVII probably died in a French prison in 1795. Like the holographs of Napoleon's son, L'Aiglon, the Dauphin's autograph is obtainable mainly in the form of unsigned pages from his youthful exercise books.

The succession of monarchs was interrupted by the French Revolution. The guillotine replaced the king! Robespierre, Danton and Marat were young

Charlemagne (signum)

Charles VII

Louis XI

Charles VIII

Francis I

Louis XII

Charles IX

Henry III

men when they came into power and young when they died. The tiny, almost feminine handwriting of Robespierre, not unlike the diminutive chirography of Madame du Barry, contrasts sharply with his strong and violent character. In the *Bibliothèque Nationale* is an appeal to the people which Robespierre was in the act of signing when his enemies burst in upon him. He had written only *Ro*— when a pistol ball struck his jaw, spattering the document with blood. The stains are still visible, as they are on the petition which Marat was reading when Charlotte Corday daggered him to death in his bath.

Signatures of Danton, Robespierre, and Marat.

Louis XIII

Marat's autograph is found in the form of unsigned pages from manuscript essays, but his letters and documents are extremely scarce. Robespierre's autograph crops up occasionally in the form of letters on ornate vignette paper, signed by him and other members of the Committee of Public Safety.

Louis XV

Louis XIV

Louis XVI

Marie Antoinette

The death of Robespierre, in 1794, ended the Reign of Terror and ushered in the era of Napoleon, whose autograph will be discussed later. "I found the crown of France in the gutter," Napoleon said, "and I picked it up with the point of my sword." Following Napoleon came the greatest anti-climax in history when Louis XVIII ascended the throne. His letters, signed as Louis Xavier Stanislas, are very plentiful. Equally abundant are autographs of his nondescript successors, Charles X, by popular demand of the French people the last of the Bourbon rulers, and Louis Philippe, who was, happily for France, the first and last representative of the House of Orleans.

At moderate cost, you may also assemble a collection of the picturesque Spanish kings. In the Spanish series occur the royal sign manuals of Ferdinand and Isabella. The cornerstone for any Americana collection, the signatures of these two great rulers are more costly when they appear on the same document. The ultimate in desirability are documents bearing the glorious date of "1492." Not long ago I had a document of Ferdinand in which he authorized the sale of Isabella's famous jewels. It is now in the collection of Dr. H. Spencer Glidden, of Andover. In the tradition of Spanish rulers, Ferdinand signed his name, "Yo el Rey" [I the King] and Isabella, "Yo la Reyna" [I the Queen]. This impersonal signature causes a little confusion, for all Spanish rulers used it. If you are unfamiliar with the signature, you may identify the monarch from the

Charles X

Louis XVIII

Signatures of Ferdinand and Isabella.

Signature of Charles V,
Holy Roman Emperor.

Two signatures of
Frederick II, "The Great."

Signature of Maximilian I,
Holy Roman Emperor.

date on the document. The huge scrawl of Philip II, who sent the Armada against England, is familiar to many collectors because of the profusion of his letters.

All Spanish signatures bear a rubric or paraph, that flamboyant flourish under or following the name. The rubric was, by Spanish law, an integral part of the signature. Even without the writer's name it was regarded as legal. Many documents and letters are signed only with the rubric.

Among the titles held by the Holy Roman Emperor Charles V was that of King of Spain. When his letters were penned in Spanish, Charles signed them "Yo el Rey," but his epistles in Latin bear a bold "Carolus" or "Carol," and those in French are signed "Charles." Like other Holy Roman emperors, he wrote vast numbers of letters. Because of the plentitude of their autographs, the Holy Roman emperors appeal to collectors. Their colorful documents, often with ornate initials and pendant seals, capture the baroque flavor of the Renaissance.

A dashing soldier with a literary penchant, Frederick II of Prussia was an intimate friend of Voltaire, exchanging verses with him. Frederick's output of letters was staggering. They were generally dictated to secretaries who indited them in a tiny script, beneath which Frederick would place a huge *Fch* or, by curious contrast, a diminutive "Federic." Frederick's knowledge of German was imperfect, and he preferred to correspond in French!

If you would like to form a collection of autographs which will make a brave display, you will find no more intriguing field, considering the modest cost, than the monarchs of Europe.

Signature of Ferdinand I, Holy Roman Emperor.

King Philip II's council of state. *Top.* Full signatures and rubrics of the council of the noted Spanish monarch. *Bottom.* Rubrics of six of the cabinet ministers whose full signatures appear above. Both documents were signed in 1576.

# 13 LETTERS OF JOHNNY REB AND BILLY YANK

THE MONTH OF MARCH HAD BEEN DAMP AND CHILLY and a persistent cold had heckled me into bed. No remedy helped.

When my wife returned from our shop at noon, she placed in my hands a quarto sheet, on the bottom of which was the signature of Robert E. Lee.

My excitement was keen as I looked upon the famous General Order No. 9, Lee's farewell to his troops! The leader of the Lost Cause had presented it to the distinguished nurse, Sally Louise Tompkins, known as "Captain Sally," the only woman to receive a commission in the Confederate army.

"The descendants of Captain Sally are asking one thousand dollars for it," explained my wife.

"Pay them the money at once!" I cried, exultantly.

That afternoon, as I read and reread Lee's moving farewell address, I felt revived and exhilarated. This glorious old manuscript succeeded where bottled compounds had failed, and by nightfall my cold had broken up.

Here is the text of Lee's farewell:

Hd. Qrs. Army of No. Va.
April 10th, 1865

Genl. Orders
No. 9
After four years of arduous service, marked by unsurpassed courage and fortitude, the Army of Northern Virginia has been compelled to yield to overwhelming numbers and resources. I need not tell the survivors of so

many hard-fought battles, who have remained steadfast to the last, that I have consented to this result from no distrust of them, but feeling that valor and devotion could accomplish nothing that could compensate for the loss that would have attended the continuation of the contest, I have determined to avoid the useless sacrifice of those whose past services have endeared them to their countrymen.

By the terms of the agreement, officers and men can return to their homes and remain until exchanged. You will take with you the satisfaction that proceeds from the consciousness of duty faithfully performed; and I earnestly pray that a merciful God will extend to you his blessing and protection.

With an increasing admiration of your constancy and devotion to your country, and a grateful remembrance of your kind and generous consideration of myself, I bid you an affectionate farewell.

R. E. LEE, Genl.

By an extravagant error on the part of a newsman who wrote up an account of my acquisition, the monetary worth was reported as twenty-five thousand dollars. It may not be many years before this evaluation is reached, since nearly every month sees an advance in the value of important Confederate autographs!

Scholars have long debated about whether an official printed copy of General Order No. 9 was issued, for none is known to exist. Precisely why the fifteen or twenty surviving signed manuscript copies are written in such a profusion of handwritings, on such a variety of stationery has also puzzled authorities. The obvious answer is that all of the surviving signed transcripts are "souvenir" copies, many of them signed within a week or two of the issuance of the original order. Had Lee sent official copies through army channels, the envelopes would survive in at least a few cases (none has been found) and the recipients would naturally have been the top brass of the Confederacy. The lack of signed copies amongst the papers of the outstanding Southern leaders indicates that such official copies were never dispatched. There are a few copies addressed to the recipients—a brigadier general, a major, a captain, and an army clerk. Obviously, these men either copied the order or had it copied, then asked Lee to sign it for them. Possibly the recipient addressed the order to himself (or had a clerk address it for him) *after* Lee had signed the transcript, thus adding a desirable personal touch. Apparently Lee signed souvenir copies for all who requested them. The copy which he signed for Captain Sally, probably in Richmond on or about April 18, bore one correction and a variant word in the text, possibly owing to the haste with which it was copied.

Speaking of Lee recalls an inflammatory letter of the guerilla fighter Colonel John Mosby which I handled many years ago. In it, Mosby made the claim that Lee, after his repulse at Gettysburg, invented a story about a spy in order to save his reputation from the onus of defeat. Mosby wrote that, in company with Pickett, he had visited Lee after the war: ". . . As soon as we got out of the room Pickett spoke very bitterly of General Lee; called him 'that old man'—said that he had his division 'massacred' at Gettysburg. I replied—'It made you immortal.'

Signature of Colonel John S. Mosby.

"Lee should be judged by the same measure that other men are. Published accounts say that the defeat was due to the absence of Gen. Stuart with the cavalry; that until a spy came in on the night of June 28th at Chambersburg and brought the news that Hooker was moving in pursuit, Gen. Lee thought that Hooker had not crossed the Potomac. The outposts of the two armies were in sight . . . .

"Lee's report says that the spy on the night of June 28th brought him the first news [of Hooker's army]. *No spy came in at Chambersburg* . . . . There is a floating legend that Gen. Lee assumed all the blame for his defeat. He did not . . . but put all the blame on Stuart and it was accepted as true. Gen. Lee is responsible for what Stuart did. Then began the criticisms of Stuart that almost broke Stuart's heart . . . ."

A summary of this letter in my catalog distressed Lee's admirers. I was fearful that a new Army of Northern Virginia would descend upon my Yankee shop in Manhattan! But everything ended on a pleasant note. The bond between me and my southern friends is now stauncher than ever!

Reminiscent of old steamboat days are the youthful letters of Robert E. Lee. He was stationed in St. Louis as a young officer, and his documents and letters of that period are often encountered. Many a collector "waiting for the Robert E. Lee" to fill out his collection hopes for a military receipt or a draft letter of the future general. Not long ago I uncovered a cache of fourteen very early letters of Lee, several written from St. Louis, and all addressed to his intimate friend and roommate at West Point, Lieutenant Jack Mackay. Full of charm and whimsey, these letters revealed the jocular side of his nature. Lee tells of adventures with the Indians, his life in the army, and extols the pretty girls with whom he was enamoured. Later, after he abandoned the "flat, stale and unprofitable life of a bachelor," Lee regarded his children as "the dearest annuals of the season," and describes how they played as he worked, "I have been

G. T. Beauregard

Braxton Bragg

made a horse, dog, ladder and target for a cannon by the little Lees since I started writing."

Lee's communications of war date are far more desirable than his earlier letters. During the six years that he survived the war he wrote many letters, all of which are highly prized. On occasions I have acquired diplomas or report cards of Washington College (now Washington and Lee) which bear his signature.

Nearly all Confederate generals are autographically rare of war date. Some are rare of any date. And some are almost unobtainable. Naturally, there is a great difference in value between a youthful letter of a distinguished Confederate general, say Beauregard, Longstreet, Bragg, or Joseph E. Johnston, and a significant or interesting letter of war date. The war letter might command a price ten or twenty times as great as the prewar letter. Letters written after the war bring only a fraction of the amount fetched by letters penned during the conflict, for collectors always seek the dramatic, and the more a letter smells of gunpowder the more eagerly it will be sought.

Among Confederate autographs that of the brilliant Thomas J. "Stonewall" Jackson is sought with impassioned eagerness. Although he served with distinction during the Mexican War he was, like most of the Southern leaders, almost unknown when Fort Sumter was fired upon. Few thought to preserve his early letters, and the slender sheaf of his correspondence which survives is mainly dated during the great conflict. The same is true of J. E. B. Stuart, A. P. Hill, and Albert Sidney Johnston, all killed in battle. Many letters of these great leaders of the Lost Cause have come my way; and a few years ago I bought a huge collection of Confederate material in which were included several letters of Jackson and Stuart. Vividly I recall a letter of the romantic Jeb Stuart. Shortly before his death at thirty- three, Stuart wrote to a young girl:

"Fitz tells me that you prized a little note of mine to him because it was *mine*. 'Tis strange what

John C. Breckinridge

J. A. Early

Richard S. Ewell

Nathan B. Forrest

John B. Gordon

Wade Hampton

William J. Hardee

Ambrose P. Hill

John B. Hood

Thomas J. Jackson

Albert S. Johnston

Joseph E. Johnston

# CHARLESTON

# MERCURY

## EXTRA:

*Passed unanimously at 1.15 o'clock, P. M., December 20th, 1860.*

### AN ORDINANCE

*To dissolve the Union between the State of South Carolina and other States united with her under the compact entitled " The Constitution of the United States of America."*

*We, the People of the State of South Carolina, in Convention assembled, do declare and ordain, and it is hereby declared and ordained,*

That the Ordinance adopted by us in Convention, on the twenty-third day of May, in the year of our Lord one thousand seven hundred and eighty-eight, whereby the Constitution of the United States of America was ratified, and also, all Acts and parts of Acts of the General Assembly of this State, ratifying amendments of the said Constitution, are hereby repealed; and that the union now subsisting between South Carolina and other States, under the name of " The United States of America," is hereby dissolved.

# THE

# UNION

## IS

# DISSOLVED!

a mystic chord binds kindred natures even though never met. He ought to have told you how much and long I gazed at your picture and asked again and again if you still looked like it . . . ." The letter was signed, "Your stranger friend, J. E. B. STUART."

Of all Confederate letters which I have handled, few were more spectacular than the last letter of Albert Sidney Johnston. Hastily scrawled in pencil, probably by campfire light on a drumhead, Johnston's letter holds the essence of drama—an order issued in the midst of a battle. "On your arrival at Monterey," he wrote to General John C. Breckinridge, "immediately put your cavalry in such a manner as to hold the country under vigilant observation towards Hamburg. Having satisfied yourself that there is no enemy in force in the direction of Hamburg, move your command in easy supporting distance of Hardee & Bragg in front, say within three miles of their rear." Opposite Johnston's message, Breckinridge had written: "Reached Monterey that night after a march through bogs, mud and rain of twenty-three miles."

Less than forty-eight hours later, Johnston was directing his troops in front of the Hornet's Nest in the Battle of Shiloh. A stray Minie ball struck his

Robert E. Lee

James Longstreet

George E. Pickett

Leonidas Polk

E. Kirby Smith

Isaac R. Trimble

Joseph Wheeler

Handwriting and signature of J. E. B. Stuart.

←The Civil War starts! Known as the first Confederate printing, this historic document is one of the most desirable of American broadsides. Because broadsides (single-page printings) are occasionally signed in ink and frequently carry significant political, military, or advertising messages, they appeal to autograph collectors.

leg, cutting an artery. Fiercely pressing the attack, Johnston ignored his wound. Within half an hour he was dead. Sadly, Jefferson Davis wrote: "The fortunes of a country hung by a single thread on the life that was yielded on the field of Shiloh."

There are other reasons besides early death which account for the rarity of Confederate autographs. N. B. Forrest, an astute general, was scarcely able to write and never touched a pen when he could avoid it. Some who lived in the shadow of death had little opportunity for writing letters. Such were Belle Boyd and W. C. Quantrill. Of the latter I have not seen even a signature.

Because of the scarcity of paper, necessary for gun-wadding, many military documents of the Confederacy were written on cheap, brown sheets which only feebly resist the incursions of time. The ink, too, was often of soot or gunpowder, a pale, grey scratching that is difficult to read and has a tendency to fade. Many letters of Lee and Pickett were penned in cheap, light-colored ink. Pickett's spidery pen adds to the washed-out appearance of his signature.

During the Georgia march, Sherman's army destroyed thousands of letters and documents, burning virtually everything in its path and leaving behind a gutted South. At the end of the war, the Confederates were forced to abandon posts with great speed; such records as they did not destroy were seized and burned by the advancing Union armies. This wholesale destruction has added to the rarity of all types of Confederate documents.

Important historical autographs of the Confederate States are not often encountered. I once owned the battered guard book of Fort Pulaski in which was recorded the heroic defense and fall of this strategic Confederate fort. This exciting record, now in the collection of Olga Mae Schiemann of Chicago, bore the scars of battle, for half a dozen blank pages were ripped when a brick, blasted by a shell from the wall of the fort, ricocheted over an opened page. General H. W. Benham, who captured the fort, had described the book in a note on the end papers, "This book was hidden at the time of the surrender and afterwards discovered by our troops." The action-packed record came to a dramatic end with the last entry:

"Yesterday at 6 1/2 O.A.M. Genl. Hunter notified Commandant to surrender the Fort—he refused at 8 O.A.M. Bombardment commenced, the fire was very heavy and without intermission until 7 1/2 P.M. then firing ceased on both sides. The South face of ft. is badly breached. 8 of our guns disabled. 8 men wounded, none killed. At 4 O'C P.M. the Federals opened fire and kept up during the night at shot intervals. Heavy

~~Sent~~ Ordered See
letter Book 15 Mar

March 14, 1863

General,

Please have
two of Anderson's brigades
moved up to the U.S. ford
as soon as the roads
will permit. And have
such disposition made
of them as will be best
calculated to prevent
the enemy from crossing
the Rappahannock.

I hope to move my Hd.
Qrs. near you on next
Monday.

I am Genl your obdt Servt
T. J. Jackson
Lt Genl

Brig Genl R. H. Chilton
Asst. A. Genl.
Hd Qrs Dept Ers & N.C.

War letter, signed, of Stonewall Jackson.

firing renewed on both sides this morning at Seven O'C A.M. The fort fast giving away. Moutton of the W.G. badly wounded. Aimes severly wounded. The bombardment continued until 2 1/2 P.M. then surrendered."

If you own original Confederate historical records, you will be interested to know that, since the Confederate States were not legally recognized by the United States, such official records are legitimate spoils of war.

Jefferson Davis' letters are abundant when written before the conflict, usually as Pierce's secretary of war, and when dated from his home at Beauvoir after the war, but during his term as President they are extremely scarce.

The letters of unknown soldiers—the privates and corporals and sergeants and captains and majors—rarely command high prices, yet they are the caviar of the historian. Such letters reveal a spirit of enthusiasm, an eagerness to beat the enemy. When defeated, the soldier felt humiliation and torment. After Bull Run many Union soldiers wrote home saying that never again would they throw down their arms and run. Next time they would die, if necessary, rather than retreat.

Often found in packets tied with ribbons, with each tan envelope bearing a reddish brown three-cent stamp, the letters of Union soldiers are very plentiful. Much scarcer are the letters of the men in gray. Often there is that last letter, scribbled before an impending battle, which bears the distressing note in another hand: "This is the last letter we received from our beloved son. He was killed on the afternoon that he wrote this letter."

I recall a correspondence of several hundred letters penned from various camps and battlefields by Captain H. Spencer Murray, a Union officer. In a letter about the Battle of Fredericksburg, Spencer described vividly how the Confederate troops, after their supply of cannon balls was exhausted, tore up a railroad and fired the rails end over end at the Union troops! In another he told of his meeting with Lincoln. Spencer was impressed with his geniality and his great height. Finally, there came a letter from Captain Murray's best friend, relating how, during an enemy attack, Spence had been struck full in the mouth by a Minie ball. At the moment he was hit, the order came to retreat. The Union troops fell back before the charging enemy, forced to leave Captain Murray's body on the field. A letter of condolence from Murray's commanding officer extolled his courage as a soldier, adding that he was killed while rallying his men. Then, strangely, there were other letters. The first, a penciled note in shaky handwriting, read, "Water, please get me water!" It was smeared with blood. With it was a letter of a Union prisoner to Mrs. Murray, explaining that her son Spencer was still alive, but fearfully wounded by a ball which had ploughed through his teeth and passed out the back of his neck. The blood-stained note was written by Captain Murray, whose mouth was so injured that he was unable to speak. Later came a letter from Spence, scrawled in a quavery hand. He had been left for dead on the battlefield, he wrote, but after his capture, a skilled rebel doctor had saved his life. Following was a letter from Captain Murray's sweetheart, describing her reaction to the news that Spence was still alive, how she half walked and half danced up and down her room, laughing and crying with joy, unable to sit down or stand still. A Hollywood scenario writer could not contrive a happier ending, for subsequent letters revealed that Captain Murray came home to Goshen, married the girl, and settled down to the tranquil life of a bank executive.

It is not possible to read a dozen letters of the men in the ranks, North or South, without finding a reference to drunken officers. One gets a pathetic picture of generals who try to direct maneuvers while half-stupefied and unable to stand or ride without aid. I recollect a letter of Braxton Bragg in which he described how the Confederates lost an important battle because the commanding general was drunk, remaining in his tent during the fighting.

"I candidly confess," wrote Bragg to General Marcus Wright, "my inability to command an army while its senior generals can remain drunk for five successive days."

By comparison with many of the heavy-drinking brass, U. S. Grant not only held his liquor, but could think and act clearly after drinking. Lincoln's remark about sending a barrel of Grant's brand of whiskey to other generals is more than a witticism, for Grant was the most competent and skilled of the Union officers. His war letters and documents are very scarce, despite the fact that he was a ceaseless correspondent and signed thousands of orders dur-

Robert Anderson

D. C. Buell

Ambrose E. Burnside

Benjamin F. Butler

John C. Frémont

Ulysses S. Grant

Henry W. Halleck

Nathaniel P. Banks

D. G. Farragut
(Admiral)

*Winfield S. Hancock*

*Joseph Hooker*

*Philip Kearney*

*Nathaniel Lyon*

*George B. McClellan*

*James B. McPherson*

*George G. Meade*

ing the great conflict.

The autographs of Sherman and Sheridan are uncommon and expensive when dated during the war, but very plentiful during the years following. Their later letters represent a splendid opportunity for the collector of limited means. Think of purchasing original letters by the great Civil War leaders for only a few dollars each! Banks, Buell, Burnside, Halleck, Hooker, and McClellan are readily available, if you are not particular about the date of the letter or document. A few of the Union generals who survived the war are moderately scarce, such as Meade and Thomas.

The only very rare Union autographs are those of officers who were killed in action. There was Lincoln's favorite, the handsome Colonel Elmer E. Ellsworth, leader of the red-pantalooned Zouaves. He was shot at the outbreak of the conflict while tearing down a rebel flag. His beautiful handwriting, once used for clerical work in Lincoln's law office, is very scarce, although the scarcity of it has been much exaggerated. There are many Union autographs much rarer, such as those of the spy, Captain Pauline Cushman.

The only signatures of Barbara Fritchie, of whom no full letter is known to exist, are on legal documents: for example, her will, preserved in the Hall of Records in Annapolis, and a slave bill of sale in the Courthouse at Frederick, Maryland. Judge Edward S. Delaplaine of Frederick has made a special study of Barbara Fritchie's autograph and reports that only half a dozen documents by Whittier's heroine are preserved in Frederick, all of them signed after the age of ninety. From descendants of her attorney Christian Steiner, I obtained another half-dozen autographs, all but two signed with X marks. Many Civil War historians have claimed that Barbara Fritchie was illiterate. "When Christian Steiner first brought her a receipt to sign," his granddaughter wrote to me, "he had arranged a place where she could put her mark. When he pointed to

*John A. Logan*

*[signature]*

Signature of Barbara Fritchie.

*[signature]*

Signature of Mathew B. Brady.

the place, she said, 'Honey, I can write my own name.' She then wrote a very large 'Barbara Fritchie' on the paper."

Of extreme rarity, too, are autographs of the great Civil War photographer Mathew Brady. Nearly all of his letters were written and signed for him by secretaries. You should be on guard against letters purportedly written by him. Perhaps the best means of identifying the signature of the camera-historian of the Civil War is to remember that he wrote a crude, virile script and, in his signature, the capital B lies open at the base and resembles an R. Brady suffered from poor eyesight and this may account for his aversion to writing.

Among the scarcest of Union autographs are those of General Nathaniel Lyon and General Philip Kearney, both killed in action. Twice wounded, with his horse killed, Lyon mounted another steed and was shot down during a cavalry charge at Wilson's Creek, Missouri, on August 10, 1861, when the war was only six months old. General Kearney, a soldier of fortune who had lost his left arm during the Mexican War, was present at the Battle of Fair Oaks when General O. O. Howard, later famous as an Indian fighter, lost his right arm. Looking up from the operating table, Howard quipped: "Well, Kearney, I guess you and I can buy our gloves together from now on." Two months later, while reconnoi-

*[signature]*

Ely S. Parker

*[signature]*

John Pope

*[signature]*

Fitz-John Porter

*[signature]*

William S. Rosecrans

*[signature]*

Winfield Scott

*[signature]*

David D. Porter
(Admiral)

*[signature]*

John Sedgwick

tering at Chantilly, Kearney penetrated behind the Confederate lines and was shot. In tribute to a former comrade whom he liked and admired, Lee sent Kearney's body to Hooker under a flag of truce.

The Civil War marked a drastic change in naval warfare. Gone were the tall and graceful vessels with sails. In their place came the black, squat, ugly "cheeseboxes on rafts"—the first ironclads. In a letter now in my possession, a former Confederate naval officer, James M. Morgan, corrects a popular error:

"Nine men out of ten believe that the first time an ironclad engaged in battle was when the memorable fight between the Monitor and Merrimac took place in Hampton Roads, when the fact is that I was in an action at the Head of the Passes of the Mississippi river when the Confederate ironclad 'Manassas' rammed the U.S. twenty-six gun sloop-of-war 'Richmond' exactly five months previous to that epoch-making battle."

Few letters are so dramatic as those on which you can almost smell the gunpowder. Such a letter, describing the engagement between the *Monitor* and the *Merrimac*, was penned by Thomas Ranson of the First Batallion of New York Mounted Rifles stationed at Fortress Monroe:

"The fight commenced on Saturday between one and two o'clock in the afternoon. The Merrimac came out from Sewel's Point followed by the Jamestown and Yorktown. Immediately upon their appearance Genrl. Wool sent the Cumberland Congress boats. Our boats fought bravely, but their shot and shell had no effect upon the rebel Merrimac, who finally ran right into the Cumberland and drove a hole into her from which she commenced to fill with water, and it was soon discovered that she was sinking. Her deck was literally covered with dead and wounded when she sunk and we were not able to rescue them . . . .

"After the Merrimac had destroyed the Cumberland she then commenced her firing upon the

Philip H. Sheridan

Edwin Vose Sumner

George H. Thomas

Lew. Wallace

William T. Sherman

Congress, which unfortunately had got aground at Newport News, and was not long dispatching her. She then commenced shelling the Newport News Camp. While all this was going on we had orders to report to Genrl. Mansfield at Newport News.

"On arriving, we met a wagon load of ladies coming from there as fast as possible, and the niggers and wenches were running like the devil, and the shells bursting all around them. The shells were flying around us in all directions and we expected every moment to be blown to pieces, as some of them burst within 15 feet of our troop . . . .

"About 50 men, all sharpshooters, went down on the bank of the river, and whenever a man came up on top of the Merrimac we shot at him. We knocked one overboard and they did not come up so often after that, for they were sure to get a ball into them some place.

"In the meantime, Saturday night, Ericsson's battery Monitor ar-rived . . . and Genrl. Wool sent it right away to Newport News to await the coming of the Merrimac on Sunday. Sunday morning about 8 o'clock the Merrimac was discovered to be coming out, also the Yorktown and Jamestown, and putting for Newport News to finish the Minnesota which lay aground there, and then to shell Newport News and land troops. They came in all confidence that the day was theirs.

"After we saddled our horses we went to look at the boats as we had a most beautiful view of the whole thing from our camp. On steamed the Merrimac in all confidence in her self and bang went a gun from her at the helpless Minnesota. But what was her surprise when she seen the little Ericsson [Monitor] which looked like a black ball on top of the water. She stopped immediately, as if thunderstruck, and then let bang at her. The Ericsson returned the shot, letting the Merrimac have one, and the Jamestown another at the same time. Both struck, and the shot went through the Jamestown which made her beat a hasty retreat and likewise the Yorktown. The Merrimac and Ericsson battery then fought like tigers for four hours until the Ericsson commenced firing steel wedges into her, which began to have some effect in putting holes into her, and it was soon discovered that the Merrimac was in a crippled condition and retreated as fast as she could . . . . She soon fired her signal gun of distress and then we seen the Jamestown and Yorktown bearing out to her assist-ance and taking her in tow. Thus ended one of the greatest naval engage-ments that has ever occurred since the beginning of the world. Two boats fighting four hours without stopping and no lives lost on our side and but 2 or 3 on the Rebels side."

This remarkable letter (in which I have corrected the spelling), is now in the collection of the Reverend Cornelius Greenway of Brooklyn.

The autographs of Civil War naval leaders are inexpensive, the most eagerly collected being those of Raphael Semmes, the Confederate raider, and Admiral David G. Farragut. When I was in school, we used a history book which carried a jaunty portrait of Farragut, under which was boldly printed: "*Never mind* the torpedoes! Full speed ahead." Since my school days, I have learned that the exact phrasing of this remark was a little more vehement!

The war cabinet which helped to guide Lincoln was the strangest in our history. At least three men in it felt that they should have been President. The paper work of the Civil War was enormous. Much of the burden of approval and disapproval of plans, applications, petitions, and appointments fell to the pens of Lincoln's cabinet members. There was the cantankerous Stanton, curt and impolitic, but so competent that Lincoln left him almost without supervision; his predecessor, the sly and unctuous Cameron; the ambitious Seward, an energetic and visionary statesman; the overreaching Salmon P. Chase, later a chief justice. These men, together with such able administrators as Montgomery Blair, W. P. Fessenden, and Gideon Welles, were prolific writers and their letters and documents of war date are often available. Oddly, Lincoln's cabinet contains several extremely scarce names—James Speed, the attorney general, and Titian J. Coffey, attorney general ad interim in 1863.

The most bloody internal struggle in world history, the Civil War was the first great conflict to produce a plethora of letters and documents, so that we are constantly revising our ideas of its history as new and significant papers come to light.

# 14 A RAMBLE AMONG THE ARTS

Sarah Bernhardt

Charlotte Cushman

Eleonora Duse

Edwin Forrest

David Garrick

THERE WAS A TIME when theatrical autographs rivaled in popularity those of the Presidents. A letter of Joe Jefferson was then worth as much as a letter of Thomas Jefferson! But the advent of motion pictures, radio, and television ended a great stage history that began with Shakespeare and his fellows.

The autographs of Elizabethan actors, especially those associated with Shakespeare, are unobtainable. Even a great library is fortunate to own a letter of Burbage or Alleyn. The earliest of the important theatrical autographs which you may hope to run across is that of Peg Woffington. The few letters which survive are mostly signed "M. Woffington." Just as rare is the signature of Nell Gwyn, mistress of Charles II. So romantic was the career of the ex-orange girl that even the most unimaginative writer can turn out a good Restoration tale simply by sticking to the facts. Nell's real name was Eleanor Gwyn. She never learned to write, and her signature was only a large, sprawling E. G., generally found on receipts for her modest pension.

The towering figures of the eighteenth century were David Garrick and Sarah Siddons. Garrick's fame has outlived that of most early actors because he had a knack for scribbling and belonged to the circle of Dr. Johnson. His letters are scarce, but of

Edwin Booth

_Joe Jefferson_

_Fanny Kemble_

_John Philip Kemble_

_Julia Marlowe_

_Sarah Siddons_

_Lola Montez_

_Nell Gwyn_

unsigned prologues and poems there survive literally hundreds.

The imperious Mrs. Siddons was painted by England's greatest artists, described in glowing adjectives by Lamb and Hazlitt, and biographized by the poet Thomas Campbell. The traits of Mrs. Siddons which her contemporaries most deplored have worked to the advantage of autograph collectors. Her arrogance and stinginess so dominated her character that she seldom overlooked an opportunity to administer a rebuff or collect a debt by mail.

Very different in her personality was the flamboyant Sarah Bernhardt. Expressing perfectly the national character of the French, Bernhardt's letters are often freighted with emotion, and despite the illegibility of her script, her appeal is universal. One of the most enthusiastic Bernhardt collectors is Harvey Fondiller.

The nineteenth century produced the Keans, the Kembles, the Booths, and a dozen other great acting families. Their autographs are very inexpensive; and in no other field of collecting will you find letters with such important contents for so small an investment.

If an actress has a scandalous career, her autograph is more appealing. Collectors prefer the spectacular! For example, in the American Hall of Fame is Charlotte Cushman, an actress of genius and virtue. Her letters are worth only a few dollars. Not in the Hall of Fame, and regarded as a mediocre performer, is the adventuress Lola Montez. After her career as a countess, she sailed to San Francisco where frantic suitors fought duels for her favors. Her letters, signed Lola Montez or with the title presented to her by Ludwig I of Bavaria, "The Countess of Landsfeld," sometimes change hands at fifty times the amount fetched by the autographs of the virtuous Charlotte Cushman.

I once owned a letter of Lola, written in sizzling and ungrammatical French, in which she excoriated the French critic Jules Janin, accusing him of "throwing around your heavy weight . . . you imagine that Lola Montez laughs at your follies, but the Countess of Landsfeld won't stand for them. I am going to the Spa. I warn you not to put foot there, for if I run into you, I will horsewhip you wherever I see you. Beware!"

If you enjoy music, you will find drama in the letters and signed excerpts of famous composers. You may not be able to read the letters of Tchaikovsky in Russian, but you can recognize the notes of music which he set down on paper. You need not read German to appreciate a musical quotation written out and signed by Wagner, or Italian to delight in a few bars of music from the pen of Puccini.

Autographs of Purcell and Palestrina are unobtainable. Scarcely less rare are musical fragments or letters of Bach and Handel, most of which were long ago absorbed into great institutional collections. Mozart's letters, often so indelicately phrased as to be unpublishable, are of extreme rarity. Not many years ago there passed through my hands the only surviving portion of the original manuscript of Mozart's "Turkish Rondo," the notes beautifully written, with not a single correction, revealing how it surged out of his creative mind.

Twenty or thirty years ago, it was easy to obtain letters or manuscripts of Beethoven, but an enthusiastic Swiss collector corralled scores of Beethoven holographs, now in the Beethoven Museum at Bonn, so that Beethoven's autograph is today among the rarest and most costly.

Bach

Berlioz

Bizet

Chopin

Debussy

Dvořák

Elgar

Enesco

Foster

*Franck*

How astonished Beethoven would be if he knew that the manuscripts which littered the floors of his studio and which he lavishly handed out to acquaintances are today valued at many thousands of dollars!

Signatures of Beethoven in Modern Roman and German script.

A favorite present of Beethoven to strangers who visited him was an original manuscript, published or unpublished.

Nearly all of the nineteenth century German composers are readily available in letters, although Schubert's autograph is usually found in the form of manuscript songs written on both sides of a sheet. Most popular are the letters of Wagner, Liszt, Mendelssohn, Johann Strauss the Younger, Richard Strauss, and Johannes Brahms. Many of Wagner's letters are complaints about singers who shriek too loudly, or who cannot master the Wagnerian range.

*Gershwin*

*Gounod*

Early signature of Richard Wagner, 1841.

Signature of Wagner in maturity.

Wagner wrote in both German and French, and his letters in French are almost as plentiful as those in German.

The letters of Brahms, generally signed with initials, occasionally baffle the most astute student of German chirography. His handwriting is so illegible that it suggests a psychopathic doodle rather than a communication. From the widow of Brahms's biographer, I purchased the earliest known autograph of the composer, a beautifully penned letter to his

*Handy*

*Haydn*

*Handel*

music teacher, written at the age of nine. The youthful Brahms promised to practice his lessons more
faithfully in the coming year.

Of the Italian composers, the most desirable is
Verdi. His letters are not uncommon, but the zeal
of collectors has made them appear rare. Verdi's
autograph is very much sought in the form of signed
music. Whenever he wrote out a few bars from one
of his operas, he usually selected *Falstaff* in prefer-
ence to the more famous *Aïda* or *Il Trovatore*.

More plentiful are autographs of Puccini, Mascagni, and Leoncavallo. Unlike Verdi, these composers selected excerpts from their most celebrated
work when approached by autograph collectors.
Puccini usually obliged with a few bars from *La Bo-
hème*, *Tosca* or *Madame Butterfly*, penned on the
verso of his visiting card. I recall a letter in which he
expressed regret that he could not find time to set
Tennyson's *Idylls of the King* to music. What an
opera he could have written about the Round Table!

The French composers are a picturesque group,
nearly all plentiful in autographs. Offenbach, Gounod, Massenet, Saint-Saëns and Meyerbeer obliging-
ly wrote out music quotations for admirers. Less

Herbert

Liszt

Mahler

Mascagni

Variant signatures of Jules Massenet.

abundant, yet frequently available, are autographs
of Bizet, Berlioz, and Debussy, whose diminutive
script, generally in blue or purple ink, is a delight to
behold but difficult to decipher.

Menotti

Meyerbeer

Mendelssohn

Mozart

Offenbach

Paderewski

Prokofiev

Rachmaninoff

Rossini

In a letter which I acquired a few years ago, Berlioz wrote of his love for the actress Henrietta Smithson:

"Hostilities have started with my parents; *hers* are doing everything in the world to tear her away from me. Happily that has produced a contrary effect. Oh, God! I can scarcely understand my happiness. We will have horrible difficulties but I would rather die than lose her."

A large collection of musical autographs arrived in my shop one day, and as I was looking through it, I ran across a few bars of music signed by Ravel. A rare item, indeed! While I was trying to decipher the music, Fred Schang, chairman of the Board of Columbia Artists Management, entered my office:

"What's that?" he asked.

"Oh, nothing very important," I answered, knowing that his collection of signed music lacked an example of Ravel.

Taking the sheet from my hands, he glanced at it and hummed the most famous notes from "The Bolero."

Musical excerpt from "The Bolero," signed by Ravel.

*From the collection of Fred Schang*

Rubinstein

Johann Strauss, the Younger

Johannes Brahms

Béla Bartók

Giacomo Puccini

Giuseppe Verdi

Signed music of noted composers.

"That will be seventy-five dollars," I said, subtracting about twenty-five dollars from the actual retail value for the information accidentally supplied me by Mr. Schang. The Ravel excerpt is now one of the stellar items in his collection.

The Russian composers hold almost a monopoly on rarity. Letters and signed music of Tchaikovsky, Prokofiev, Moussorgsky, Rimsky-Korsakov, and Borodin are rarely encountered. Tchaikovsky's sig-

Saint-Saëns

Signature of Tchaikovsky in Russian script.

Signature of Tchaikovsky in Modern Roman script.

Schubert

Schumann

Johann Strauss, the Elder

Richard Strauss

nature, like those of other Russian composers, occurs in Roman as well as Russian script. The autographs of Edvard Grieg, who wrote many letters explaining that his name was Edvard and not Edward, are very abundant. Plentiful, too, are letters of Paderewski.

The autograph of the American composer, Stephen Collins Foster, is among the great musical rarities. Letters in his beautiful and fluent script are rarely offered for sale. Other American composers like McDowell and Nevin are of little interest to the modern collector, and despite the scarcity of their letters, the price asked is generally modest.

This is not the case with George Gershwin. Regarded as America's greatest composer, his letters are avidly pursued by discerning collectors. His popularity increases from year to year, and the supply of autographs dwindles. Gershwin never wrote a letter when there was any way to avoid it.

Among opera stars, the most appealing to collectors are Caruso and Jenny Lind, whose letters are

Sibelius

Jenny Lind

very plentiful, especially when signed Jenny L. Gold-
schmidt. A man of extraordinary talents, Caruso
could have achieved distinction as an artist had he
elected to study painting, for he drew many delightful caricatures of himself and his friends.

If you collect the autographs of composers you
will find signed photographs of special interest.
Some, like those of Tchaikovsky and Wagner, are
very rare. One of the finest collections of signed photos of composers is owned by my brother Bruce, who
has spent many years in assembling it. Another outstanding collection is that of Charles D. Russell, of
Tulsa. James Van Heusen of Los Angeles, a distinguished composer himself, is rapidly adding to his
assemblage of framed musical excerpts.

The letters of artists, like those of composers,
may reveal how or why a work was created. Many of
van Gogh's famous paintings were first set down as

Sullivan

Deems Taylor

Toscanini

Wolf

Stravinsky

Self-portraits of Feodor Chaliapin (*left*) and Enrico Caruso (*right*).

Boucher

Botticelli

Braque

Buffet

Cellini

sketches in letters to his intimate friends. Often van Gogh marked his ink sketches with notations of the colors he planned to use. If you cannot afford to buy original paintings by the world's great artists, you will find an original letter or document more exhilarating than a reproduction.

The dictates of fashion set the price which the letters of an artist command in the manuscript market. Today the Impressionists are in vogue. An enormous sum would be asked for any letter of van Gogh, however trivial the contents. On the other hand, letters of Reynolds and Gainsborough, once fiercely dueled for in the auction rooms, are at present modestly priced.

If you are wealthy, you can start your collection with the colossi of the Renaissance. At long intervals there appear documents indited in the strikingly beautiful script of Michelangelo and Raphael. Raphael's chastely formed writing is as artistic as his paintings. Not in many years has an autograph of Da Vinci turned up. In his notebooks, he used a "mirror" script, writing backwards. The devil-may-care Cellini is represented in a few American collections with letters about the crude gold and silver needed for his craft.

*From an American collection*

Sketch incorporated in a letter of van Gogh.

Except for Hogarth, whose autograph is extremely rare and obtainable only on ornate receipts, letters of the English artists may be found without a prolonged search. Gainsborough's letters fetch two or three times as much as those of Reynolds and Romney; but some figures of this period, such as Sir Thomas Lawrence, are so modestly priced that they offer a unique opportunity.

The autographs of Boucher and Fragonard would be collected if they were available, but only once in a decade does a letter of either come along. As for the mid-nineteenth century French artists, their autographs are so plentiful that you need anticipate no difficulty in acquiring all or most of the distinguished figures, such as Gérôme, Detaille, Delacroix, Corot, Millet, and Breton.

The only letters of Cézanne available are a handful to his critic-friend Geoffroy. Monet, Manet, and Renoir are easy to find, but examples of Gauguin and Picasso do not turn up often. Despite the early death of Toulouse-Lautrec, his immense correspondence to his mother was dispersed and has greatly alleviated the rarity of his autograph. Amusing and intimate, Lautrec's letters to his mother are generally signed with an initial "H," or less frequently, "Henri" or "Your boy Harry," in a humorous affectation of English which may have been a private joke between Lautrec and his mother. In one of the few letters of Rouault to come my way, the modern painter commented wryly on Da Vinci's *Mona Lisa:* "People have seen so much mystery that it would be

Chagall

Corot

Dali

Daumier

Degas

Delacroix

Dufy

Gauguin

Fragonard

Goya

Hicks

difficult without seeming a little singular to say that it hasn't any."

Delectable and startling are the letters of Dali, written in a fractured French based on individual phonetics. Those who delight in the paintings of Dali will find his letters of extraordinary interest. Whatever his defects, he is never pedestrian.

Some of the most unusual autographs discovered in recent years have come from Bucks County, Pennsylvania, long a source of "finds" for the lovers of antiques and rare books and manuscripts. Sergeant John Mitchell, of the Pennsylvania State Police, has a talent for turning up beautiful examples of early *Fraktur*. It is always enjoyable to have a visit from him. Recently, after showing me some historical documents, he placed on my desk a small bundle of letters. Not recognizing the handwriting, I asked:

"And what are these?"

"A few months ago," he explained, "I obtained an enormous mass of papers of John Watson, of

Hogarth

Marc

Lawrence

Michelangelo

Manet

Millet

Monet

Picasso

C. Pissarro

Pissarro

Raphael

Rembrandt

Bucks County, an unimportant local figure of the early 1800's. I went through carton after carton searching for papers of interest."

"What did you find?"

"What I discovered is lying in front of you—a group of letters and documents by and about the great primitive painter, Edward Hicks. They were the only documents of value in the collection, but they will more than repay my effort in wading through pounds of old letters."

Hicks lived and died unknown, and I had never before seen his handwriting. The value of Sergeant Mitchell's find may be gauged by the fact that, save in the hands of descendants of Hicks, there were no letters of this great artist known to exist. I lost no time in buying the collection from the genial trooper. It covered every phase of Hicks's career, ranging

Renoir

Reynolds

Rodin

Romney

Toulouse-Lautrec

Stuart

Trumbull

Utrillo

Da Vinci

Da Vinci (mirror signature)

Vlaminck

West

Sketch by Picasso

from his religious opinions, carriage building and sign painting, to the creative work for which he is remembered. Ironically, Hicks asked in one letter that Watson take his paintings, *The Peaceable Kingdom* and *Penn's Treaty*, to pay the interest on some loans or else sell the two paintings for fifteen dollars!

The caustic epistles of James McNeill Whistler are often signed with a device known as "the butterfly signature," but it is hard to detect any resemblance to a butterfly. Occasionally Whistler used both his written and butterfly signature. His letters are remarkable for their brevity. When his former friend, the poet Theodore Watts, added the name Dunton to give himself a triple appellation, Whistler inquired sarcastically in one of the shortest letters on record: "Theodore, Watts Dunton?"

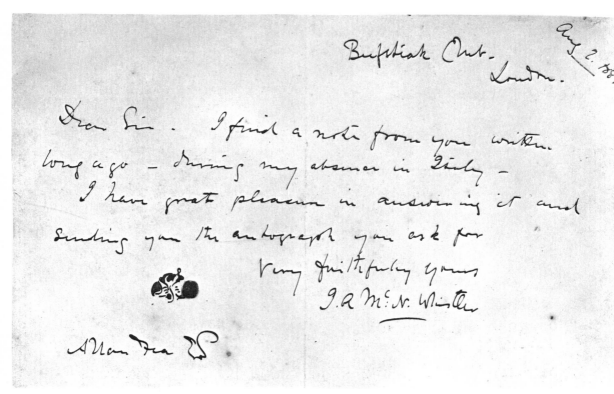

Letter of James McNeill Whistler. On the left of the signature is a characteristic "butterfly signature."

# 15 THE MAN OF DESTINY

"I ALWAYS KNEW THAT MAN WOULD COME TO A BAD END," said the Emperor Francis I of his son-in-law, Napoleon. "He wrote such a villainous hand!"

The scratch of Napoleon's quill was heard around the world. At the height of his power he could, by a single pen stroke, unseat a king or change a nation's boundaries. No task was too great, no odds too many for him.

Not long ago, Junzo Imamichi, visiting the United States, called at my shop. After selecting a number of presents, including a letter of Baudelaire for one of Japan's leading poets and a Lincoln note for the Japanese ambassador, he picked out an early letter of Napoleon.

"I have chosen this letter," he explained, speaking through an interpreter, "as a gift for a dear friend who may never see it, since he is totally blind. But the mere ownership of so intimate a relic of the great man who did not know the meaning of the word 'impossible' will inspire and perhaps give new hope to him."

Napoleon was history's most energetic letter writer. He left an abundance of autographs and a bewildering variety of imperial scrawls. He signed his name at least a dozen different ways, always illegibly. At times

1785, Second Lieutenant          1793, Captain

1794, Brigadier General

1795, Retired General

he assaulted a sheet of paper with such impetuosity that the nib of his quill split, showering the page with ink. He was a master of what Pope called "the last and highest art—the art to blot." Apologizing for his weird chirography, Napoleon said to his aide, General Gourgaud: "My ideas outspeed my pen—then goodbye to the letters and lines!"

Full autograph letters of The Man of Destiny are very rare and costly. Often his penned words seem to be engulfed by the ink, as though Napoleon were trying to blot out the very thoughts he was putting on paper. Some of his most important communiqués have never been completely deciphered. His facetious definition of history as "a fiction agreed upon"

Napoleon's handwriting in the third year of his reign. Words are formed from the first letters only; there is no punctuation; the orthography is without precedent; and the improvised elision blends the words into a succession of weird hieroglyphs which often only the Emperor could decipher.

would be true if we were obliged to depend upon his own unreadable holographs! Most of Napoleon's letters were dictated to aides. He would

1796, Commander, Army of Italy

1797, General

1798, Commander, Army of Egypt

often rise in the night, dictating until his secretary was exhausted and had to be replaced by an assistant. At times, he dictated to five or six secretaries at once, moving from one to another as his rapid-fire speech was being recorded. He would emerge from a personal bout with the inkpot un-wearied, but with his white doeskin breeches splattered by ink. "Among Bonaparte's singular habits," wrote his aide, Bourrienne, "was that of seating himself on any table which happened to be of a suitable height for him. He would often sit on mine, resting his left arm on my right shoulder, and swinging his left leg, which did not reach the ground; and while he dictated to me he would jolt the table so that I could scarcely write."

The rarest form of Napoleon's signature is the Italian style—Buona-parte—employed when he was a youth and during his early years in the army. This was the signature with which the cocky young officer signed his letters and documents during the bloody years of the French Revolu-tion and in the early days when he was forcing his way up through the ranks in the Republican army. On February 23, 1796, Napoleon was ap-pointed general-in-chief of the Army of Italy. Six days later he jettisoned the *u* from his name and thenceforth used the French form "Bonaparte" exclusively. Taking command of a ragged, underfed, ill-disciplined Re-publican army, he speedily gained a succession of brilliant victories which sent the larger forces of Austria reeling and left their commanders dazed and confused. As Bonaparte, he signed his innumerable letters and dis-patches from Italy, Egypt, and during the years of the Consulate. His signature became increasingly illegible and, as his power grew, the "nap" in Bonaparte became larger, foreshadowing the day when that rapidly scrawled abbreviation of "Napoleon" would alter the course of history.

1800, First Consul

1801, First Consul

1802, First Consul

1803, First Consul

His early letters are often written on ornate vignette stationery. You may find it interesting to assemble an example of each variety. If you collect Napoleon by "periods," you will discover that letters from Corsica, Russia, Elba, and St. Helena are the rarest.

Napoleon's early holograph letters were signed *Bp*, and, as emperor, *Np*. There is a legend that he signed with his initials, *N. B.*, an error caused by the fact that the paraph under the terminal *p* makes that letter appear like a *B*. No letter is known which is signed *N. B.*

On May 18, 1804, Napoleon was proclaimed Emperor of the French. His signature expressed itself in many variants, of which the scarcest is the full "Napoleon," reserved for important documents or letters to sovereigns. Letters to his marshals and generals were most often signed *Np*, *Nap*, or *Napol*. Some of his stationery as emperor is watermarked with his profile portrait and the imperial eagle. It is usually gilt-edged.

The size and grandeur of Napoleon's signature varied according to his fortunes. During his first years as emperor it was large and bold, becoming even more so as his power expanded, but after the disasters at the Battle of the Nations and Waterloo, it shrank, contracting to a shaky replica of itself at St. Helena. I once owned Napoleon's abdication, dated from Fontainebleau in 1814 and signed with an uncertain "Nap."

Even the most trivial communications of Napoleon are touched with his amazing genius for terse, forceful expression. In spite of the dispersal in recent decades of a huge number of Napoleonic documents, his autograph has increased in value. The sale of Napoleon's correspondence with his two secretaries of war, Berthier and Clarke, consisting of thousands of letters, temporarily glutted the market, but the oversupply has been absorbed by new collectors. Recently the famed Andre de Coppet collection

1803, First Consul

1804, Emperor

1806, Emperor

1807, Emperor

1808, Emperor

1808, Emperor

of Napoleona was put up at auction in England. The sale, in ten parts, realized £196,454—more than half a million dollars!

Napoleon's first wife, Josephine, had a warm and yielding nature which made her an easy target for all who sought favors. Nearly all of her letters request help for unemployed or indigent persons. Josephine's autograph in its earliest forms—la Citoyenne Beauharnois [*sic*], veuve Lapagerie, and veuve Beauharnais—is of extreme rarity. Usually her letters are signed "Lapagerie Bonaparte" (after her marriage to Napoleon) or "Josephine Bonaparte" (during the Consulate); or "Josephine" (as empress

Autograph Note Signed by Josephine as Empress.

Signature of Josephine as wife of the First Consul.

and ex-empress). Letters signed "Josephine" are the most desirable. Like her husband, Josephine dictated most of her letters. Her full holographs are scarce, although much less so than Napoleon's. A curious habit of Josephine was to run her sentences to the very edge of the right margin

1809, Emperor

1810, Emperor

1812, Emperor

1813, Emperor

1813, Emperor

of the paper and cram or curve the words to avoid a hyphen. According to graphologists, this habit indicates thrift, but Josephine's profligacy is too well known to require comment. Napoleon might also prove a bit bewildering to graphologists, for he often neglected to cross his *t*'s, allegedly a sign of cowardice!

Signature of Joseph Bonaparte, King of Spain.

The marshals and generals of Napoleon were the heroes of a thousand charges! It was during a battle that Napoleon first met Junot, who had brought him a dispatch. In those days, blotters were seldom used, and it was the custom to sprinkle gold or silver sand on ink to dry it. Sitting at his field desk, Napoleon glanced at the message.

"Take back this reply," he said, scribbling several lines on the paper. As he handed the document to Junot, a shell burst, showering them with dirt. When the air cleared, the members of Napoleon's staff were hugging the ground. But Napoleon and Junot had not moved. As Junot took the paper, he shook the dirt from it, remarking: "Good! Now we won't have to sand it!"

The autographs of Napoleon's marshals are easily obtainable, with the exceptions of Lannes and Poniatowski. It is an odd fact that Lannes

Signatures of Marshals Lannes and Poniatowski.

is rarer in America than in France, and Poniatowski is rarer in France than in America! There is a simple explanation. It was an alert American who, many years ago, discovered in Poland a cache of Poniatowski documents, and these papers, mostly dated between 1807 and 1810, relieved the scarcity of what had previously been an "impossible" autograph.

If you collect Napoleon, you will be interested also in his two great antagonists—Nelson and Wellington. The letters of Nelson are rather scarce. He had two very different handwritings, used before and after the

1815, after Elba

1815, after Elba

loss of his right arm in 1797. Wellington's letters are rare only of war date. After 1815, they are so plentiful that examples are found in the most modest collections.

Signature of Lord Nelson with his right hand.

Signature of the Duke of Wellington.

Signature of Lord Nelson, Duke of Bronte, with his left hand.

# 16 FROM THE PENS OF FOREIGN AUTHORS

SEVERAL YEARS AGO A GERMAN REFUGEE handed me a bundle of letters of the German poet, Rainer Maria Rilke. All to an intimate friend, the letters were badly stained. The odor which clung to them was not of perfume!

"How badly these letters have been cared for!" I said, adding facetiously, "Somebody must have had a grudge against Rilke!"

"You are right," replied my visitor in excellent English. "Somebody did have a grudge against Rilke—the Nazis!"

"During the war," he went on, "I was put in a Nazi labor battalion. We were sent into Austria. There we had the job of clearing out the magnificent home of a woman who had just died in a Jewish internment camp. The Nazis wanted the building and grounds for their officers. One day as I was burning a pail of garbage, I saw in it this bundle of letters. I read the signature on one of them, and realized that it was written by Rilke. God knows what the Nazis would have done to me if they had caught me taking anything, even from the garbage, but I hid the letters in my shirt. I could not bear to burn them. Later I dried them out and carried them with me until the war was over. I would not offer them for sale now, only I need money badly."

Youthful signature of Rilke.

182 /

Signature of Rilke in his last years.

Charles Baudelaire

Hans Christian Andersen

Casanova

Colette 1953

Dostoievski

After this touching tale, I could not refuse to buy the letters. The high sum I paid—I later sold them almost at cost—was influenced by my respect for the man who, at the risk of his life, had saved them from destruction.

The spokesman of a disenchanted generation, Rilke's lyrics are often quoted. Another German author whose work was born out of disillusionment was Erich Maria Remarque, author of *All Quiet On the Western Front*. An autograph collector himself, Remarque is not a prolific letter writer. His letters, like those of other German authors, often have dramatic contents, but many of us feel like one of the struggling figures in *The Laocöon* when we wrestle with a German sentence!

Most universally desired of early German autographs is that of Goethe. As he lived to an advanced age, his letters are numerous. Often he signed them G. Sometimes he wrote in German script, some-

Signatures of J. W. von Goethe in German and Modern Roman script.

times not. During his later years, he relied upon a secretary, and most of his letters are merely signed by him. He had an unusual custom of signing printed first editions of his poems. Such signed broadsides are rare and desirable.

The autograph of Goethe's friend, Schiller, who often signed his letters "Sch," is extremely scarce. Of particular appeal to Americans are the letters of Heinrich Heine, lyric poet and satirist. Like Goethe, Heine used two scripts. His letters in French, as fre-

Alexandre Dumas père

Alexandre Dumas fils

André Gide

Signature of Heinrich Heine in German script.

Two signatures of Heine in Modern Roman script.

_Maksim Gorki_

_Victor Hugo_

_Immanuel Kant_

quently encountered as those in German, were signed "Henri Heine"—the name that is carved on his tomb in Paris. Unsigned original manuscripts, nearly always bearing extensive corrections, often turn up, but the price is apt to be high.

Although most Scandinavian authors are not collected in America or England, Henrik Ibsen and Hans Christian Andersen are notable exceptions. I know of no script more beautiful than Ibsen's, exact and precise as copperplate. Ibsen's letters frequently

_Signature of Henrik Ibsen._

_Nikolai Lenin (Ulyanov)_

were penned in German. You will find, too, that Andersen preferred the language of Goethe. The warm-hearted Danish author never failed to oblige his admirers with an autograph poem or quotation, his favorite being, "Life is the most beautiful of all fairy tales." Andersen's autograph has become rare in recent years and Ibsen's, by contrast, seems to be more abundant.

A curious fact about the autographs of Russian authors is that there is no middle ground between the plentiful and the unobtainable. The reason for this phenomenon is that the authors who corresponded with friends in Europe or who spent considerable time in traveling on the Continent or in America left many autographs outside of Russia, today available to collectors. There are other writers who lived only in Russia and who corresponded only with Russian friends. Nobody knows whether their letters are common or rare—only that they are un-

_Martin Luther_

_Thomas Mann_

_Charles Perrault_

_Karl Marx_

_Variant signatures of Ivan Turgenev._

Signature of Leo Tolstoi in Russian script.

Pushkin

Two signatures of Tolstoi in Modern Roman script.

obtainable outside of Russia. In twenty years I have seen but two letters of Dostoievski, and of Pushkin, only an unsigned fragment. But of those titans Lermontov, Gogol, and Chekhov, I have never set eyes on so much as a quill scratch! On the other hand, Turgenev's letters—in German, French, and English, are often met with. So are those of Gorki, who wrote in German or Russian. Most of Tolstoi's letters are in Russian, on spiritual and inspirational matters, but he handled German and French with facility. One of the most revealing letters of Tolstoi, dictated in English to his daughter, passed through my hands some years ago. Writing to George Bernard Shaw, Tolstoi castigated the dramatist for not making full use of his great talents:

"I see the desire to astonish, to astound the reader with your great erudition, talent and cleverness; whereas all this is not only unnecessary for the solution of the questions you touch upon, but very often distracts the attention of the reader from the essence of the subject, attracting it by brilliancy of exposition . . . ."

This great letter is now in the Harvard University library, a famed repository for European autographs, especially Italian and French.

How many books were written by the inexhaustible Frenchman, Alexandre Dumas, nobody knows. He claimed a total that ran into the hundreds! As if to prove the prodigality of his pen, his autograph is

Marcel Proust

Rimbaud

Rousseau

Marquis de Sade

George Sand

August Strindberg

Spinoza

probably the most abundant of any major nineteenth-century author. If he had received a sou for each time he dipped his quill in an ink pot he would have acquired a fortune to rival the Rothschilds.

Almost as plentiful are letters of Victor Hugo, who often signed his letters "Victor H." or merely "V. H." Readily available, too, are letters of Jules Verne, Chateaubriand, George Sand, and Lamartine, with a shadow of scarcity falling upon De Musset and De Vigny. Balzac loathed writing letters. Those he wrote were often signed DeBc, an abbreviation which saved time but which does not appeal to the collector.

Full and initialed signatures of Honoré de Balzac.

The unconventional literary figures are always rarest in autographs. Few people bothered to save their letters. It was obvious that the letters of Hugo and Dumas would have value and were worth saving. But Baudelaire, Verlaine, Rimbaud, Corbière, Laforgue, and others of the Symbolist group acquired great reputations only after they were dead. The rarest is Rimbaud, whose career reads like the plot of one of Dumas' colorful romances. After the age of twenty, Rimbaud ceased to write poetry, commenting sarcastically that "books are good only to cover the foul leprosies on old walls." He had already penned the lyrics which were to change the course of literature when he began the wild adventuring which ended with his early death after a fall from his horse. His autograph occasionally occurs in the form of documents signed while he was a trader in gold and ivory in Harrar, the unofficial advisor to the emperor of Abyssinia. The letters of Rimbaud's friend, the satyr-poet Paul Verlaine, are moderately scarce. The original manuscripts of his poems are often stained with absinthe.

Voltaire

Jules Verne

Of the modern French authors, such as Anatole France, Jean Cocteau, and Romain Rolland, there is an inexhaustible supply of autographs! But of the earliest of France's great authors, there is a great dearth. François Villon, né Montcorbier, hero of Friml's operetta, *The Vagabond King*, left not a single scrap of handwriting. Until the middle of the last century, no autograph of Rabelais was known to exist. The discovery of a letter stirred a controversy over whether it was an original or a copy. The controversy was settled by the subsequent discovery of several undoubted Rabelais originals which proved that the first specimen was a copy. Only a few years ago, a manuscript of Montaigne, author of the famous *Essays*, was sold at auction in New York, fetching a price in five figures.

Paul Verlaine

Zola

Amusing and lively are the letters of Voltaire. Frequently corresponding with his friend, Frederick the Great, or with James Boswell, Voltaire turned out huge numbers of letters. His holograph letters are often signed V, but those dictated to a secretary (whose handwriting closely resembled Voltaire's) are signed "Voltaire." Many delightful letters of the great satirist have passed through my hands, but one in particular I recall, in which he commented to a friend: ". . . Verses are not made so easily as you suppose. Never think that one may write poems like you create children. I had rather plant a thousand trees than write a thousand lines of poetry!"

Sketch of Arthur Rimbaud by Paul Verlaine

# 17 THE SCAMP JUPITERS

THE MOST FASCINATING OF ALL SCOUNDRELS are "the scamp Jupiters," the ruthless kings and fuehrers and assassins. Just why the demon-heroes of history intrigue us is hard to explain. Perhaps because there is, as Baudelaire said, some strange and perverse beauty in evil. Or perhaps because evil is a form of hypnosis.

Not long ago a pleasant young man walked into my office. He told me of his interest in Judaica, then suddenly asked, "What do you have of Adolf Hitler?"

His question did not astonish me, for many of the leading collectors of Nazi autographs are Jewish.

Only that morning I had purchased an interesting document signed by both Hitler and Goering. When I showed it to him, he exclaimed enthusiastically, "Exactly what I want! It's perfect for framing. I'm going to hang it in my den."

I asked why he had selected a document of Hitler to ornament his wall.

"Didn't I tell you?" he said. "I'm starting a rogue's gallery and this will be the stellar piece!"

Shrewd and hard, without a political conscience, Hitler was the greatest conqueror of modern times, perhaps of all times. Dominated by a hysterical patriotism, his sole aim was the glorification of Germany. "I would sign a treaty today," he once wrote, "and break it tomorrow, if it would serve my purpose."

When the allied armies swept into Germany, they bombed and blasted and burned their way through every city, destroying archives as they went. The Germans retreated so quickly that they were unable to

Martin Bormann

Dr. Hans Frank

carry off or destroy their files. In those grim days, I waded through many abandoned records (at the risk of being booby-trapped) in the hope of uncovering interesting Nazi documents. All I found were routine military directives signed by minor officers.

Oddly enough, Hitler's autograph, in the form of military commissions and appointments, is far from rare. Such documents are ornate and impressive. Usually bearing an embossed Nazi seal, they are signed by Hitler under the text, while the countersigner, any one of his powerful henchmen, signed in the lower right. Hitler's tiny signature is something of an enigma. In his early years he signed in full, but with the increase of

Rudolf Hess

R. Heydrich, "The Hangman"

Heinrich Himmler

Wilhelm Keitel

Albert Kesselring

Dr. Hans Lammers

4. 3. 41

Franz von Papen

Walther von Brauchitsch    *Nazi signatures are from the collection of H. Keith Thompson*

his power, his signature degenerated into an illegible, "Af. Hitler," the *Af* being the German abbreviation for Adolf.

Hitler's full holograph letters, penned only to his intimates, are of great rarity. They are signed "Adolf," a signature so hurriedly written that, with its open A and *d*, it appears to read "Wolf." So rare is the autograph of Hitler's mistress, Eva Braun, that only one specimen of her autograph, a signed photograph, has ever passed through my hands.

Of the many Hitler autographs which I have handled, perhaps the most unusual was a brief signed statement dated early in his career:

"We desire nothing except to build up a strong and free Germany on

18. Oktober 1935.

Dr. Joseph Goebbels

Erich Raeder

Karl Doenitz

Walther von Reichenau

*Joachim von Ribbentrop*

Dr. Fritz Todt

Alfred Rosenberg

Heil Hitler!
Ihr sehr ergebe...

terms of equality with other nations. This Germany will be a better guarantor of peace than a Reich and a people suffering political and economic hardships and being ever a new source of unrest."

There are many apocryphal relics of Hitler. You should be wary of postcard paintings or architectural drawings purporting to be Hitler's. Even while he was alive, his early drawings were extensively forged, and Hitler himself denounced the fabrications!

Of Hitler's associates, only documents of Heinrich Himmler are abundant. Himmler's sharp, angular signature, almost like a harrow, was often affixed to ornate awards of storm-trooper medals or daggers. Rather scarce

Holograph greeting signed by Hitler

Hitler's signature, 1914

Hitler's signature, 1940

**Variant signatures of Adolf Hitler.**

*Karl von Rundstedt*

*Heil dem Führer!*

Erwin Rommel          *Generaloberst.*

are documents bearing the undecipherable signature of Goering. His fu
holographs are extremely rare, but not long ago I obtained a group c
postal cards written as a prisoner-of-war to his children's nurse. Goerin
warned her against going into the Russian zone!

If you collect Nazi autographs, you will search a long time befor
finding a document of Goebbels. Rarer still are letters of Rudolf Hes
Hitler's secretary, who secretly flew to England in the hope of negotiatin
peace. The autographs of the other top Nazi officials—Ribbentrop, vo
Rundstedt, Keitel—are all scarce, as are the letters of the colorful Fiel
Marshal Rommel, most brilliant military figure of World War II. Ron

Variant signatures of Hermann Goering.

World War I ace, 1918

**Heil Hitler?**

On his visiting card, 1935

Generalfeldmarschall.

On a war directive, 1940

Fascist leaders.

Benito Mussolin

Italo Balbo

Count Galeazzo Ciano.

mel never joined the Nazi party, and in spite of his ill-concealed aversion to Hitler, he rose to a high position in the German military hierarchy. Most of Rommel's personal papers and letters were kept intact by his widow; and many of his military papers were destroyed when the Nazi armies retreated from Africa.

Rommel's letters from Africa are signed in pencil, perhaps because ink evaporated so quickly in the desert sun. In a letter dated from Africa, May 6, 1942, the "Desert Fox" wrote: "Soon the time is coming when we will test our strength again. We hope that it will bring final victory." Only a few weeks later, he captured Tobruk!

A masterpiece of strategy was disclosed when I discovered the original top-secret Nazi plans for the conquest of Holland and Belgium. They had belonged to General Paulus, and some of the directives were in his hand. The Nazis had foreseen every move of the enemy. No contingency was overlooked. Realizing that the Dutch would flood their country by opening the dykes, the Germans provided their advance troops with rubber rafts, so that the efforts of the Dutch to stop the invaders actually worked to the Nazis' advantage! From these documents, dated four or five months before the attack, it was clear that the swiftest conquest in history was also the best planned!

There is a quality of mystery about the occasional autographs which come out of Russia. The only document of Ivan the Terrible ever offered for sale in America appeared in one of my catalogs a few years ago. Signed with a weird scrawl by the monarch who slew his son in a fit of temper, it bore the Czar's red wax seal and authorized an abbot to purchase tax-free salt. Now and then you will encounter a letter of Peter the Great, usually addressed to another sovereign and adorned with paper seals. Much commoner are documents of Catherine the Great, readily obtainable in the form of military commissions on parchment, with woodcut borders, and bearing the Russian form of her signature, "Ekaterina."

Few dictators have wielded the immense power of the uncouth monk, Rasputin. Though he could barely write, the crudely penned "Grigori" with which he signed his communications was enough to open or close any door, to bring death or grant reprieve. Surmounting his orders with a tiny cross, Rasputin would write, "Beloved, Do it! Grigori." When someone asked why he was not more explicit in giving important instructions, Rasputin answered: "Why should I write more. The person to whom I give the letter knows to whom he is to take it. The recipient knows it is for him when he receives it. And the person who delivers it knows my instructions and will make sure that they are followed. To write more would be a sinful waste of time."

Julius Streicher

Signature of Peter the Great.

Signature of Catherine the Great in Russian script.

Signature of Catherine the Great in Modern Roman script.

Signature of Ivan the Terrible (Ivan Vasilievich).

Signature of Pancho Villa.

The most remarkable letter of the astute hypnotist ever to come to light was sold at auction in London (1956), under unusual circumstances. My wife was bidding at the sale. Just as the auctioneer offered the Rasputin letter, a sudden cloudburst distracted most of the bidders sitting near a cracked skylight. In the confusion, the letter was knocked down to Doris for a fraction of its value. A London reporter was present, and the incident so amused him that he wrote an account of it, saying that "an American woman in a periwinkle blue suit laughed merrily as the rain fell."

In the letter, one of the few surviving of Rasputin, he wrote in crude, almost verbless Russian, to:

My dear beloved:

Sinister signs of terrible despair that will befall the earth. The world of the mother of God lying in nightly silence and no escape. Terrible wrath and where can you escape to? The hour has come to end our world in blood. A dark night of terrible suffering before us. Soon my own hour will come. There will be much suffering for faith, and brother will slay brother. The earth will shake, and famine and disease will rule the world. I shall pray for the whole world . . . . Salvation and joy will come to the earth due to the mercy of the Saviour and

GRIGORI

Even as he wrote, predicting the Russian Revolution and his own death, Rasputin's enemies were plotting the scheme which ended in his murder.

Autograph note, signed, of Rasputin: "Beloved, Do it! Grigori."

Signature of Henri Christophe

Signature of Toussaint l'Ouverture.

On the magic-ridden Isle of Haiti, the ruthless Negro emperor, Henri Christophe, built a great stone fortress to shut out the vengeance of his people. But there was no refuge for him, and in a final dramatic gesture, he shot himself with a silver bullet. His career inspired Eugene O'Neill's drama, *The Emperor Jones*. Christophe's autograph, as soldier and later as emperor, is very rare. There is now much interest in him and in his predecessor, Toussaint l'Ouverture, and their autographs have moved up sharply in value. Rare, too, are the letters of the Mexican bandit, Pancho Villa, most of whose autographs occur in the form of military passes bearing a gigantic "Francisco Villa."

Even more violent than Pancho Villa were the assassins who took the lives of Lincoln, Garfield, and McKinley. Looked upon as the most execrable murderer of history, John Wilkes Booth, the misguided idealist who shot Lincoln in Ford's Theatre on the night of April 14, 1865, is of great rarity in autographic material. A popular stage idol, Booth carried on a vast correspondence, but there was a wholesale destruction of his letters after he murdered Lincoln.

Signature of John Wilkes Booth.

Four or five eyewitness accounts of Lincoln's assassination have come my way in the past few years. Perhaps the most interesting was that of George C. Maynard, published here through the courtesy of its present owner, Robert K. Black:

"While the play was progressing, a sharp pistol shot rang out, & Booth suddenly slid down from the front of the presidential box on to the stage, dragging the flag decorations with him, made some exclamation I did not understand, hastily ran diagonally across the stage and disappeared. He did not make a clear jump from the box . . . .

"His whole demeanor was that of a cowardly, sneaking murderer in frantic endeavor to escape danger. Had Booth paused for five seconds he would have been a dead man in five minutes, and he knew it. A lady leaned over the front of the box crying out, 'The President is shot, the President is shot.' Intense excitement ensued. Several men hastened to the door of the box, while an officer in military uniform climbed up the front and entered it. I saw and heard nothing to warrant the picturesque descriptions of Booth's heroic performance that have been published. He did not face the audience, nor brandish his knife before the spectators, nor make any heroic speech. He acted like a man who was most anxious to get out of the building."

Recently I bought the papers of John K. Porter, the United States prosecuting attorney in the trial of Charles J. Guiteau for the murder of Garfield. Among them, I found a number of Guiteau documents, including his original confession, taken from his pocket on the day of the shooting.

A demented attorney, Guiteau had stalked Garfield for weeks before an opportunity came to kill him without injuring any "innocent" person. On the day of the attempt, Guiteau obtained a fine sheet of laid stationery. On opposite sides, so that the document could be reproduced or displayed with ease, he confessed his guilt of the crime not yet committed, and outlined his reasons for slaying the President. Then he hired a cab and had the driver take him to the railroad station to wait while he shot Garfield. He planned to go at a gallop to the jail afterward and give himself up to the authorities. The syllogisms of his confession show clearly that Guiteau's mind was unhinged.

In jail, Guiteau carried on a large correspondence, alternately damning and praising his critics. He signed his autograph for collectors upon payment of one dollar; but, if no money was forthcoming, he gave his signature without charge. During his trial, he announced his candidacy for the Presidency! Guiteau's signature is fairly common, valued at only a few dollars, but his letters, especially when significant or revealing, often change hands at high prices.

Two decades after Guiteau was hanged, early in the morning of September 6, 1901, a young laborer tumbled out of his bed in a cheap boarding house in Buffalo. Carefully he washed and brushed his teeth, then put on his best suit and his only clean shirt. He was a handsome youth, with a quiet, determined manner. He had never committed a criminal act or even an unkind deed. Declared a former landlady: "He hadn't the heart to kill a fly. He used to catch them and then let them go." Almost illiterate, this twenty-eight-year-old youth was unemployed, still living on the wages he had saved from a six-year job as wire winder in a Cleveland mill. He was so painfully shy that he never went out with girls and even crossed the street to avoid meeting young women whom he knew. On this fateful morning, he put in his pocket his last remaining dollar and a 32-calibre Iver Johnson revolver.

Taking a trolley to the Pan-American Exposition grounds, Leon F. Czolgosz waited around the Temple of Music for President McKinley's scheduled visit. His plan was to kill the President, not because he disliked him personally or disapproved of his policies, but because McKinley was a "ruler" and therefore (to Czolgosz's aberrated mind), a tyrant. McKinley arrived and began to shake hands with a long queue of people. Czolgosz got into line. In his right hand he gripped his revolver, with a handkerchief wrapped around it. To the President's guards, he appeared to be a young man with an injured hand. Reaching McKinley, Czolgosz did not shake hands, but fired two quick shots. McKinley dropped. His guards, aided by a huge Negro porter, piled Czolgosz to the floor before he could fire a third shot. A few hours later, in the Buffalo police station, Czolgosz agreed to write a confession. His hand shook terribly, so he dictated a brief statement to a reporter named Storey, then placed on it the date and his signature—the last signature he was to sign and perhaps the only example of his handwriting in existence:

> I killed President McKinley because I done my duty. I didn't believe one man should have so much service and another man should have none.
>
> September 6th 1901
>
> LEON F. CZOLGOSZ

This remarkable document is one of the most grisly items which I have ever owned. Czolgosz subsequently repudiated his confession, even denying that he knew how to write. After he was electrocuted, his clothes and all of his effects were burned.

Recent assassins. Signatures of Lee Harvey Oswald in English and in Russian, and signature of Jack Ruby.

> Washington July 2nd 1881
>
> To the White House
>
> The President's tragic death was a sad necessity, but it will unite the Republican party and save the Republic. Life is a flimsy dream and it matters little when one goes. A human life is of small value. During the war thousands of brave boys went down without a tear.
>
> I presume the President was a Christian and that he will be happier in Paradise than here.
>
> It will be no worse for Mrs Garfield, dear soul, to part with her husband this way, than by natural death. He is liable to go at any time, any way.
>
> I had no ill will toward the President.
>
> His death was a political necessity.
>
> I am a lawyer, theologian, and politician.
>
> I am a Stalwart of the Stalwarts.
>
> I was with General Grant and the rest of our men in New York during the canvass.
>
> I have some papers for the Press which I shall leave with Byron Andrews, and his co-Journalists, at 1420 N.Y. ave where all the reporters can see them.
>
> I am going to the Jail. Charles Guiteau

> I killed President McKinley because I done my duty. I didn't believe one man should have so much service and another man should have none.
>
> to A September 6th 1901.
>
> Leon F. Czolgosz

*From the collection of Elsie O. and Philip D. Sang*

Signed confessions of two Presidential assassins. *Top.* The original holograph signed confession of Charles Guiteau, found in his pocket after he shot Garfield. *Bottom.* Confession of anarchist Leon F. Czolgosz, signed on the day he murdered McKinley.

# 18 TAKE A FASCINATING BYPATH

"I'D LIKE TO START AN AUTOGRAPH COLLECTION," said my young visitor, "but all the interesting autographs cost so much—Presidents, Signers, composers, Lincoln, Napoleon, American authors and statesmen—I can't afford to compete with rich collectors who get all the choice rarities. Why, even if I spent every penny of my salary for a year, I would not have enough for a document signed by Button Gwinnett!"

I felt sorry for this discouraged young man. I recalled the first autograph I had ever purchased, for which I paid fifty cents—my allowance for five weeks!

"Why should you want to collect Signers or Presidents?" I asked him. "Why not do a little pioneering? The obvious is always expensive because everybody wants it; but if you have imagination—and use it—you have more than a millionaire can buy."

"What sort of a collection do you recommend?"

"If you want to form an interesting historic collection, why not pick the Spanish-American War? The colorful personalities, like Theodore Roosevelt and Admiral Dewey and Captain Hobson, are very inexpensive. With a modest budget you could assemble a significant collection.

*Signature of Admiral George Dewey.*

"Or why not go in for American financiers? Jay Gould, Commodore Vanderbilt, James Fisk, John Jacob Astor—all of them are modestly priced. To add a little zest, you will find it hard to get John D. Rockefeller, Sr. and Henry Ford.

"Or you might try African explorers. For the price of a fine letter of Washington, you can assemble a complete collection of the heroes of the Dark Continent, including the scarcest and most desirable, Dr. David Livingstone. There are a few others which are a bit costly, such as Mungo Park, James Bruce, and Sir Richard Burton. But even Henry M. Stanley is not expensive!"

My youthful friend leaned forward in his chair. He had suddenly realized that there were vast and unexplored possibilities in autograph collecting.

The specialist collector, like the specialist dealer, often blazes his own bypath. Dr. John A. Murray, of Patton, Pennsylvania, has a partiality for significant Revolutionary and Civil War newspapers; Ralph E. Becker, of Washington, delights in Presidential campaign matter; Norman H. Strouse adds to his Ruskin and Carlyle collections the letters of modern printers; Professor Philip A. Shelley, of Pennsylvania State College, gathers up Bayard Taylor and his circle.

The universities and libraries seek specialized material. The Indiana University Lilly library, headed by Professor David Randall, is assembling letters of Wordsworth and his friends. Bern Dibner, at the Burndy Library in Norwalk, Connecticut, has accumulated a valuable archive of letters and books relating to electricity; the William H. Clements Library, at the University of Michigan, directed by Howard H. Peckham, possesses a noteworthy collection of letters and manuscripts representing the British and Hessian side of the Revolutionary War; and the University of Texas has stressed Latin Americana and the Emperor Maximilian.

Among autograph dealers there are only a few specialists. Dr. Milton Kronovet, of Brooklyn, and

Signature of Maximilian of Mexico, as Ferdinand, Archduke of Austria.

Signature of Maximilian as Emperor.

Marie Curie

Mary Baker Eddy

Paul Ehrlich

Alexander Fleming

W. C. Gorgas

William Harvey

Dr. John Hunter

Charles T. Jackson

*Signature of the elder J. Pierpont Morgan.*

*Signature of John Jacob Astor.*

*Signature of John D. Rockefeller, Sr.*

2, RICHMOND TERRACE,
WHITEHALL, S.W.

May 3d 1899

Dear Sir

Pray observe the Correction
to be made - carefully, and before
you strike off 1,500 (Fifteen hundred)
Copies, we should save time if you
were to bring to me personally 2 clean,
revised Copies tomorrow morning
about 10 o'clock.

You have finally planned
the letter very nicely.

Yours faithfully
Henry M. Stanley

be forwarded
in a few days

I took the
liberty of recom-
-mending Rev
Mr. Helmore to
apply to you
for any beads
he might need
for Africa

Yours &c
David Livingstone

*Letters of Henry M. Stanley and David Livingstone.*

Conway Barker, of La Marque, Texas, emphasize less costly material, a great help to the impecunious collector; Julia S. Newman, of Battle Creek, Michigan, handles only Americana; and Robert K. Black, of Upper Montclair, New Jersey, offers mainly literary and historical autographs.

Even more varied are the specialties of New York's rare-book and autograph dealers. John Kohn and Mike Papantonio at the Seven Gables Bookshop deal in American and English literature, as do those affable brothers, Jim and Marston Drake, of James F. Drake, Inc.; the American West is the province of Edward Eberstadt and Sons; Margaret Cohen at House of Books, Ltd. is an expert in modern literary books and autographs; Rosejeanne Slifer at B. Altman and Co. displays letters and documents framed with portraits; George W. Stair in the Rare Book Department of Brentano's inserts autographs in first editions and finely bound sets; and Harold Graves at Scribner's Rare Book Department stresses scientific books and autographs.

There has recently been an increase of interest in medical autographs. Letters of Edward Jenner, Joseph Lister, William Osler, and Harvey Cushing are now much sought. Few modern autographs are more desired than that of Louis Pasteur. Rarest of American medical autographs are those of W. C. Gorgas and Walter Reed.

I recall the late Dr. Max Thorek, one of America's most distinguished surgeons, who had devoted many years to his unusual autograph collection. Shortly before his death he telephoned from Chicago to tell me, elatedly, "I have just acquired a document of Ambroise Paré, the great Renaissance

Edward Jenner

Dr. Robert Koch

Joseph, Lord Lister

Anton Mesmer

Sir William Osler

Ambrose Paré

Florence Nightingale

**Institut Pasteur**

25, Rue Putot

Paris, le 7 Août 1891

Variant handwritings of Louis Pasteur. Pasteur's script varied according to his mood and both of the illustrated handwritings are characteristic examples.

surgeon." Dr. Thorek's acquisition marked the end of a long quest, for Paré's autograph is of the utmost rarity. Still young at eighty, Dr. Thorek's love for his hobby kept him buoyant despite a heavy schedule of work which would have exhausted a much younger man. Dr. Victor R. Turner, of Dayton, Ohio, exhibits similar enthusiasm for medical autographs and it is always a pleasure to locate a new rarity for his collection.

The beautiful handwriting of Thomas A. Edison is a delight to look upon. Although the great inventor employed a sloppy script in his hastily written laboratory notes, his formal hand is notable for its legibility. In a letter written from Edison's laboratory, the inventor's biographer, W. H. Meadowcroft, commented: "Mr. Edison's handwriting was cultivated when he was a telegraph operator many years ago. He found by using it that he could write with great rapidity. In forming the signature, he makes the down stroke of the 'T' first, and then adds the sweeping flourish before writing the remainder of his name." In an old album I recently discovered a transcript by Edison of "Mary had a little lamb," the first words he ever spoke into the phonograph. It is now in the scientific collection of Rex Beasley, of Dallas, Texas.

In one of the most interesting Edison letters ever to come my way, the inventor thanked a friend for presenting him with a holograph letter of Michael Faraday. Adding that he intended to frame the letter and hang it in his laboratory, Edison described Faraday as the world's "greatest experimenter in electricity." Faraday's letters, penned in a fluent, legible script, are very common. The same cannot be said of some of his predecessors. Galileo's letters are extremely rare, valued in the hundreds of dollars, and there is no lack of interest whenever one appears for sale. Nearly as scarce are letters of Isaac Newton; but fortunately for admirers of the great English scientist, he left many unsigned memoranda, mainly excerpts in Latin from the writings of others. Such unsigned fragments are highly prized by collectors. Much sought are letters of Ampère and Volta, both of whom are moderately scarce. Ampère used two styles of writing, one very legible and prim, the other sloppy and rapidly scrawled. Volta's signature is most often found affixed to documents relating to scholastic matters at the University of Pavia, where he was a professor for twenty-five years. The discoverer of X rays, Wilhelm Konrad Roentgen, was also a professor at various German universities and his rare autograph generally turns up on academic papers. Pierre and Marie Curie represent a husband-and-wife combination which greatly appeals to collectors, but the autograph of Pierre, who died at forty-seven, is much scarcer and more costly than that of his equally celebrated wife.

Very plentiful are the letters of Humphry Davy, the spelling of whose

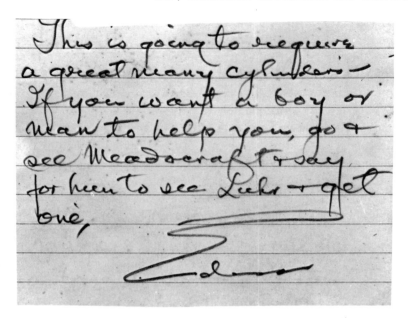

*This is going to require a great many cylinders — If you want a boy or man to help you, go & see Meadocraft & say for him to see Luer & get one,*

*Boston Feby 3d 69*

*Received of Samuel W Ropes Jr The sum of Thirty 30 dollars — being full amount received from him ——*

*Thomas A Edison*

*Mary had a little Lamb its fleece was white as snow*

*and everywhere that Mary went the Lamb was sure to go*

*How do you get that now.? Hello! Hello!*

*Thomas A Edison*

Variant handwritings of Thomas A. Edison. *Top.* Laboratory instructions regarding phonograph cylinders, hurriedly written and signed by Edison. *Center.* Printlike handwriting of Edison when a telegraph operator. *Bottom.* The first words ever spoken into the phonograph, meticulously written out and signed in Edison's beautiful script.

name has long proved vexing to cataloguers. To aid my secretary, I devised this little couplet:

*There is no "e"*
*In Humphry Davy.*

Perhaps the most influential thinker of the nineteenth century was Charles Darwin and, as might be expected, his letters, becoming less abundant every year, are avidly gathered both by private collectors and institutions. When a boy, Darwin was himself fascinated by autographs and collected franking signatures. His acquisitive instincts ultimately took a botanical turn, and from this youthful scientific collecting developed the keen sense of observation which made him the outstanding naturalist of modern times. Had he continued as an autograph collector, he might well have become a great librarian! Darwin's letters are extremely interesting, but a challenge to decipher!

In recent years there has been a great surge of interest in the autographs of American inventors. Especially sought are the letters of Robert Fulton, a prolific and fascinating correspondent. Nearly all of his letters concern his inventions—or the alleged attempt of other inventors to infringe upon his patents. By contrast, in the many letters of Eli Whitney I have run across, I do not recall a single mention of the cotton gin! Almost always his letters concern the manufacture or sale of muskets, for which Whitney devised the first interchangeable parts.

There is no more intriguing pursuit than gathering letters and documents about spies. To form a representative collection requires patience and money. Obviously, secret agents are wary of paper and ink. Incriminating messages have a way of falling into the hands of the wrong people. The autographs of the English spy, John André, mostly early letters dated before the war, appear for sale on rare occasions; but our American spies, like Nathan Hale and Enoch Crosby, left hardly any writings. The best collection of Nathan Hale (whose autograph is sometimes confused with that of his cousin of the same name) is in his alma mater, Yale University. Still another espionage collection has been presented to Harvard University by James N. B. Hill, of Boston.

Signature of Enoch Crosby.

The rarity of spies' autographs is even more acute when we consider the espionage and counterespionage of the Civil War, a conflict in which military intelligence played a vital role. Among the most noted secret agents were Lafayette Baker, Major Pauline Cushman, and Belle Boyd. The autographs of both women are of superlative rarity. The only exam-

Signature of Belle Boyd.

ple of Belle Boyd I ever acquired is now in the Confederate collection of Lucius S. Ruder. It is a receipt for five hundred dollars in gold which Jefferson Davis gave her for a special mission to England. Contrary to popular belief, Belle Boyd was a homely woman with a thin face and a hatchet nose.

More glamorous was the modern Delilah, Mata Hari. Her real name was Gertrud Margarete Zelle, and she was born, not in romantic Bali, but in prosaic Holland. Her dancing was exotic. Swaying voluptuously, with a live snake in her hands, and nude save for a jeweled brassière, Mata Hari enchanted audiences throughout Europe. When World War I broke out, she was the mistress of the Crown Prince of Germany and cast her lot with the Germans. Her information,

Signature of Mata Hari.

obtained from unsuspecting French and British officers, was of great value to the German high command. The French finally suspected her trips across the border and she was arrested and shot by a firing squad. Her prison doctor later wrote a brief narrative in which, with a lack of discretion rarely found among the French, he explained why Mata Hari never danced without a brassière. "I cannot understand why she wore it," he wrote blandly, "because there was nothing to cover."

Many of Mata Hari's letters were seized by French officials at the time of her arrest, but an energetic search netted me a small sheaf of nine letters about a refresher course in dancing. There was another pathetic letter, penned from prison on cheap brown paper, in which the once glittering dancer, now writing as plain Margarete Zelle, beseeched the jail officials to allow her a nightgown and a few undergarments. Mata Hari's original passport is in the espionage collection of my friend Colonel Walter L. Pforzheimer.

Unique among spies' letters are those of the Chevalier d'Éon. Writing in French, D'Éon (whose sex was a mystery to his contemporaries and who even fought duels as a woman) signed his title in masculine or feminine gender, depending upon his whim or purpose.

Another attractive but very different field is that of the chief justices of the Supreme Court. Most desirable are letters of John Marshall and John Jay. Letters of Taney and Chase are very abundant. If you seek full

Signatures of John Marshall and R. B. Taney.

holographic letters of the chief justices, you will find only one which is very elusive, Edward D. White. Among associate justices there are few rarities. By far the most popular are letters of the picturesque Oliver W. Holmes, Jr., son of the famous poet.

It is a short step from America's great jurists to their predecessors who literally "held the law in their hands." Such were the Colonial governors. Their age was one of plots and counterplots, dark intrigues, and wars with the Indians. There is no more dramatic period than when the tree of liberty was taking root in the new continent.

Signature of Oliver W. Holmes, Jr.

Of particular interest are autographs of the royal governors of Massachusetts. John Carver, William Bradford, John Winthrop, John Endicott—what a galaxy of brilliant personalities! On the rare occasions when a letter of one of these founding fathers appears for sale, the price fetched is generally high. Less valuable are letters of their successors. Signed documents of Francis Bernard, Thomas Hutchinson, and William Shirley are modestly priced. Much of Shirley's vast correspondence deals with the frontier wars in which he played a significant role.

Signature of William Bradford.

Signature of William Shirley.

One of the most eagerly collected of early American autographs is that of William Penn, who bequeathed to posterity an abundance of letters. Signed land grants, adorned with his handsome signature and a red wax peppercorn seal, may be found without difficulty.

Signature of William Penn.

Crackling with action, the diaries of the French and Indian War have all the ingredients of the perfect adventure tale. One of the most exciting to come my way was the journal of Lieutenant Colonel Thomas Williams, brother of the founder of Williams College, and commander of Fort Edwards. Through its pages moved the romantic figure of Major Robert Rogers. This journal, unpublished and unknown when it turned up, is now in the archives of the New York State library.

Among the more interesting epochs of American history is the War of 1812. Andrew Jackson, who defeated the British at New Orleans, William Hull, who surrendered Detroit to the British, and William Henry Harrison, who defeated Tecumseh, were professional soldiers, and during their long military careers signed thousands of documents. Among naval heroes is the courageous Stephen Decatur, killed in a duel with Commo-

Signature of Oliver Hazard Perry.

Signature of Stephen Decatur.

dore James Barron. "Old Ironsides" was commanded by Isaac Hull, whose autographs, like those of Barron and Decatur, are not particularly scarce. The outstanding rarity is James Lawrence, who uttered the order, "Don't give up the ship," and then lived just long enough to see his ship surrendered.

If you wish to form a collection that will test your ingenuity, I recommend an assemblage of noted antagonists or famous lovers. Antagonists could include Burr and Hamilton, Wellington and Napoleon, and Wolfe and Montcalm. Among lovers whose autographs may be obtained are Nelson and Lady Hamilton, Napoleon and Josephine, Elizabeth Barrett and Robert Browning, and Louis XV and Madame du Barry.

Signatures of James Wolfe and the Marquis de Montcalm.

Signature of Lady Emma Hamilton.

Autograph note signed by Madame du Barry.

If curiosities appeal to you, you might form a collection of ornate signatures and handwritings. Among the former, the frenetic flourishes of Francis E. Spinner are well known. The illegible script of Horace Greeley has elicited many squibs. Mark Twain once spent hours trying to decipher a note in Greeley's hand, only to conclude that it read: "Washing with soap is wholly absurd." It is said that Greeley wrote an irate note to an employee, discharging him for incompetence, but the man used the letter as a recommendation. A rival editor, baffled by Greeley's penmanship, quipped: "If Belshazzar had seen Greeley's handwriting on the wall, he would have

Signature of General F. E. Spinner.

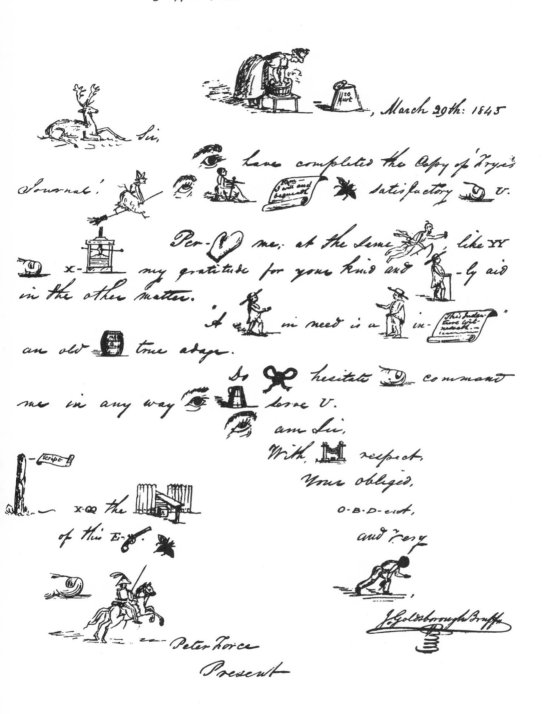

Rebus letter of J. Goldsborough Bruff, artist of the gold rush.

been a good deal more frightened than he was." If you wish to test your ability to read Greeley's script, see the illustration on page 213. A transcript of the letter is included here.

The letter of Greeley reads:

Private
New York
July 5, 1872
Dear Sir:
Your letter with extract came safe to hand.
Our news from every quarter is cheering, and promises an overwhelming triumph.

> Yours,
> Horace Greeley

The letters of the genius of humbug, P. T. Barnum, are full of vitality. In one of the most delightful of his letters to come my way was a discussion of a rival "white elephant":

"The opposition white elephant . . . was a common elephant painted white in Liverpool. It died the other day according to its owner's declaration, but it was 'dyed' already, and its only death consisted in rubbing off the white paint and restoring it to its original color! . . . my elephant stands the test of all intelligent people. But 'the masses' whom a writer called 'them asses' believe in nothing short of a snow white elephant all over, and therefore don't think much of mine . . . ."

Barnum readily sent his signature to admirers, but the famous strong man Eugene Sandow, whose muscles awed the women of America, invariably and with great earnestness, declined to send his autograph, put-

Eugene Sandow refuses to send his autograph!

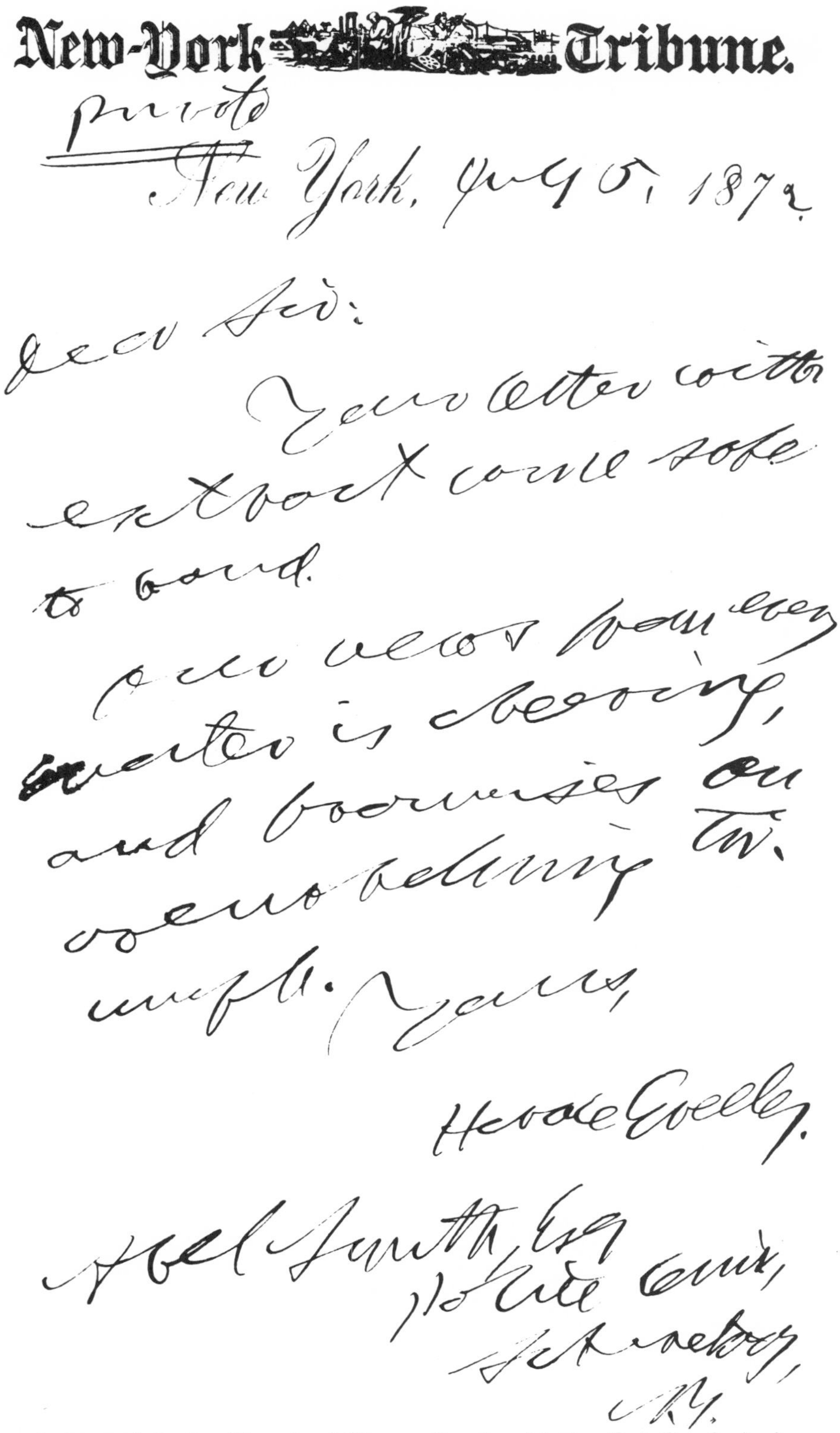

**New-York Tribune.**

*[handwritten letter in Horace Greeley's hand]*

New York, July 5, 1872.

Dear Sir:

Your letter with extract came safe to hand.

*[illegible handwritten text]*

Truly Yours,

Horace Greeley.

Abel Smith Esq
*[illegible address]*

Autograph Letter Signed, of Horace Greeley. Notice that Greeley's *r*'s resemble *o*'s, and his *p*'s appear to be *f*'s. A transcript of this letter appears on page 212.                    *From the collection of the New York Public Library*

ting a bold signature to his refusal!

Few collections are more dramatic than an assemblage of the challengers of the sky. The autographs of the early balloonists are very rare. Signed tickets to balloon ascensions by Blanchard and Leonardi are greedily collected. Much sought, too, are the letters of John Wise, American aeronaut who planned the first Atlantic crossing by balloon.

The autographs of the Montgolfier brothers, inventors of the balloon, sometimes turn up on political documents. The letters of Jacques Étienne Montgolfier, a commissary during the French Revolution, are much commoner than those of his brother Joseph. An almost comparable degree of rarity prevails in the case of the Wright brothers. The let-

Jacques Étienne Montgolfier

Joseph Michel Montgolfier

Otto Lilienthal

Francesco Zambeccari

Baron von Richthofen

The Wright Brothers

ters of Wilbur are scarcer than those of Orville. During his later years, Orville signed many photo-reproductions of the first flight at Kitty Hawk in 1903. Despite their abundance, these souvenirs of the great inventor are much prized.

I once obtained a correspondence of Bishop Milton Wright, father of the Wright brothers, in which he told his friend Belle Mosier of his sons' early experiments. Included was a twenty-four-page pamphlet in the original brown wrappers, entitled "Christian Giving," which was printed by the Wright brothers on their job press in Dayton, about 1893.

On the campus of New York University in the Bronx is the Hall of Fame for great Americans. Since

Alexander Graham Bell

Louis Daguerre

Charles Darwin

James B. Eads

Michael Faraday

Robert Fulton

Robert Houdin

Guglielmo Marconi

Gregor Mendel

C. H. McCormick

Samuel F. B. Morse

Isaac Newton

Joseph Priestley

Alessandro Volta

Astronaut John H. Glenn, Jr.

W. C. Roentgen

Eli Whitney

the eligibility requirement is that a nominee be dead for twenty-five years, Wilbur is already elected but Orville has yet to have his bust placed among the illustrious. Many members are autographically inexpensive, such as George Bancroft and Phillips Brooks, but there are others whose letters are very elusive. To form a complete collection requires much patience and a substantial bank account, for in the Hall of Fame are such costly rarities as Stephen Collins Foster, Jonathan Edwards, Daniel Boone, Edgar Allan Poe, and Roger Williams. A few enterprising collectors have already embarked upon the difficult task. The group formed by Carl Haverlin, president of Broadcast Music, Inc., is now only a few names from completion.

The wives of the Presidents are a colorful group and merit your attention. Some were noted for charm, others for beauty; but with two or three exceptions they were not distinguished for writing a large number of letters! Many of them—Martha Washington, for example—were pen-shy. This adds zest to the pursuit. It is almost impossible to form a complete set of First Ladies! There are fifty letters of George available for every one of Martha. Not long ago I owned a letter in which she observed, with that homey directness which marked her character, "Worms is the cause of all complaints in children." Letters of Mrs. Lincoln, signed either "Mrs. A. Lincoln" or "Mary Lincoln," are more often encountered. Usually they are replete with self-pity and full of complaints about the ill-treatment accorded her by an ungrateful world, a striking contrast to the uncompromising, outspoken letters of her husband.

A few of the First Ladies rank among the most

Louisa C. Adams

Rachel Jackson

Anna Harrison

Julia G. Tyler

Sarah C. Polk

Martha Washington

Abigail Adams

Martha Jefferson

Dolley P. Madison

Elizabeth Monroe

Margaret Taylor

Abigail Fillmore

Caroline C. Fillmore

Jane M. Pierce

Mary Lincoln

*Eliza Johnson*

Elizabeth Johnson

*Julia D Grant*

Julia D. Grant

*Lucy W. Hayes*

Lucy W. Hayes

*Lucretia R. Garfield*

Lucretia R. Garfield

elusive of American autographs. Martha Jefferson, for instance! I know of only one example from her pen. Even harder to find, if such is possible, are autographs of Eliza Monroe and Hannah Van Buren. In thirty years I have not seen even a cut signature of these distinguished ladies, and even after several years of searching I was unable to locate a facsimile of Hannah Van Buren to reproduce in this volume. Almost as scarce are the autographs of Margaret Taylor and Eliza Johnson. The only example of Mrs. Taylor to come my way is now in the First Lady collection of Professor Jack Pollman, of Lansing. Rare, also, are the autographs of Caroline Fillmore, Ida McKinley, Ellen Arthur, Rachel Jackson, and Anna Harrison.

Refreshingly plentiful are the letters of Dolley Madison, who was not the first hostess to serve ice cream in the White House. That distinction, as I recall from a receipt I once owned, was Mrs. Washington's. Dolley (that is the way *she* spelled her first

*E. L. H. Arthur*

Ellen Arthur

*Ida Saxton McKinley*

Ida S. McKinley

*Frances Cleveland.*

Frances F. Cleveland

*Edith Roosevelt*

Edith K. Roosevelt

*Carrie S. Harrison*

Carrie S. Harrison

*Helen H. Taft*

Helen H. Taft

*Mary Lord Harrison*

Mary Lord Harrison

*Edith Bolling Wilson*

Edith Bolling Wilson

Florence Kling Harding

Florence Kling Harding

Grace Coolidge

Grace Coolidge

Lou Henry Hoover

Lou Henry Hoover

name) usually wrote her signature, "D. P. Madison."

If you relish ornate documents, you might assemble old stock certificates. Since Americans as a nation enjoy gambling, you will never lack for specimens of defunct stock issues. Generally speaking, the more worthless the stock the more ornate is the engraved certificate!

One of the best ways to understand the history of American business is through old invoices, receipts, indentures, and ledgers. There is scarcely an

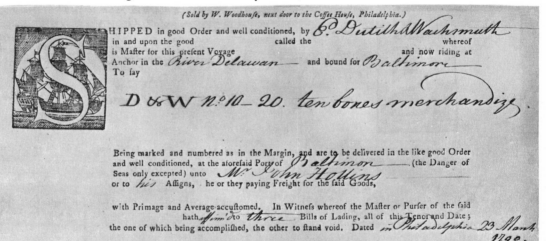

Early American bill of lading, Philadelphia, 1790.

old document which does not tell an interesting story. You may trace the development of insurance companies through early policies, many of them adorned with deliciously quaint engravings. If your taste leans to the law, you will find an inexhaustible supply of early legal documents, curiously phrased, which furnish amusing details on the legal tangles faced by our ancestors.

Eleanor Roosevelt

Mamie Doud Eisenhower

Bess W. Truman

Lady Bird Johnson

Jacqueline B. Kennedy

Patricia Nixon

# 19 THE MAIL MUST GO THROUGH—FREE!

"Here's a little trophy that may interest you."

My visitor, Alden S. Condict, a distinguished executive, pulled a pale blue envelope from his pocket, continuing: "It recalls the toughest selling job of my life—the day I tried to persuade the President of the United States to break the law!"

A noted autograph collector, Mr. Condict seemed in a confidential mood. I suspected that he was about to reveal some strange secret.

"I had done several favors for Franklin D. Roosevelt," he went on, "but I had never asked anything in return. That was in the thirties when Roosevelt needed all the support he could get.

"After he was elected President, there *was* one thing that I did want from him, and wanted desperately. But I just couldn't work up the nerve to ask for it.

"You know, of course, that no President of the United States since U. S. Grant has had the franking privilege, or the right to send mail free by just signing his signature on the envelope. That privilege was abolished in 1877. Today the President, as when Franklin D. Roosevelt was at the helm, uses a governmental post free envelope imprinted with the words 'Official mail. Penalty for private use, $500.' Ex-Presidents now receive the free-franking privilege, but the President must use postage on his personal mail.

"What I hoped to get from Roosevelt was a bona-fide Presidential frank in the upper right corner of a postmarked White House envelope. Not a penalty envelope of the official sort, but a White House envelope like the President uses for personal mail. Think of it! A franking signature by a President not authorized to use the frank! Can you imagine any item more exciting?

"Finally I decided to beard the lion in his den—and Roosevelt could be a lion at times, you know! During one of his visits to Hyde Park I dropped in on him. We chatted for a while, and then, with a thumping heart, I sprang the big question, 'I wonder, Mr. President, if you would mind letting me have your signature in the upper right corner of a White House envelope?'

"I put the question casually, as though it weren't important, but Roosevelt was an autograph and stamp collector, and he knew instantly that I was asking for a 'frank.' His genial manner left him abruptly, and his face became hard. His eyes flashed, and he said icily, 'You're asking me to break the law.'

"If only I could have dropped through the floor! But I had to stand there, after having asked the awful question, with the President of the United States giving me the coldest look I had ever got from any mortal. He saw that I was squirming inside, so he began softly opening and closing the drawers in his desk. Presently he said, almost in a friendly tone, 'Odd, but I don't seem to have any White House envelopes around.'

"A few moments later, still embarrassed, I shook his hand as I prepared to leave his office. He seemed to be his amiable self again, and his last words were: 'Speak to my secretary about that signature.'

"I expected, of course, that he was giving me the run-around, but I sought out his secretary and said, 'I asked the President for a postmarked, franking signature on a White House envelope and he told me to speak to you about it.' His secretary seemed very astonished at my request, but promised to find out what, if anything, could be done for me.

"I was sure I had bungled the matter hopelessly, and hadn't the remotest chance to get a Presidential franking signature from Roosevelt. Weeks passed, and I gave up all hope. Then, about two months later, I received through the mail a large stamped White House envelope. Afire with eagerness, I opened it up, and inside I found two magnificent White House envelopes, each boldly franked by the President in his familiar blue ink, and each bearing a very clear Washington, D.C. postmark, dated the very day he was elected for a third term. Here was something of unbelievable rarity, something no other collector possessed!"

My visitor paused, dramatically placing the envelope in my hands.

The unique or nearly unique is always exciting, and many a collector would willingly exchange pistol shots with a competitor to obtain such a rarity.

Said Mr. Condict: "What do you think I was once offered for that little envelope?"

I declined to venture a guess.

Presidential franking signatures. *Top.* The extremely rare frank of Franklin D. Roosevelt. *Center.* Franking signature of Thomas Jefferson. *Bottom.* The only known franking signature of Rutherford B. Hayes as President.

"Not long afterward, when I needed money badly, I was offered ten thousand dollars. Yes, ten thousand dollars! You see, the Republicans wanted it for propaganda. They wanted to prove that Franklin D. Roosevelt had no respect for the laws of this country, and even franked his mail when he had no legal right. Of course, I refused the offer. I couldn't violate the President's confidence."

I was delighted when this rare frank passed into my possession. For nearly a week I had the pleasure of admiring it before it disappeared into one of America's outstanding franking collections.

Few autographs remain so briefly in a dealer's files as a fine or rare franking signature. The full envelope (or cover sheet) of the letter—not just the face of it or the cut signature—is sought. Scarce, unusual, or especially clear postal markings add enormously to the value. A franked envelope without postal markings is not worth much more than a signed document. Because of the postal interest, a franked cover forms a common ground between the philatelist and the autograph collector. The leading stamp dealers, such as John A. Fox, of New York, and Herman Herst, Jr., of Shrub Oak, New York, regularly offer franking signatures at auction.

Imagine franking thirty hounds through the mails, or forwarding "two male-servants going out as laundresses" to your correspondent! Fantastic though it sounds, such objects were "mailed" in the early days of the frank. Introduced more than three hundred years ago in England, during the reign of James I, the frank was granted to members of Parliament and certain of the nobility, who were permitted to send mail without charge under their covering signature. Before long, the right to frank had developed to the point where the post office was collecting almost no revenue. Servants of government officials sold franks to make up their wages. Possessors of the frank handed out to their friends or sold to banking houses great batches of letter covers inscribed with their franking signatures. Men, women, even cattle were sent to distant parts of the world under the frank. The mailing of live deer, turkeys, or haunches of venison was a daily occurrence.

Perhaps the oddest British use of the frank (though perhaps not so odd in a nation of whiskey drinkers) was by a drunk who franked his way home, accompanied by a postal messenger!

After nearly one hundred years of flagrant abuses, franked mail was limited to packets weighing two ounces or less. It was not long before swindlers discovered another use for the frank. Because of the enormous numbers of blank cover sheets in circulation, on which possessors of the franking privilege had written only the word *free* and their signature, leaving the address to be filled in by the sender of the letter, forgers could turn the frank to dishonest purposes. Erasing the word *free*, they would then write an I. O. U. above the franking signature. In some cases they actually borrowed or collected money on these spurious promissory notes. Several forgers were hanged, but their dexterous-fingered brethren were not discouraged. The result was that possessors of the frank introduced a variety of signatures to prevent forgery. Instead of signing in the customary way—"Free. John Jones," they turned to new and curious methods, such as "John Free Jones," or "Colchester John Jones Essex," inserting the signature between the names of their town and county. Others circled their signature or drew heavy lines above and beneath it, or even scratched a line entirely through their name. The famous "B. Free Franklin" frank of "the first civilized American" was used, not to express his love of liberty, as some historians have claimed, but to forestall forgers.

How franking signatures were used by forgers.

Letter cover addressed and franked by author William Cobbett (Peter Porcupine). Notice that Cobbett took no precautions to forestall the illegal use of his frank.

The same franking signature of Cobbett, removed from the letter cover and transformed into an I. O. U. bearing Cobbett's actual signature.

The franking privilege was once considered the mark of eminence and prosperity, and every sort of cajolery was used to obtain it. One millionaire, who could have bought out the English post office, refused to write letters because he did not have the right to frank and it embarrassed him to pay postage.

In 1840, when Sir Rowland Hill introduced the penny postage system, the franking privilege was officially abolished by the English Parliament. Only Queen Victoria and a very few government officials were permitted to send post-free letters, with the result that the art of correspondence went into a decline. When the "élite" of English society found that it cost them money to gossip by mail, they kept their letters brief!

In America, the frank was first used in Colonial days. The earliest I recall was on a letter of Governor Hunter of New York in 1709. It had no postal markings. Exactly when the first franking signatures with postal indicia were used in America is not known. There is a free franking signature of Jeffrey Amherst on a cover bearing the notation, "On His Majesty's Service" and a straight-line New York postmark which purportedly dates from 1759, but I have personally examined the cover and in my opinion the date should be approximately ten years later. Some of the rare franking signatures of Benjamin Franklin as deputy postmaster-general of the Colonies (1753–74) also bear the stamped word *Free* in a circle.

At the outbreak of the Revolutionary War, in 1775, Congress granted the franking privilege to members of the Continental Congress and to military personnel, thus allowing the speedy flow of official mail by either civil or military couriers. Of special interest and value are franks of the Signers of the Declaration of Independence and the more noted generals of the Revolution. Later the privilege was accorded to cabinet members.

Extremely popular are franking signatures of the Presidents, all of whom, from Washington to Grant, enjoyed the privilege while in office. Not long ago a collector insisted that I find for him a Revolutionary War franking signature of Washington with postal markings.

"Unfortunately," I explained, "Washington used military couriers almost exclusively, merely writing 'Public Service' and his signature, or perhaps 'Free' and his signature, or just his signature on the cover of his letters. I doubt if the postmarked cover you are seeking exists."

"Well, if you can't get me a Revolutionary frank of Washington with indicia, maybe you can get me a frank signed 'Go: Washington' as President."

"Again you have asked for the impossible. Although Washington's letters during his presidency often bear straight line postmarks, they are

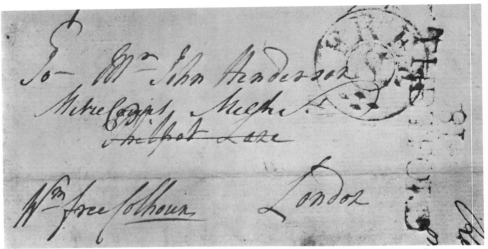

Placing the word *free* between the first and last names.

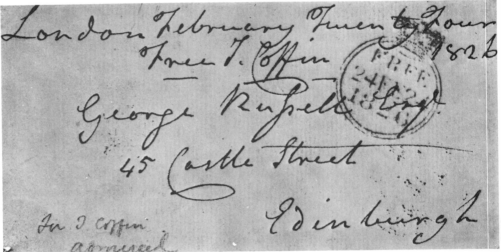

Writing the frank between the date and the address.

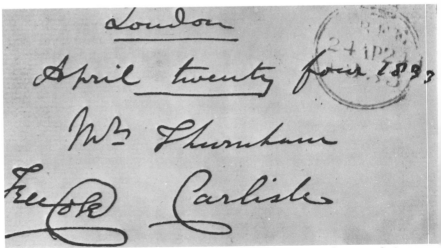

Incorporating the word *free* into the actual signature

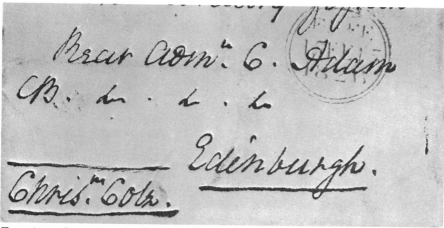

Drawing a line above and below the signature.

Writing the first and last names on different lines.

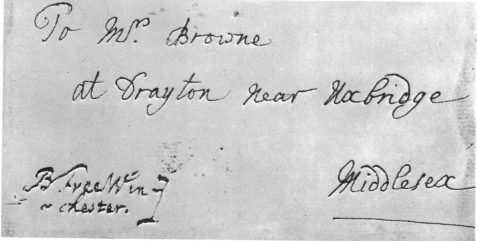

Placing the word *free* between the first and last names and also hyphenating the surname. The Bishop of Winchester, who franked this cover, had once been victimized by a forger and took this extreme precaution to prevent a recurrence.

franked 'President U.S.' or 'Pres. U.S.' Practically the only postmarked, full signature 'franks' of Washington are on letters dated during his retirement."

Washington's successor, John Adams, held many posts in which he enjoyed his franking privilege, but his frank is most distinguished for the amazing contrast between the bold, early franks, "J. Adams" or "John Adams" and the strange and spidery, almost unreadable, "J. Adams" of his last years, usually written, not in a corner of the letter cover, but between the lines of the address. This was a precaution against the use of his signature for any illicit purpose.

Like the franks of Madison, Monroe, J. Q. Adams, Martin Van Buren, and James Buchanan, Jefferson's franks are very plentiful as secretary of state. But Jefferson's franking signature as President is unique and scarce: "free. Th: Jefferson Pr. U.S." Such franks of the author of the Declaration of Independence command prices many times greater than franks dated before or after his Presidential terms.

Of Presidential franks dated during their term of office, those of Zachary Taylor, James K. Polk, and Andrew Johnson are extremely scarce, especially Johnson (his son often franked his mail for him), and that of William Henry Harrison is unobtainable, with only a single example known.

An interesting sideline of Presidential franks is to assemble franked covers by the Presidents during their earlier or later careers. What a variety of postmarks one encounters in the early military letters franked by Zachary Taylor, Andrew Jackson, or William Henry Harrison, often written from our Western frontier or during the Indian campaigns. Intriguing, too, are the franks of such multi-officed statesmen as James Monroe, James Madison, and John Quincy Adams.

Just as Lincoln's autograph is perhaps the most universally desired by collectors, so his franking signatures bring out all the acquisitiveness of postal specialists. No more piquant bit of Americana can be conceived than a frank as postmaster of New Salem! Highly valued, too, are franking signatures of Lincoln on covers dated during his tenure as Congressman (1847–49). They are scarcer than his Presidential franks, which are far from common and are valued at three or four times as much as comparable franking signatures of Washington. In 1863, Lincoln's secretaries Hay and Nicolay were accorded the franking privilege, and very few envelopes were personally franked by the President after that year.

All of the Presidents who followed Grant are extremely rare in franking signatures. Some are unobtainable. Garfield franked many covers while a Congressman, but none as President. Cleveland, Woodrow Wilson, Benjamin Harrison, William McKinley, and Franklin D. Roosevelt never had the franking privilege, for although both Harrison and McKinley were Congressmen, their tenure of office was during a period when official stamps or penalty envelopes were used for government mail.

In 1877, owing to abuses of the franking privilege, the right to send mail under signature was abolished by Congress. Everything from machinery and garden tools to boulders and even snakes had been dispatched under the free frank. Congressmen sent their laundry home and got it back again without a cent passing into government coffers.

In 1891, the free frank was again extended to Congressmen, and in 1895 to the Vice President who, as president of the Senate, enjoyed the same privilege as senators. Both Theodore Roosevelt and Calvin Coolidge had the right to frank their mail when Vice President, but the privilege was withdrawn when they succeeded to the Presidency. Former Presidents Herbert Hoover and Harry S. Truman were accorded the frank by Congress in 1958. Warren G. Harding had the franking privilege when senator. Nearly all of the franks of the last half-century were printed, and it is an interesting commentary upon Harding's honesty that he put a postage stamp over his printed frank when writing personal letters. The same cannot be said for some of our earlier Presidents. Washington not only wrote letters for his wife, even signing them "Martha Washington" in his own hand (did ever a woman have so illustrious a secretary!) but even franked them for her. John Adams franked Abigail's personal letters. Madison and Lincoln also used the free frank on letters of their spouses. Apparently this was a general practice and despite the wording of the law, which explicitly limits the frank to official correspondence, such misuse was not frowned upon by officials.

Evidence of Warren G. Harding's honesty.

Widowed First Ladies have, with the exceptions of Caroline Fillmore, Julia G. Tyler, and Eliza M. Johnson, been granted the franking privilege by special act of Congress. To a stranger who wrote to Grover Cleveland, asking whether he or his wife had ever possessed the frank, the former President penned a wry answer: "I have no postal frank, nor does Mrs. Cleveland. I believe franks do not go to the wives of the Presidents until they become widows, and I am not anxious to hasten that day."

Only three franks of Martha Washington, who had the franking privilege for two years, are known to exist. Of Margaret Taylor, no example is known to me. Of the other First Ladies who survived their husbands and were granted the frank, those of Ida McKinley, Anna Harrison, Sarah Polk, and Louisa C. Adams are all very scarce. Oddly, although Florence

K. Harding lived for only ten months after getting the franking privilege, her franks are not rare. Of the recent First Ladies—Mary Lord Harrison, Edith Bolling Wilson, Helen H. Taft, Grace Coolidge, and Eleanor Roosevelt—it may be observed that all are common in franking signatures. A word of caution! By special concession of Congress, these First Ladies have been allowed to use a facsimile franking signature, so that, as a rule, only those franks which were signed for collectors are authentic originals. Rubber stamp or printed signatures, whether of First Ladies or Presidents, are of relatively small value, except in the case of Theodore Roosevelt, Calvin Coolidge, and Warren G. Harding, where they serve to fill up what might otherwise be a gap in the franking series of Presidents.

Facsimile franking signatures of recent First Ladies and Presidents. *At top.* Rubber stamp franking signatures of Edith Bolling Wilson and Eleanor Roosevelt, with a printed franking signature of Jacqueline Kennedy. *At Bottom.* Metered franking signatures of Herbert Hoover and Dwight D. Eisenhower.

# 20 HOW TO EVALUATE
## AND SELL YOUR AUTOGRAPHS

EVERY YEAR THOUSANDS OF IMPORTANT OLD DOCUMENTS are destroyed because the owners fail to recognize their value!

Perhaps the best test for those who wish to determine the worth of their autograph material is this: are the documents interesting? If they intrigue you and your friends, they would also intrigue an autograph collector. A collection of old deeds, mortgages, receipts, and property transfers is not apt to excite anybody. But a diary or group of letters describing a frontier settlement, Indian fighting, whaling, politics, Civil War battles, or early American industries would make interesting reading and would have monetary value.

Except for routine documents such as land grants, an expert's estimate of value cannot be given without a careful examination of the actual autographs. No person ever wrote exactly the same letter or document twice, and every autograph presents a different problem in evaluation. Factors like contents, condition, length, date, name of addressee, place where written, size of signature, brightness of ink, and postal markings all affect value.

It would be easier for a physician to diagnose a patient's illness over the telephone, or for a real estate agent to evaluate a house after looking at a photo of it, than for an autograph dealer to estimate the value of letters or documents without seeing them. However, there are certain types of autographs which have very little value:

(1) Signatures cut from documents or letters, or signatures on cards. With a few exceptions, plain signatures are valueless. The advanced collector, who acquires autographs by purchase, desires letters and documents in their original and complete form.

(2) Signatures and signed photographs of movie stars, sports heroes, current stage favorites, popular singers, and contemporary senators and congressmen.

(3) Autograph albums containing signatures of popular figures of the sport and theatre world—or autograph albums dated between 1870 and 1920 which contain signatures of the minor authors and statesmen of the period.

(4) Lithographic, copperplate, or wood-engraved facsimiles. Only original autographs are desired by the experienced collector, and most facsimiles are without value.

Among the autographs of monetary value are:

(1) Complete letters and documents of almost any person whose name may be found in a biographical dictionary, such as Presidents, statesmen, military leaders, jurists, authors, composers, poets, scientists, explorers, and Western personalities.

(2) Letters and diaries of persons unknown to fame, but who have written about interesting or important subjects. Examples are letters and diaries relating to any significant phase of American history. Also desired are early hand-drawn maps, printed handbills, broadsides, original sketches by noted artists, and inscribed books.

Autographs are subject to the law of supply and demand. When the demand is strong and the supply limited, the price is certain to be high. If there is no demand, the autograph has little value. If the demand is very strong, no matter how common an autograph may be—Lincoln, Washington, and Napoleon are extremely common in autographic form—then the value is substantial. If the demand is only moderate, but the autograph itself is extremely rare, then its worth may still be high.

It is *not* true that the longer an autograph is held the more valuable it gets. Thirty years ago letters of Coolidge were bringing five or six times as much as today. While it is impossible to predict accurately what the value of Coolidge's autograph will be in the future, it is probable that it will decrease in value as more of his letters pour on the market and the available supply increases. Remember, too, that, like stocks and bonds, autographs are subject to fluctuation in value. The time to sell is when the price is up.

And now, a word of caution! Do not heed the advice of well-meaning persons who know nothing of autograph values and who are not familiar with the current autograph market. They may tell you that your treasured letter of Daniel Webster, written to your great-grandfather, is worth a fortune, while in reality Webster letters are extremely common. They may suggest that a document signed by Button Gwinnett is worth five hundred dollars, and recommend that you ask that price for it; but any document bearing the signature of this signer of the Declaration of Independence is worth closer to five thousand dollars.

A letter or document penned by a distinguished person does not necessarily have a high value. King George III of England and the poet William Blake were contemporaries; both lived to an advanced age, and yet there is a great difference in the monetary value of their autographs. A dealer would pay a relatively small sum for a routine letter of George III, but he would cheerfully give many times as much for a letter of the relatively obscure William Blake. The span is one of rarity, not of greatness, for George III's autograph is very common and Blake's is very rare.

Another word of caution. Do not attempt to repair autographs unless you are an expert. You may seriously damage or totally ruin the document you are trying to mend. The value of autographs which are amateurishly repaired is generally much less than before the repairs were attempted. If you insist upon making repairs, do not use any self-sealing adhesive, such as Scotch tape, for it may so utterly ruin the document that it will be unsalable at any price.

A good maxim to follow is: Do not repair anything and do not destroy anything before consulting a reliable dealer or expert. You may inadvertently throw out, or give away, the most valuable material.

I am frequently asked by those who own or have inherited a collection of rare letters or family papers: "What is the best way to sell my autographs?"

If you know a private collector, especially a collector interested in your autographs, you might offer them at what you consider a fair price, or suggest that he make an offer.

You might wish to sell your material to your local historical society for a token payment. Very few historical societies are amply endowed, and if your autograph collection supplements their other material, it would be suitable to give it to them.

If your collection is extensive and valuable, the best methods of disposal are through an auction house or by selling direct to a dealer. Should you choose to consign your collection to auction, your material will be cataloged by the auction house, then sold publicly to the highest bidder. You may realize a very high price, or, if the auction is not well attended, a very low price. For those who enjoy speculation, the auction method is excellent. However, some of the disadvantages are that the charges of the auction house, including insurance, run to about twenty-five per cent of the total amount fetched; it may be six months or more before your collection is sold and you receive any money, and no accurate forecast of the amount you may realize is possible.

Most of the larger dealers prefer to buy material outright. This method insures that you will receive immediate cash for your collection. You need have no hesitancy in entrusting your autographs to the mails provided you have confidence in the dealer to whom you are sending them. The dealer knows how to care for the collections which reach him daily. If you elect to mail your autographs, be sure to pack them carefully between corrugated board so that they will not be damaged. The dealer will usually make an offer, subject to your approval, and will mail your material back if you do not accept.

As many owners of family papers are aware, autographs which are paid for by collectors or institutions are more treasured than those which are gifts. The owner who sells his treasures to an autograph dealer or institution knows that since a cash value has been established for them, they will be cared for and guarded. Some archivists look casually upon gifts and tend to store such acquisitions in the basement.

Scarcely a week passes but what I am asked: "Does publication or photostating of family papers affect their monetary value?"

Emphatically, yes! It not only affects value, but, in some cases, destroys it. Suppose, for instance, that your grandfather was a noted statesman, and that you have come into possession of a trunkful of his official papers. Unless the papers are written or signed by famous persons, they will be valuable only so long as they are unpublished and unphotostated. If you permit a historical society or library to photostat or microfilm them, the value will be affected, except for such documents as bear the signatures of noted people. Although most archivists and librarians will frankly tell you that autograph dealers or collectors will hesitate to purchase your family papers once they have been photostated or microfilmed, there are unfortunately a few librarians who, in their eagerness to obtain copies, may neglect to mention this important fact. Remember that whenever any document is copied, it becomes available to scholars and historians, and the original is no longer needed. If you wish to keep the originals of your family papers for sentimental reasons, by all means allow your local historical society to make photostats or microfilms. But if you wish to sell your papers, be sure to consult an expert before you dispose of them or permit anyone to make copies.

# 21 EPILOGUE—
## THE FUTURE OF AUTOGRAPH COLLECTING

"THE TIME IS NOT FAR DISTANT," a collector wrote to me, "when important letters and manuscripts will no longer be available to the collector. Consider that enormous numbers of fine autographs have been swallowed up by institutions and are not being replaced with new material. Most letters today are typed on wood-pulp paper which will disintegrate in a few years. The telephone has already partly supplanted the letter, and, in a short time, much of our communication will be by television. People may even forget how to write."

"Nonsense!" I wrote back. "As our world expands, more and more we must seek a permanent record for our thoughts and activities— whether in literature, diplomacy, science, or business.

"No technological improvements can replace the written word—the most exact and concise record of man's achievements and the means by which he passes on what he has learned to each succeeding generation. When Bell invented the telephone, some predicted that it would mark the end of the mails. When Edison devised the phonograph, some said that the spoken word would supplant the written word. But more letters are written today than ever before in history.

"In his last years, the Signer Charles Carroll, of Carrollton, admitted that he had destroyed many letters from his associates 'because they referred only to the passing events of the time.' But so historically aware are we today that it is hard to imagine anyone throwing away a letter of Eisenhower or Mahatma K. Gandhi or Charles de Gaulle. Future biographers and historians will find their path paved with enlightening manuscript records."

Our leading periodicals frequently make use of original documents.

/ 235

Signatures of Mahatma K. Gandhi and Charles de Gaulle.

Almost daily there are discoveries of manuscripts which add to, or change, our view of the past. Early in 1960, I purchased an old document in Dutch. Although only a scrawl on a tiny piece of paper, apparently of little consequence, it was to prove a significant historical discovery. Suspecting its importance, I obtained the services of a specialist to translate it:

16 July 1625
The ship, the *Endracht*, arrived about half-past
five in the afternoon with the following:

| | |
|---|---|
| A pile of woolen blankets, value | ƒ 60 |
| Two chests with clothing for the soldiers | ƒ 80 |
| A chest with snaphances | ƒ180 |
| Armor and other diverse straps | ƒ 40 |
| Diverse goods to carry on trade with the Indians | ƒ100 |
| Total | ƒ460 |

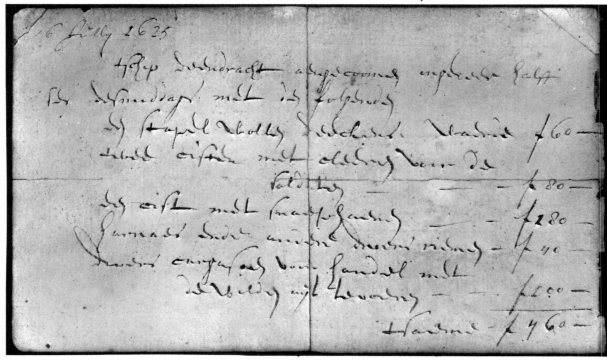

The earliest known document written in New York. Mentioned in this earliest American bill of lading are "goods to be traded to the Indians." Possibly some of the "goods" were used nine months later in the purchase of Manhattan.

*From the collection of Elsie O. and Philip D. Sang*

My belief that this tiny paper was of American origin was confirmed. Before me lay the earliest-known document written in New York. Predating by three years any other Dutch-American document, it disproved the statement in history books that the vessel *New Netherland* brought the first settlers to New York in 1624. Our entire knowledge of the landings by the first Dutch settlers is based upon two depositions of Caterina Trico, made about threescore years after her arrival with the first group. Madame Trico said that the name of her vessel was the *Eendracht*, but she did not recall the exact year of her arrival. Not finding any confirming record of the *Eendracht*, historians believed that she was in error and attributed her statements to the voyage of the *New Netherland*, a vessel which arrived the previous year but which probably carried no settlers. The early histories of New York must now be rewritten.

"It is quite possible," declared Professor Richard B. Morris, of Columbia University, who confirmed my findings, "that part of the 'goods to be traded to the Indians' was used for the purchase of Manhattan Island about nine months later!"

Spurred by the desire to preserve manuscript records for a better understanding of man's past and future, collectors, historical societies, and colleges vie in gathering illuminating letters and documents. There is the Clements Library at the University of Michigan, with its Colonial and Revolutionary collections; the Columbia University assemblage of Alexander Hamilton and John Jay material; the Lincoln collection in Brown University; and the assemblage of English literary material at U.C.L.A.'s William Andrews Clark Library.

The acquisitiveness of Yale augurs a great future for this progressive university. Its manuscript holdings of American and English Literature, Western Americana, and such specialized fields as the papers of James Boswell, Benjamin Franklin, and the aeronautical collection being formed by Colonel Richard Gimbel indicate a wide cultural horizon. Significance is added to Yale's activities through the efforts of James Marshall Osborn in assembling English literary autographs of the eighteenth century, and the generosity of Edwin J. Beinecke in building a collection of Robert Louis Stevenson's letters for the library. Part of the program of Yale includes ease of access to rare manuscript material. "The effort to make manuscripts available takes up a good deal of staff time," Professor Robert F. Metzdorf, University Archivist and a collector of Thackeray letters, wrote me recently, "but it is worthwhile in that it offers a chance to teach younger scholars not only how to use manuscripts, but also how to treat them."

The growing appreciation of our youth for the living documents of the past has induced some of America's great collectors to create special libraries. Such an endowment was the recent gift of C. Waller Barrett to the University of Virginia—a library of American literature with 250,000 items, representing rare books and autograph letters and manuscripts of more than one thousand authors. The worth of a collection so rich and varied can be computed only in terms of dollars, for its cultural value is beyond computation. If collectors of the future follow the example of Mr. Barrett, as I believe they will, the manuscript heritage of our country will be placed beyond jeopardy.

The most effective ideas in the use of manuscript material are now being developed by Brandeis University, where the Shiffman Humanities Center and the Olin-Sang American Civilization Center are being constructed. Dedicated to a new principle, these two centers will replace the old-fashioned blackboard by a series of lounges surrounded by original manuscripts and portraits.

The Olin-Sang Civilization Center, incorporating the historical collections formed by Elsie O. and Philip D. Sang, will comprise a Four Freedoms Hall, a Lincoln Room, a Washington Room, an Ethnic Room, a Legislative Hall, and a Congressional Hall, with a Town Meeting Room. The concept is daring and progressive. Here will be classes in American history, conducted in the presence of the very autograph letters and manuscripts which have influenced or changed the course of our nation. The furnishings and portraits are planned to create an atmosphere in keeping with the studies.

This great project will be a model for universities of the future and, as the number of autograph and manuscript collectors increases, there will come a deeper respect and admiration for our cultural heritage and a fresh understanding of the problems which face each generation.

History awaits from autographs its final verdict!

# APPENDIX

*The Care and Preservation of Autographs*

AMONG THE MOST DURABLE OF HEIRLOOMS, autographs sometimes out-last stone and brass. Often you will find parchment or rag paper of the fourteenth and fifteenth centuries which is still in pristine condition, the writing as bright and clear as the day it was set down. Early papers are strong and sturdy, usually creamy white after the lapse of five centuries. Letters of the American Revolutionary era turn up in fine condition. It is not passing years, but scissors and glue and Scotch tape which destroy old documents. Even more devastating are the inroads of fire and the ignorance of owners who throw away valuable papers which they do not appreciate or understand. Mice and insects, too, play their role. Excessive dampness or heat from attic or cellar will crumble or rot even the staunch-est of papers.

It is a good plan to keep autographs where the temperature is not subject to violent fluctuations. Paper is sensitive to temperatures. It should not be stored too near a radiator or stove, or where the atmosphere is humid.

If a document is brittle because of prolonged exposure to heat, place it near a window during a rain or leave it out on a humid day. This pro-cedure will sometimes give fresh strength to brittle paper.

You should not attempt complicated repairs without practice. Un-less necessary, avoid trimming the margins of old papers. Never make any repairs with Scotch or masking tape or rubber cement. In the course of a few years, these will destroy even the sturdiest paper.

For minor repairs, use thin strips of ordinary tissue paper applied by common, white library paste. It is best to remove old letters from the envelopes, so that the creases will not become worn. Press letters or documents flat and place them loosely in a box, or in a manila folder, or hinge them lightly with library paste in an album. Do not completely seal out the air.

Many collectors use cellulose acetate folders, obtainable in any stationer's. These serve to display and at the same time protect documents.

Old documents may be removed from previous mountings or albums by soaking in cold or tepid water. Always immerse the entire document, otherwise the dampened portion may become stained. It is a little hazardous to plunge into water a document penned in aniline blue ink like that used by Dickens, Bryant, Louisa May Alcott and a few other writers of the nineteenth century. But documents penned in iron gall ink and written between the fourteenth and nineteenth centuries may be soaked in water without adverse effects. Wax seals should never be put into water, nor should parchment. The best method to straighten the crinkles in old parchment is by exposing the document on a very humid day, afterwards pressing it under a heavy weight.

If you acquire a document on which Scotch tape, rubber cement, or some other destructive adhesive was applied, you may be able to remove the Scotch tape in humid weather by peeling it off slowly, working toward the margin. But if Scotch tape has been on for several months or more, the best way to remove it is by bathing the document in benzene. Be sure to use chemically pure benzene. Since benzene is toxic and dangerous, work in an outdoor area so that there will be no danger of inhaling the deadly fumes. Benzene is extremely effective in dissolving the gummy residue of Scotch tape.

There is no reason why you should not frame letters or documents. Ordinary library paste should be used to hinge the autograph in place. It should be backed by pure rag paper. Corrugated paper should never be put next to the autograph and no glue or adhesive tape of any kind should be used. Framed documents should never be displayed where the direct rays of the sun can hit them, for this will cause the ink to fade; nor should they be hung over radiators or near fireplaces where the heat may dry out the framed autograph and make the paper brittle. If these precautions are observed, framed autographs will remain attractive for generations.

### Standard Catalog Abbreviations

(All reliable dealers guarantee authenticity
and offer material on an approval basis.)

THE ABBREVIATIONS in American and British catalogs are: A.L.S., Autograph Letter Signed (all in the hand of the writer); L.S., Letter Signed (the body of the letter typewritten or in the hand of a secretary, with the signature only in the hand of the writer); A.D.S., Autograph Document Signed; D.S., Document Signed; A. Verse S., Autograph Verse Signed; A.Ms.S., Autograph Manuscript Signed; A.N.S., Autograph Note Signed; T.L.S., Typewritten Letter Signed; n.d., no date; n.p., no place; Signer, Signer of the Declaration of Independence; M.O.C., Member of the Continental Congress; sig., signature; p., page; pp., pages; Pres., President; Sec., Secretary; fol., folio; 4to, quarto; 8vo, octavo; 12mo to 24mo, a very small sheet.

The terms folio, quarto, and octavo are used very laxly today. Originally they referred to the folding of a large sheet by the printer. The folio sheet when folded four times made four quarto sheets and when folded eight times made eight octavo sheets. Today by folio is meant any sheet from about eight by eleven inches upward in size, but generally a folio sheet is any sheet of a very large size, with such terms as elephant folio, giant folio and atlas folio used to designate enormous pages. By quarto is meant a sheet ranging from about seven by nine inches to around nine by twelve inches. The term octavo describes a sheet from about five by seven inches to around six by nine inches.

In French catalogs, the abbreviations are: L.A.S., Autograph Letter Signed; L.S., Letter Signed; P.A.S., Autograph Document Signed; P.S., Document Signed; Mss., Manuscript; s.l., no place; s.l.n.d., no place or date; Billet, note; Pièce, document; Belle, fine.

In German catalogs, the abbreviations are: E.Br.m.U., Autograph Letter Signed; Br.m.U., Letter Signed; S., signature; E. Albumblatt m.U., Autograph Album Quotation Signed; O.O.u.D., no place or date; S., page; Gr., large; Pergament, parchment; Gedicht, poem; Urkunde, document.

In Italian catalogs the abbreviations are: L.a.f., Autograph Letter Signed; l.c.f.a., Letter Signed; f., signature; Doc. con f.a., Document Signed; pp., pages; rr., lines; s.d., no date; in perg., on parchment; doc., document.

## Presidents' Widows Granted the Franking Privilege by Act of Congress

| | |
|---|---|
| Martha Washington | April 3, 1800 |
| Dolley P. Madison | July 2, 1836 |
| Anna Harrison | September 9, 1841 |
| Louisa Catherine Adams | March 9, 1848 |
| Sarah Polk | January 10, 1850 |
| Margaret Smith Taylor | July 18, 1850 |
| Mary Lincoln | February 10, 1866 |
| Lucretia R. Garfield | December 20, 1881 |
| Julia D. Grant | June 28, 1886 |
| Ida S. McKinley | January 22, 1902 |
| Frances F. Cleveland | February 1, 1909 |
| Mary Lord Harrison | February 1, 1909 |
| Edith Carow Roosevelt | October 27, 1919 |

# ALPHABETS.

| Modern Gothic. | Old English. | Set Chancery. | Common Chancery. | Court Hand. | Secretary. | German Alphabet | SECRET ALPHABETS. | |
|---|---|---|---|---|---|---|---|---|

# A CONCORDANCE OF THE FRENCH REPUBLICAN AND THE GREGORIAN CALENDARS

| Year of the Republic. | I. | II. | III. | IV. | V. | VI. | VII. | VIII. | IX. | X. | XI. | XII. | XIII. | XIV. |
|---|---|---|---|---|---|---|---|---|---|---|---|---|---|---|
| | 1792. | 1793. | 1794. | 1795. | 1796. | 1797. | 1798. | 1799. | 1800. | 1801. | 1802. | 1803. | 1804. | 1805. |
| VENDEMIAIRE 1 | Sept. 22 | Sept. 22 | Sept. 22 | Sept. 23 | Sept. 22 | Sept. 22 | Sept. 22 | Sept. 23 | Sept. 23 | Sept. 23 | Sept. 23 | Sept. 24 | Sept. 23 | Sept. 23 |
| BRUMAIRE 1 | Oct. 22 | Oct. 22 | Oct. 22 | Oct. 23 | Oct. 22 | Oct. 22 | Oct. 22 | Oct. 23 | Oct. 23 | Oct. 23 | Oct. 23 | Oct. 24 | Oct. 23 | Oct. 23 |
| FRIMAIRE 1 | Nov. 21 | Nov. 21 | Nov. 21 | Nov. 22 | Nov. 21 | Nov. 21 | Nov. 21 | Nov. 22 | Nov. 22 | Nov. 22 | Nov. 22 | Nov. 23 | Nov. 22 | Nov. 22 |
| NIVOSE 1 | Dec. 21 | Dec. 21 | Dec. 21 | Dec. 22 | Dec. 21 | Dec. 21 | Dec. 21 | Dec. 22 | Dec. 22 | Dec. 22 | Dec. 22 | Dec. 23 | Dec. 22 | Dec. 22 |
| | 1793. | 1794. | 1795. | 1796. | 1797. | 1798. | 1799. | 1800. | 1801. | 1802. | 1803. | 1804. | 1805. | |
| PLUVIOSE 1 | Jan. 20 | Jan. 20 | Jan. 20 | Jan. 21 | Jan. 20 | Jan. 20 | Jan. 20 | Jan. 21 | Jan. 21 | Jan. 21 | Jan. 21 | Jan. 22 | Jan. 21 | |
| VENTOSE 1 | Feb. 19 | Feb. 19 | Feb. 19 | Feb. 20 | Feb. 19 | Feb. 19 | Feb. 19 | Feb. 20 | Feb. 20 | Feb. 20 | Feb. 20 | Feb. 21 | Feb. 20 | |
| " 10 | ..... | ..... | ..... | Feb. 29] | ..... | ..... | ..... | ..... | ..... | ..... | ..... | [Feb. 29] | ..... | |
| GERMINAL 1 | *March 21* | March 21 | March 20 | March 21 | March 21 | March 21 | March 21 | March 22 | March 22 | March 22 | March 22 | March 22 | March 22 | |
| FLOREAL 1 | April 20 | April 20 | April 20 | April 20 | April 20 | April 20 | April 20 | April 21 | April 21 | April 21 | April 21 | April 21 | April 21 | |
| PRAIRIAL 1 | May 20 | May 20 | May 20 | May 20 | May 20 | May 20 | May 20 | May 21 | May 21 | May 21 | May 21 | May 21 | May 21 | |
| MESSIDOR 1 | June 19 | June 19 | June 19 | June 19 | June 19 | June 19 | June 19 | June 20 | June 20 | June 20 | June 20 | June 20 | June 20 | |
| THERMIDOR 1 | July 19 | July 19 | July 19 | July 19 | July 19 | July 19 | July 19 | July 20 | July 20 | July 20 | July 20 | July 20 | July 20 | |
| FRUCTIDOR 1 | Aug. 18 | Aug. 18 | Aug. 18 | Aug. 18 | Aug. 18 | Aug. 18 | Aug. 18 | Aug. 19 | Aug. 19 | Aug. 19 | Aug. 19 | Aug. 19 | Aug. 19 | |
| 1. GENIE | Sept. 17 | Sept. 17 | Sept. 17 | Sept. 17 | Sept. 17 | Sept. 17 | Sept. 17 | Sept. 18 | Sept. 18 | Sept. 18 | Sept. 18 | Sept. 18 | Sept. 18 | |
| 2. TRAVAIL | Sept. 18 | Sept. 18 | Sept. 18 | Sept. 18 | Sept. 18 | Sept. 18 | Sept. 18 | Sept. 19 | Sept. 19 | Sept. 19 | Sept. 19 | Sept. 19 | Sept. 19 | |
| 3. BELLES ACTIONS | Sept. 19 | Sept. 19 | Sept. 19 | Sept. 19 | Sept. 19 | Sept. 19 | Sept. 19 | Sept. 20 | Sept. 20 | Sept. 20 | Sept. 20 | Sept. 20 | Sept. 20 | |
| 4. RECOMPENSES | Sept. 20 | Sept. 20 | Sept. 20 | Sept. 20 | Sept. 20 | Sept. 20 | Sept. 20 | Sept. 21 | Sept. 21 | Sept. 21 | Sept. 21 | Sept. 21 | Sept. 21 | |
| 5. OPINION | Sept. 21 | Sept. 21 | Sept. 21 | Sept. 21 | Sept. 21 | Sept. 21 | Sept. 21 | Sept. 22 | Sept. 22 | Sept. 22 | Sept. 22 | Sept. 22 | Sept. 22 | |
| 6. REVOLUTION | ..... | ..... | Sept. 22 | ..... | ..... | ..... | Sept. 22 | ..... | ..... | ..... | Sept. 23 | ..... | ..... | |
| Year of the Republic. | I. | II. | III. | IV. | V. | VI. | VII. | VIII. | IX. | X. | XI. | XII. | XIII. | XIV. |

Complementary Days according to Thiers (see opposite).

The Gregorian Calendar was resumed in France on and after January 1, 1806 (Nivôse 10, Year XIV., or December 31, 1805, being the last day of the Republican Calendar).

*The year I. of the Republican Calendar was retrospective only.*

| | |
|---|---|
| Florence Kling Harding | January 25, 1924 |
| Edith Bolling Wilson | March 4, 1924 |
| Helen H. Taft | June 14, 1930 |
| Grace Coolidge | June 16, 1934 |
| Anna Eleanor Roosevelt | May 7, 1945 |

## Members of the Federal Constitutional Convention[1]

Those whose names are in capitals signed the Constitution; those whose names are in italics attended the Convention but did not sign; and those whose names are in roman were elected or appointed, but did not attend.

### CONNECTICUT

WILLIAM SAMUEL JOHNSON
ROGER SHERMAN
*Oliver Ellsworth*
Erastus Wolcott

### DELAWARE

RICHARD BASSETT
GUNNING BEDFORD, JR.
JACOB BROOM
JOHN DICKINSON
GEORGE READ

### GEORGIA

ABRAHAM BALDWIN
WILLIAM FEW
*William Houstoun*
*Nathaniel Pendleton*
*William Pierce*
George Walton

### MARYLAND

DANIEL CARROLL
DANIEL OF ST. THOMAS
  JENIFER
JAMES McHENRY
Charles Carroll of Carrollton

Gabriel Duval
Robert H. Harrison
Thomas Sim Lee
*Luther Martin*
*John Francis Mercer*
Thomas Stone

### MASSACHUSETTS

NATHANIEL GORHAM
RUFUS KING
Francis Dana
*Elbridge Gerry*
*Caleb Strong*

### NEW HAMPSHIRE

NICHOLAS GILMAN
JOHN LANGDON
John Pickering
Benjamin West

### NEW JERSEY

DAVID BREARLEY
JONATHAN DAYTON
WILLIAM LIVINGSTON
WILLIAM PATERSON
Abraham Clark
William C. Houston
John Neilson

[1] This list, based upon the findings of Dr. Frederick M. Dearborn, a collector for sixty years, was published originally in "The Collector" of Walter R. Benjamin Autographs (1958).

NEW YORK

ALEXANDER HAMILTON
*John Lansing, Jr.*
*Robert Yates*

NORTH CAROLINA

WILLIAM BLOUNT
RICHARD DOBBS SPAIGHT
HUGH WILLIAMSON
Richard Caswell
*William R. Davie*
Willie Jones
*Alexander Martin*

PENNSYLVANIA

GEORGE CLYMER
THOMAS FITZSIMONS
BENJAMIN FRANKLIN
JARED INGERSOLL
THOMAS MIFFLIN
GOUVERNEUR MORRIS
ROBERT MORRIS

JAMES WILSON

SOUTH CAROLINA

PIERCE BUTLER
WILLIAM JACKSON, Secretary[2]
CHARLES PINCKNEY
CHARLES COTESWORTH
  PINCKNEY
JOHN RUTLEDGE
Henry Laurens

VIRGINIA

JOHN BLAIR
JAMES MADISON
GEORGE WASHINGTON,
  President
Patrick Henry
Richard Henry Lee
*James McClurg*
*George Mason*
Thomas Nelson, Jr.
*Edmund Randolph*
George Wythe

*Revolutionary War Generals*

Allen, Ethan. Maj. Gen., 1778.
Armand, Charles T. Brig. Gen., Mar. 26, 1783–Nov. 3, 1783.
Armstrong, John, Sr. Brig. Gen., Mar. 1, 1776–Apr. 4, 1777.
Arnold, Benedict. Brig. Gen., Jan. 10, 1776–Feb. 17, 1777; Maj. Gen., Feb. 17, 1777–Sept. 25, 1780.
Baylor, George. Brig. Gen., from Sept. 30, 1783.
Borre, Prudhomme de. Brig. Gen., from Dec. 1, 1776.
Brodhead, Daniel. Brig. Gen., from Sept. 30, 1783.
Butler, Richard. Brig. Gen., from Sept. 30, 1783.
Cadwalader, John. Brig. Gen., Feb. 21, 1777; declined the appointment.
Clark, George Rogers. Brig. Gen., from 1782.
Clark, Thomas. Brig. Gen., from Sept. 30, 1783.
Clinton, George. Brig. Gen., Mar. 25, 1777; Maj. Gen., from Sept. 30, 1783.
Clinton, James. Brig. Gen., Aug. 9, 1776–Sept. 30, 1783; Maj. Gen., from Sept. 30, 1783.
Conway, Thomas. Brig. Gen., May 13, 1777–Dec. 13, 1777; Maj. Gen., Dec. 13,
  [2] Not a delegate.

Crane, John. Brig. Gen., from Sept. 30, 1783.

Davidson, William. Brig. Gen., 1780.

Dayton, Elias. Brig. Gen., Jan. 7, 1783–Nov. 3, 1783.

Du Coudray, Philippe. Maj. Gen., Aug. 11, 1777–Sept. 15, 1777.

Duportail, The Chevalier Louis Lebegue. Brig. Gen., Nov. 17, 1777–Nov. 16, 1781; Maj. Gen., Nov. 16, 1781–Oct. 10, 1783.

Elbert, Samuel. Brig. Gen., from Nov. 3, 1783.

Febiger, Christian. Brig. Gen., from Sept. 30, 1783.

Frye, Joseph. Brig. Gen., Jan. 10, 1776–Apr. 23, 1776.

Gadsden, Christopher. Brig. Gen., Sept. 16, 1776–Oct. 2, 1777.

Gates, Horatio. Brig. Gen., June 17, 1775–May 16, 1776; Maj. Gen., May 16, 1776–Nov. 3, 1783.

Gibson, John. Brig. Gen., from Sept. 30, 1783.

Gist, Mordecai. Brig. Gen., Jan. 9, 1779–Nov. 3, 1783.

Glover, John. Brig. Gen., Feb. 21, 1777–July 22, 1782; Maj. Gen., from Sept. 30, 1783.

Greaton, John. Brig. Gen., Jan. 7, 1783–Nov. 3, 1783.

Greene, Nathanael. Brig. Gen., June 22, 1775–Aug. 9, 1776; Maj. Gen., Aug. 9, 1776–Nov. 3, 1783.

Gunby, John. Brig. Gen., from Sept. 30, 1783.

Hand, Edward. Brig. Gen., Apr. 1, 1777–Sept. 30, 1783; Maj. Gen., from Sept. 30, 1783.

Haas, John Philip de. Brig. Gen., Feb. 21, 1777–Sept. 30, 1783; Maj. Gen., from Sept. 30, 1783.

Hazen, Moses. Brig. Gen., June 29, 1781–Jan. 1, 1783.

Heath, William. Brig. Gen., June 22, 1775–Aug. 9, 1776; Maj. Gen., Aug. 9, 1776–Nov. 3, 1783.

Hogan, James. Brig. Gen., Jan. 9, 1779–Jan. 4, 1781.

Howard, John E. Maj. Gen., Dec., 1776.

Howe, Robert. Brig. Gen., Mar. 1, 1776–Oct. 20, 1777; Maj. Gen., Oct. 20, 1777–Nov. 3, 1783.

Huger, Isaac. Brig. Gen., Jan. 9, 1779–Nov. 3, 1783.

Humpton, Richard. Brig. Gen., from Sept. 30, 1783.

Huntington, Jedediah. Brig. Gen., May 12, 1777–Sept. 30, 1783; Maj. Gen., from Sept. 30, 1783.

Irvine, William. Brig. Gen., May 12, 1779–Nov. 3, 1783.

Jackson, Henry. Brig. Gen., from Sept. 30, 1783.

Jackson, Michael. Brig. Gen., from Sept. 30, 1783.

Kalb, Baron John de. Maj. Gen., Sept. 15, 1777–Aug. 19, 1780.

Knox, Henry. Maj. Gen., Nov. 15, 1781–June 20, 1784.

Kosciuszko, Thaddeus. Brig. Gen., Oct. 13, 1783–Nov. 3, 1783.

Lafayette, Marquis de. Marie Jean Paul Joseph Roche Yves Gilbert du Motier. Maj. Gen., July 31, 1777–Nov. 3, 1783.

Lamb, John. Brig. Gen., from Sept. 30, 1783.

Laumoy, Monsieur de. Brig. Gen., from Sept. 30, 1783.

Learned, Ebenezer. Brig. Gen., Apr. 2, 1777–Mar. 24, 1778.

Lee, Charles. Maj. Gen., June 17, 1775–Jan. 10, 1780.

Lee, Henry. Maj. Gen., 1778.

Lewis, Andrew. Brig. Gen., Mar. 1, 1776–Apr. 15, 1777.

Lincoln, Benjamin. Maj. Gen., Feb. 19, 1777–Oct. 29, 1783.

Marion, Francis. Brig. Gen., 1780.

Mathews, George. Brig. Gen., from Sept. 30, 1783.

Maxwell, William. Brig. Gen., Oct. 23, 1776–July 25, 1780.

McDougall, Alexander. Brig. Gen., Aug. 9, 1776–Oct. 20, 1777; Maj. Gen., Oct. 20, 1777–Nov. 3, 1783.

McIntosh, Lachlan. Brig. Gen., Sept. 16, 1776–Sept. 30, 1783; Maj. Gen., from Sept. 30, 1783.

Mercer, Hugh. Brig. Gen., June 5, 1776–Jan. 11, 1777.

Mifflin, Thomas. Brig. Gen., May 16, 1776–Feb. 19, 1777; Maj. Gen., Feb. 19, 1777–Feb. 25, 1779.

Montgomery, Richard. Brig. Gen., June 22, 1775–Dec. 9, 1775; Maj. Gen., Dec. 9, 1775–Dec. 31, 1775.

Moore, James. Brig. Gen., Mar. 1, 1776–Apr. 9, 1777.

Morgan, Daniel. Brig. Gen., Oct. 13, 1780–Nov. 3, 1783.

Moultrie, William. Brig. Gen., Sept. 16, 1776–Oct. 2, 1777; Maj. Gen., Oct. 15, 1782–Nov. 3, 1783.

Moylan, Stephen. Brig. Gen., from Nov. 3, 1783.

Muhlenberg, Peter. Brig. Gen., Feb. 21, 1777–Nov. 3, 1783; Maj. Gen., from Sept. 30, 1783.

Nash, Francis. Brig. Gen., Feb. 5, 1777–Oct. 17, 1777.

Neuville, The Chevalier de la. Brig. Gen., Aug. 14, 1778–Dec. 4, 1778.

Nevil (or Neville), John. Brig. Gen., from Sept. 30, 1783.

Nicola, Lewis. Brig. Gen., from Sept. 30, 1783.

Nixon, John. Brig. Gen., Aug. 9, 1776–Sept. 12, 1780.

Ogden, Mathias. Brig. Gen., from Sept. 30, 1783.

Parsons, Samuel Holden. Brig. Gen., Aug. 9, 1776–Oct. 23, 1780; Maj. Gen., Oct. 23, 1780–July 22, 1782.

Paterson, John. Brig. Gen., Feb. 21, 1777–Sept. 30, 1783; Maj. Gen., from Sept. 30, 1783.

Pickens, Andrew. Brig. Gen., 1781.

Pinckney, Charles Cotesworth. Brig. Gen., from Nov. 3, 1783.

Pomeroy, Seth. Brig. Gen., June 22, 1775; declined the appointment.

Poor, Enoch. Brig. Gen., Feb. 21, 1777–Sept. 8, 1780.

Pulaski, Count Casimir. Brig. Gen., Sept. 15, 1777–Oct. 11, 1779.

Putnam, Israel. Brig. Gen., June 19, 1775–June 3, 1783.

Putnam, Rufus. Brig. Gen., Jan. 7, 1783–Nov. 3, 1783.

Reed, James. Brig. Gen., Aug. 9, 1776–Sept., 1776.

Reed, Joseph. Brig. Gen., May 12, 1777–June 9, 1777.

Rochefermoy, The Chevalier Mathieu Alexis de. Brig. Gen., Dec. 1, 1776–Sept. 14, 1777.

Russell, William. Brig. Gen., from Nov. 3, 1783.

St. Clair, Arthur. Brig. Gen., Aug. 9, 1776–Feb. 19, 1777; Maj. Gen., Feb. 19, 1777–Nov. 3, 1783.

Schuyler, Philip. Maj. Gen., June 19, 1775–Apr. 19, 1779.

Scott, Charles. Brig. Gen., Apr. 1, 1777–Nov. 3, 1783; Maj. Gen., from Sept. 30, 1783.

Sheldon, Elisha. Brig. Gen.

Shepard, William. Brig. Gen.

Smallwood, William. Brig. Gen., from Oct., 1776; Maj. Gen., from Sept., 1780.

Spencer, Joseph. Maj. Gen., Aug. 9, 1776–Jan. 13, 1778.

Stark, John. Brig. Gen., Oct. 4, 1777–Nov. 3, 1783; Maj. Gen., from Sept. 30, 1783.

Stephen, Adam. Brig. Gen., Sept. 4, 1776–Feb. 19, 1777; Maj. Gen., Feb. 19, 1777–Nov. 20, 1777.

Steuben, Baron von, Friedrich Wilhelm August Heinrich Ferdinand. Maj. Gen., May 5, 1778–Apr. 15, 1784.

Stewart, Walter. Brig. Gen., from Sept. 30, 1783.

Stirling, Lord (William Alexander). Brig. Gen., Mar. 1, 1776–Feb. 19, 1777; Maj. Gen., Feb. 19, 1777–Jan. 15, 1783.

Sullivan, John. Brig. Gen., June 22, 1775–Aug. 9, 1776; Maj. Gen., Aug. 9, 1779–Nov. 30, 1779.

Sumner, Jethro. Brig. Gen., Jan. 9, 1779–Nov. 3, 1783.

Sumter, Thomas. Brig. Gen., from Oct. 6, 1780.

Swift, Herman. Brig. Gen., from Sept. 30, 1783.

Thomas, John. Brig. Gen., June 22, 1775–Mar. 6, 1776; Maj. Gen., Mar. 6, 1776–June 2, 1776.

Thompson, William. Brig. Gen., Mar. 1, 1776–Sept. 3, 1781.

Tupper, Benjamin. Brig. Gen., from Sept. 30, 1783.

Van Cortlandt, Philip. Brig. Gen., from Sept. 30, 1783.

Van Schaick, Goose (or Gozen). Brig. Gen., from Sept. 30, 1783.

Varnum, James M. Brig. Gen., Feb. 21, 1777–Mar. 5, 1779.

Vose, Joseph. Brig. Gen., from Sept. 30, 1783.

Ward, Artemas. Maj. Gen., June 17, 1775–Apr. 23, 1776.

Warren, Joseph. Maj. Gen., June 14, 1775–June 18, 1775.

Washington, George. Gen. and commander-in-chief, June 15, 1775–Dec. 23, 1783.

Wayne, Anthony. Brig. Gen., Feb. 21, 1777–Sept. 30, 1783; Maj. Gen., from Sept. 30, 1783.

Webb, Samuel B. Brig. Gen., from Sept. 30, 1783.

Weedon, George. Brig. Gen., Feb. 21, 1777–June, 1783; Maj. Gen., from Sept. 30, 1783.

Whitcomb, John. Brig. Gen., June 5, 1776; declined the appointment.

Wilkinson, James. Brig. Gen., Nov. 6, 1777–Mar. 6, 1778.
Williams, Otho Holland. Brig. Gen., May 9, 1782–Jan. 16, 1783.
Woedtke, Baron de, Friedrich Wilhelm. Brig. Gen., Mar. 16, 1776–July 28, 1776.
Woodford, William. Brig. Gen., Feb. 21, 1777–Nov. 13, 1780.
Wooster, David. Brig. Gen., June 22, 1775–May 2, 1777.

*Washington's Aides-de-Camp and Secretaries*[3]

Baylies, Hodijah. Extra aide-de-camp, from May 14, 1782.
Baylor, George. Aide-de-camp, from Aug. 15, 1775.
Cary, Richard. Aide-de-camp, from June 21, 1776.
Cobb, David. Aide-de-camp, from June 15, 1781.
Custis, John Parke. Aide-de-camp, 1781.
Fitzhugh, Peregrine. Aide-de-camp.
Fitzgerald, John. Aide-de-camp, 1777.
Gibbs, Caleb. Aide-de-camp, from May 16, 1776.
Grayson, William. Aide-de-camp, from August 24, 1776.
Hamilton, Alexander. Aide-de-camp, from Mar. 1, 1777.
Hanson, Alexander Contee. Assistant Secretary, from June 21, 1776.
Harrison, Robert Hanson. Aide-de-camp, from Nov. 5, 1775; secretary, from June 21, 1776.
Humphreys, David. Aide-de-camp, from June 23, 1780.
Jackson, William. Aide-de-camp, 1781.
Johnston, George. Aide-de-camp, Jan. 20, 1777.
Laurens, John. Extra aide, from Sept. 6, 1777; aide-de-camp, from Oct. 6, 1777.
Lewis, George. Aide-de-camp, from May 16, 1776.
McHenry, James. Assistant Secretary, from May 15, 1778.
Meade, Richard Kidder. Aide-de-camp, from Mar. 12, 1777.
Mifflin, Thomas. Aide-de-camp, June 23–Aug. 14, 1775.
Moylan, Stephen. Aide-de-camp, from Mar. 5, 1776.
Palfrey, William. Aide-de-camp, from Mar. 6, 1776.
Penet, Pierre. Aide-de-camp, from Mar. 6, 1776.
Randolph, Edmund. Aide-de-camp, from Aug. 15, 1775.
Reed, Joseph. Secretary, from July 4, 1775.
Smith, Benjamin. Aide-de-camp, 1776.
Smith, William Stephen. Aide-de-camp, from July 6, 1781.
Thornton, Peter Presley. Extra aide-de-camp, from Sept. 6, 1777.
Tilghman, Tench. Aide-de-camp, from June 21, 1780.
Trumbull, John. Aide-de-camp, from July 27, 1775.
Trumbull, Jonathan, Jr. Secretary, from June 8, 1781.
Varick, Richard. Recording Secretary, from May 25, 1781.

[3] This list comprises Washington's aides and secretaries, but does not include the many individuals who were temporarily employed as amanuenses.

Walker, Benjamin. Aide-de-camp, from July 25, 1782.
Walker, John. Extra aide-de-camp, from Feb. 19, 1777.
Webb, Samuel Blatchley. Aide-de-camp, from June 21, 1776.

## The Best Books About Autographs

### Books On Collecting

Of the dozens of volumes about autographs, only a few are sufficiently detailed or accurate to merit study. A few, like the memoirs of Joline and Hill, are reminiscences mainly notable for the letters of celebrities quoted in them. Others, like the books of Sims and Williams, are very inaccurate. The following list comprises the outstanding books on the subject, all of which are recommended.

Benjamin, Mary A. *Autographs: A Key to Collecting*. New York, 1946. By far the best and most reliable manual, with detailed discussions of some of the complicated aspects of collecting.

Broadley, A. M. *Chats on Autographs*. London, 1910. Written in a pedestrian style, with many out-of-date prices quoted, this book has the merit of accuracy and is enhanced by numerous illustrations.

Charnwood, Lady. *An Autograph Collection*. New York, about 1932. A charming and nostalgic volume by a collector who, if not the most knowledgeable, was one of the most enthusiastic.

Madigan, Thomas F. *Word Shadows of the Great*. New York, 1930. Zestful introduction to autograph collecting by one of America's great dealers.

Scott, Henry T. *Autograph Collecting*. London, 1894. The charter manual on autographs, crammed with details, with many facsimiles and a long-out-of-date guide to prices.

### Books With Important Sections On Collecting

Newton, A. Edward. *The Amenities of Book-Collecting and Kindred Affections*. Boston, 1918. A delightful reconnaissance into the world of books and manuscripts by a charming essayist.

Rosenbach, A. S. W. *Books and Bidders*. Boston, 1927. An exhilarating account of the chase by America's greatest rare book dealer.

Storm, Colton and Howard Peckham. *Invitation to Book Collecting . . . With Kindred Discussions of Manuscripts . . . .* New York, 1947. An illuminating and helpful guide by two distinguished librarians.

### Periodicals

Most of the great autograph periodicals of the past were issued by dealers, such as the publications of Charavay in Paris, and the American Autograph Shop in Merion Station, Pennsylvania. These are of some interest but of relatively small value to the modern collector.

*Hobbies Magazine* (Chicago, Illinois, 1949 ff.). Contains a monthly article on autographs by Charles Hamilton or Doris H. Hamilton.

*The Collector*, published by Walter R. Benjamin and edited by Mary A. Benjamin (New York, 1887 ff.). An autograph bulletin, published irregularly, containing introductions on various phases of collecting.

*The Month*, published by Goodspeed's Book Shop (Boston, 1934 ff.). A delightfully written bulletin, offering books and autographs for sale, with useful facsimiles.

## Books on Facsimiles

There are immense numbers of books which contain facsimiles, and there are many volumes exclusively devoted to facsimiles. But such works as *Illustrated Classics Manuscripts* and various other volumes published in France and especially in Germany during the last century are too specialized to interest the contemporary collector. The same objection may be made of certain American facsimile volumes, such as the *Centennial Book of the Signers*.

More important to the collector are the illustrated catalogs issued by Maggs and Spencer in London, Charavay in Paris, and Stargardt in Marburg, Germany, as well as the catalogs issued by auction firms like Sotheby's in London and Parke-Bernet in New York.

*Appleton's Cyclopaedia of American Biography*, 6 vols., with a rare seventh volume. New York, 1886–89. In the absence of a book devoted exclusively to American facsimile autographs, *Appleton's Cyclopaedia* is a valuable reference, containing hundreds of signatures of celebrities.

Bovet Catalog [edited by Étienne Charavay]. *Lettres Autographes Composant la Collection de M. Alfred Bovet*. Paris, 1884–85. Published in three parts, with a separate index to each part, this scholarly catalog of the collection of a great French enthusiast is one of the most useful of all volumes of facsimiles.

Geigy, Charles. *Handbook of Facsimiles of Famous Personages*. Basle, 1925. The best work on facsimiles available, but with only a small section devoted to American celebrities.

# INDEX

*Collecting Autographs and Manuscripts* makes use of the two major printing processes, letterpress and offset lithography, to insure the maximum fidelity of reproduction to the hundreds of signatures contained in the book. The text was set in Electra, the late W. A. Dwiggins' highly original design for the Linotype Company, and printed by letterpress on large sheets. Then each signature and illustration was individually positioned on the page. When all illustrative matter was in place, the sheets were photographed a final time and offset plates were made. The finished book, combining the text and the illustrations, was printed by offset.

 UNIVERSITY OF OKLAHOMA PRESS : NORMAN